MW01097054

UNSTOPPABLE

UNSTOPPABLE

The story of asset-based finance and leasing in Canada

BETH PARKER

BARLOW

Library and Archives Canada Cataloguing in Publication data available upon request.

ISBN 978-0-9917411-9-9 (print)
ISBN 978-0-9937656-2-9 (ebook)

Printed in Canada

ORDERS:
In Canada:
Jaguar Book Group
100 Armstrong Avenue, Georgetown, ON L7G 5S4

In the U.S.A.:
Midpoint Book Sales & Distribution
27 West 20th Street, Suite 1102, New York, NY 10011

SALES REPRESENTATION:
Canadian Manda Group
165 Dufferin Street, Toronto, ON M6K 3H6

Cover design: Luke Despatie
Interior design: Kyle Gell Design
Page layout: Kyle Gell Design
Project management/production editorial: At Large Editorial Services

For more information, visit **www.barlowbookpublishing.com**

Barlow Book Publishing Inc.
96 Elm Avenue, Toronto, ON, Canada M4W 1P2

BARLOW

Contents

Foreword

ASSET-BASED FINANCE and leasing is based on a premise that is simple in concept but endless in its variety of applications: you don't have to own a vehicle to drive it, and you don't need to own that computer, software, truck, or airplane to profitably use it.

This book tells the story of the asset-based finance industry in Canada in a way that leaves no doubt about why this industry has become integral to our country's financial system and economic well-being. Its innovative approaches have evolved over the past half-century through the work of entrepreneurial leaders who developed an entirely new industry.

It is estimated that asset-based finance in Canada finances about $300 billion worth of vehicles and equipment in this country, making it the largest provider of credit and capital to Canadian businesses and consumers after traditional lending. This type of finance is much larger than most Canadians realize and has become increasingly entrenched in the economy, expanding the pool of available capital and offering a competitive choice to businesses and consumers.

This is the story of how and why the asset-based finance industry carved its unique niche in Canada's business landscape. It is a story that has not been told before. You will read about the products and services that didn't exist until entrepreneurial minds with vision and determination invented them. Most importantly, you will read about the people—both the pioneers and those carrying on their legacy—who have made this industry work. Leaders, both past and present, have had much in common. They are risk-takers. They all have the capacity to innovate and apply new technology. They're good at pricing risk. They know how to re-market assets efficiently. They're flexible and are able to operate competitively in an unregulated marketplace.

These talents have been ingrained in the industry's DNA and are personified by many of the industry's leaders, starting with Canadian Ned Mundell, founder of what is considered to be Canada's first independent leasing company, Canadian Dominion Leasing (and later CEO of the giant U.S. Leasing, the first independent leasing company south of the border)."In the early days of the leasing business, there were no rules," Mundell said. "You were free to try anything because you weren't tied down with traditional patterns or rules.... This meant you were free to innovate. The mantra of the business was: 'What do we need to create now?' as opposed to 'business as usual.'"

The asset-based finance industry has faced many obstacles, including a global financial crisis and several recessions. It has weathered dramatic changes in the marketplace, technology, the mechanics of funding, and the market reach of the industry. The industry has survived a rollercoaster ride thanks to leaders who were innovative, determined, and resilient enough to take risks and guide the industry through transformation and renewal.

Steve Hudson, founder of Newcourt Credit Group and later CEO of Element Financial Corporation, put it this way: "You can knock down the asset-based finance and leasing industry, but it is always going to come back in one way or another."

Hence, the title of this book: *Unstoppable*.

Asset-based financing is offered by banks, credit unions, insurance companies, government financial institutions, manufacturer finance companies, independent finance companies, and vendors. But asset-based finance is not the same as a classic loan. The industry complements the work of conventional lenders but stands alone as its own, alternative way of financing.

As its name suggests, asset-based finance is the financing of a specific asset—a vehicle or piece of equipment—commonly by way of a lease, loan, conditional sales contract, or line of credit. In the early days, this financing was chiefly available by way of a lease, but in later years, it has also been increasingly offered by way of a loan, conditional sales contract, or line of credit. The customer doesn't actually own the equipment or vehicle; the company owns it until the customer either buys it or returns it. The asset is the principal collateral for the customer's obligation to make regular payments.

This has implications for both the financing company and the customer. It affects the way a financing company decides on credit applications. The essential determining factor is not customer net worth, as it would be in conventional lending, but cash flow. Can the customer afford the monthly payments? Can the business customer generate sufficient revenue by using the asset? From the customer's point of view, this form of finance offers an advantage: it allows them to use vehicles or equipment without using up their regular bank credit.

Being both creative and complex, the industry's very nature demands a number of specialized skills from the people who work in it. First and foremost, they must understand the equipment or vehicle and its value at every stage of its useful life.

From receipt of the customer's credit application to the asset's return or repossession, the finance company must know what the asset is worth. This is crucial for the company to safeguard its position. In the case of a lease, finance companies must accurately forecast the value of the asset in the event they get it back several years later.

Second, finance companies build multiple relationships, not just with customers but with vehicle and equipment manufacturers, their distributors, and dealers. They do this both to gain a deep understanding of the value of the asset and to become an indispensable part of the selling process. By providing financing and specialized knowledge, they help the buyer to buy and the seller to sell.

In my years with the Canadian Finance & Leasing Association, I have admired the industry's professionalism and entrepreneurial drive and the sheer brainpower steering it all. Above all, the passion for business and commitment within this industry is remarkable. Very few people planned a career in this industry. Most found it by happy accident and prospered. But those who arrived mostly stayed, sometimes working together as colleagues or competing as rivals over thirty to forty years, changing companies as they were merged, consolidated, or closed. And companies were always re-emerging, with colleagues working under a new corporate banner, bringing their experience and expertise to boost and expand the business. When banks and credit unions offer asset-based financing, they usually entrust the job to people who have made their careers in this business.

In closing, I want to thank author Beth Parker and editor Bernard Simon, who have managed the challenging double feat of producing a book about a little-known industry that is both informative and entertaining. Beth started with a blank canvas because there is so little written about this business. Her extensive interviews with so many who have generously and enthusiastically given their support are yet another reflection of the people who played an integral role in this industry over the decades.

This book began as a project to mark the fortieth anniversary of the founding of the Canadian Finance & Leasing Association, the industry's trade association. But it quickly became much more: *Unstoppable* is a celebration of Canadian business at its best and of the Canadians who made it happen.

David Powell, President and Chief Executive Officer
Canadian Finance & Leasing Association
Association canadienne de financement et de location
Toronto, Ontario
September 2014

Preface

FROM THE START, it was clear that *Unstoppable: The Story of Asset-Based Finance and Leasing in Canada* would be a history told by the men and women who guided the industry from its inception. If nothing else, the research and writing for this project demonstrated that just because you can't find it with Google doesn't mean it didn't happen.

The process began over lunch with two successful, now retired Canadian businessmen, both in their eighties—Bill Bell, a former president of Pitney Bowes Leasing Canada, and Ben Young, former vice-president and part of the founding family of The Hamilton Group. Many interviews later, the pieces of a vibrant and fascinating industry began to take shape.

The most inspiring part was uncovering the qualities of the people who developed the industry. It is a story of pioneers, leaders, mentors, and inventors. Personal respect and professionalism permeate the industry, despite fierce competition and high pressure. In hindsight at least, most competitors were considered worthy opponents. Honesty and straight talk prevailed. There was no holding back of information or wrapping the industry in mystique.

The industry definitely has its heroes—and their counterparts: some successful in the short-term but fading over the long haul; others foolhardy opportunists who pushed the envelope too far, reflecting poorly on the industry and triggering government reaction. This is a business where serious profits are to be made and a lot of money could be lost. The temptation to increase risk for the sake of profit is described by some as a kind of addictive drug. Industry leaders, policymakers, regulators, accountants, and lawyers have laboured to understand the constantly evolving industry and bring order to aspects of its freewheeling nature.

Those interviewed presented a "warts and all" picture of what worked and what failed. When I asked billionaire Jimmy Pattison to comment on his tremendous success, he replied, "Well, I got a lot of scars on my back from doing the wrong thing." Yet there was always a pervasive sense of optimism—an ongoing "we'll work it out" attitude that emerged even when someone had bounced, by circumstances beyond his or her control, from acquired family business to merged conglomerate.

Finally, I can't emphasize enough the generosity of each individual in taking time to share information and explain it to a novice. These are busy people, many working at senior levels in Canadian banks and other financial institutions or running Canada's (and in many instances North America's) largest companies.

At the top of the list is CFLA president David Powell, who trusted me with the project and reached out to his vast network to encourage participation. During the course of my interviews, Powell was praised without exception for his intelligence, diplomacy, and leadership.

Roman Oryschuk, former vice-president of General Electric Company and the president and CEO of GE Capital Solutions

Europe, provided a "soup to nuts" picture of the industry. Stanley Hartt, one of Canada's most respected lawyers, businesspeople, and political thinkers, welcomed the challenge of explaining the 2008–09 global financial crisis. Steve Hudson candidly reflected on turning points in his remarkable—and still unfolding—career. So many of you patiently reviewed my emails that asked you, one more time, to explain ever-evolving leasing terms, interpret an arcane tax ruling, or recall a complex round of acquisitions. Without exception, your responses were prompt, helpful, and encouraging.

The effort was worth it. These are your stories, and they now represent a vital part of your industry's history.

Beth Parker

Acknowledgements

IN ADDITION TO the interviewees named below, the Canadian Finance & Leasing Association (CFLA) would like to thank Tracy Bordian, John Jackson, Liz Milroy, Doug Moore, Trevor Mosley, Sarah Scott, Bernard Simon, Geordie Smith, Robin Somerville, Gary Thompson, and the staff at the CFLA.

The following participants generously donated their time and expertise in the writing of this book:

Steve Akazawa
Peter Andrew
Angela Armstrong
Ginter Baca
Larry Baldesarra
Eugene Basolini
Bill Bell
Fred Booth
John Carmichael
Jim Case
David Chaiton
Al(bert) Clarke
Michael Collins
Moe Danis
Paul Frechette
Mike Goddard

Bob Graham
Barbara Hannesson
Stanley Hartt
Peter Horan
Bob Hunkin
Nick Logan
Serge Mâsse
Doug McKenzie
Larry Mlynowski
Ned Mundell
Jim Pattison
Tom Pundyk
Luc Robitaille
Debbie Sands
Tom Simmons
Hugh Swandel
Ben Young
Jim (James) Halliday
Jeff Hartley
Tom Hopkirk
Steve Hudson
Joe LaLeggia
Jack Marandola
Richard McAuliffe
Michael Meighen
Owen Moher
Roman Oryschuk
David Powell
Peter Ringler
Ron Rubinoff
Ralph Selby
Hugo Sørensen
Gordon Thompson

We have endeavoured to tell the most comprehensive story possible of the people and products that built and sustained Canada's asset-based finance and leasing industry. With little published information available, we have relied principally on the memories of those active in the industry over the years. If you notice an error or serious omission from the narrative—whether a person or an event—please email details and any relevant comments to **unstoppable@cfla-acfl.ca**.

chapter 1

Asset-Based Finance: A Pillar of the Economy

Take a look out at the highway; take a look at the trucks, trailers and cars passing by. Now ask yourself: What's in those trucks? The appliances, equipment, machine parts, vehicles, computers, network systems, microchips.... The leasing industry finances so much outside the financial world that people don't realize, and through the decades it has become part of every industry and come to support every business.

Richard McAuliffe, senior vice-president and chief operating officer, Key Equipment Finance Canada

MENTION ASSET-BASED finance and only a few Canadians will have any idea what you are talking about. Ask them what they know about leasing and they are likely to think no further than their car or the office photocopier.

Yet leasing and other asset-based finance techniques have been with us for a long time, becoming a pervasive part of our everyday lives. Some argue it started 4,000 years ago with the ancient Sumerians, who marked leases on clay tablets for agricultural tools, land and water rights, and oxen and other animals.[1] Canada's first telephones for commercial use were leased to Prime Minister Alexander Mackenzie in 1877. And until a 1982 regulatory ruling, Canadians were simply not allowed to have a telephone through any other arrangement except a lease.[2]

Today, estimated at $300 billion, **asset-based finance**, including leasing, is the largest source of debt financing to businesses and consumers in Canada outside of traditional bank and credit union lending. This form of financing has made a widespread contribution to economic growth and improved living standards. In both its 2004 and 2014 reports, the Centre for Spatial Economics examined the linkages between the financial services sector, productivity, and economic growth. The 2004 study concluded that CFLA member financing had boosted Canadians' living standards by 2.3 percent between 1992 and 2002, equal to about 8 percent of the total increase in Canada's living standards during that decade.[3]

Noting that the asset-based finance industry provides access to capital outside traditional banking, the report added that "the analysis ... confirms that, in the absence of the asset-based finance industry, capital formation would be adversely affected, growth in equipment investment would be lower—and Canadian living standards would suffer."[4]

Two of Canada's prominent economists agreed. Jim Stanford, chief economist for the Canadian Auto Workers union (now Unifor), and Jack Mintz, then chief executive of the C.D. Howe Institute, both reviewed the report. Mintz remarked:

> *This unique study overwhelmingly demonstrates the importance of asset-based financing to Canada's economic growth by supporting greater financial product choice and innovation. The industry contributes a disproportionate share to higher living standards.*[5]

Ten years later, the Centre for Spatial Economics completed another multinational analysis of economic data that further supported this conclusion. The 2014 study found that the $34 billion of new equipment and commercial vehicles financed in 2013 by the public and private sector is estimated in that year to have added $14.2 billion to Canada's gross domestic product (GDP), to have supported an initial 100,000 jobs for that year, and to have provided governments with an additional $4.3 billion in revenue. In subsequent years, the use of machinery, equipment, and commercial vehicles financed by this 2013 spending will each year add an average of $8.9 billion to the GDP, support 27,800 long-term jobs, and provide governments with an additional $0.7 billion in revenue.[6]

These figures speak directly to the strength and importance of this industry.

Dynamics of a healthy economy

Asset-based financing is an important determinant of investment spending, economic growth, and improved standard of living. Such forces are linked and asset-based financing is an important contributor to a healthy economy. Healthy, functioning financial markets are necessary to ensure that needed investment takes place so as to improve productivity, to support new jobs, and to raise the standard of living in Canada and for all other nations.[7]

Looking to asset-based financing? The choices are endless.

Driven by imagination and resolve, the scope of asset-based finance these days has almost no bounds. The everyday items we usually associate with this type of financing—cars, trucks, and office equipment—are far from the only items to be financed in this way. The ingenuity of this type of financing now extends to airliners, golf carts, turf-building equipment, ice-making machines, spa chairs, magnetic resonance imaging

(MRI) systems, railway cars, lobster traps, casket-lowering devices, dairy cows, hotel room key card entry systems, and fleets of branded delivery vehicles for everything from pizza to pet grooming. The list includes not only aircraft but the wheels attached to them; not only computers but the software that drives them, keeping wide swaths of the economy running smoothly and giving many companies their competitive edge.

And there is more. Asset-based finance companies have created a "one-stop shop" by adding an array of other useful services. A leasing deal now covers such essential services as repairs and maintenance, insurance, training packages, freight, installation, and technology upgrades covering both hardware and software. "We not only lease the trucks," said one company executive. "We provide the safety training for the drivers."

Unstoppable progress

A hallmark of asset-based finance is the industry's never-ending drive to renew and reinvent itself, regardless of the obstacles. Instead of stepping back when economic slowdown altered the business environment, leaders found ways to turn crisis into opportunity: new channels for credit were uncovered and visionaries launched new products and services. As Roman Oryschuk, chief executive of GE Capital Canada Equipment Financing from 1993 to 2003, noted, "The defining moments in the asset-based finance industry *have been* the economic recessions."

During the competitive 1980s, a new technique known as **securitization** further stimulated growth by reducing providers' cost of funding and diversifying risk among a broader group of investors. When the 1989 federal budget severely restricted **capital cost allowance (CCA)** benefits and created a more complex tax mechanism, industry leaders wasted no time in coming up with new strategies and marketing programs.

More recently, the industry staged a robust recovery from the damage caused by the 2008–09 global financial crisis. Initially tarred from fears spreading from other asset classes in the global securitization market, the industry stepped up to be part of the solution. Leaders were steadfast in their argument that the securitization freeze was caused by ripple effects from other corners of the financial markets, not by inherent defects in the industry. And as the story unfolded, history proved them right. Canadian business thrives because of the asset-based finance industry.

Financing options to business

Asset-based financing expands the financing options available to businesses in Canada. Without the ability to lease, many businesses would find it more difficult, more risky or impossible to acquire equipment. Consequently, business choice would be restricted to either buying the equipment and financing the purchase through internal or borrowed funds, or not acquiring the equipment at all.[8]

Setting the stage for financial innovation

Asset-based financing in North America has its origins in the quest by businesses to gain access to essential but costly equipment without having to rely on typically risk-averse and slow-moving traditional lenders.

Among the early pioneers were railroad companies, which turned to outside investors to finance their railcars. The railroads were not interested in long-term control or ownership of the railcars. So investors pooled their funds, bought the cars from the manufacturer, and then allowed the railroads to use them under short-term contracts in the form of "equipment trust certificates" or leases. At the expiry of a previously agreed term, the car and its title would revert to the investor, or lessor. Both sides benefited from these arrangements: the railroads gained the use of a piece of vital equipment for a fraction of its useful life and at a fraction of its total cost while the outside investors retained ownership and—most important—reaped substantial tax benefits.

Commercial lending vs. leasing

Commercial lending and leasing are different products, each with an important role to play in offering alternative forms of financing to Canadian businesses and consumers. Leasing is not simply a form of passive lending. It is a separate, very pro-active commercial discipline. It is an asset management–based business.[9]

Two big steps forward

The attractions of asset-based financing were immediately clear, but two additional factors played a big role in nurturing this young sector:

1. *Tax benefits*. Until 1976, Canadian and U.S. tax laws allowed 100 percent of lease payments to be treated as expenses for accounting purposes, thus making them fully tax-deductible. This meant companies could defer large amounts of taxable income through a capital cost allowance on lease portfolios and equipment purchases if they were considered to be the owner of the asset. Sometimes such transactions were carried out by wealthy individuals who would typically create consortiums among themselves by buying a costly piece of

equipment, such as an aircraft, and then leasing it to a company, such as an airline. Each investor could write off its portion of the purchase for tax purposes, a practice that worked particularly well on long-term assets.

2. *Banking laws.* Until 1979, the Bank Act kept Canadian banks out of leasing because regulators deemed the business to be too risky for financial institutions funded by individual depositors. These restrictions cleared the way for a group of imaginative and ambitious entrepreneurs to create other means of financing vehicles and other equipment. These pioneers helped spur the massive growth in asset-backed financing, especially in the second half of the twentieth century. The law was not relaxed until 1980, and even then it allowed banks to offer lease financing of equipment and large vehicles only, not passenger cars.

Acceptance and sales finance companies

"Big ticket" leasing, involving financings of $1 million or more, began as a specialty of acceptance companies (also known as sales finance companies), which were key players in the sector until the early 1980s.[10] They helped an ever-widening range of businesses finance the acquisition of costly industrial and transport equipment, including locomotives, ships, mining and logging equipment, buses, shipping containers, and aircraft. As described by Hamish Smith, who pursued big ticket leasing throughout his career in numerous asset-based finance and leasing companies, "Big ticket people have to think and innovate continuously. It's a thinking business."

The acceptance companies were not initially set up to handle lease transactions. General Motors, the venerable Detroit carmaker, formed the first acceptance company in Canada in 1919—General Motors Acceptance Corporation (GMAC)—to make new cars affordable to the average family. GMAC (since superseded by General Motors Financial Company) enabled GM dealers to offer instalment loans at a time when banks would not put up money for such a supposedly risky purchase. GMAC did business by buying unpaid customer accounts at a discount from dealers, then collecting monthly payments from the new car owner. As Bob Hunkin, whose father worked at GMAC from its beginning and remained there thirty-two years, explained, "The word acceptance stemmed from the concept that the accounts had been 'accepted.'"

First applied to vehicles and appliances, the acceptance business later spread to heavy industries. Acceptance companies gradually expanded their services from small loans and conditional sales contracts, which were considered a type of loan and therefore came with no tax benefits.

By the 1960s, most had added various forms of leasing,[11] under which they could claim the capital cost allowance as soon as they acquired the asset. Numerous sales finance companies had emerged by this time. The largest were Industrial Acceptance Corporation (IAC), Delta Acceptance, and the ill-fated Atlantic Acceptance Corporation; others included Canadian Acceptance Corporation, Traders Group, and Laurentide Financial Corporation (which set up Union Acceptance).

Their customer lists included governments as well as large industrial and transportation companies such as Canadian Pacific, Canadian National Railway, and Air Canada. At a time when the economy was expanding and business was thriving, leasing gave companies a way to meet their widening needs as well as shelter their growing profits from taxes.

Vehicle leasing

As a growing number of North Americans yearned for a car in the 1920s, the Detroit carmakers realized that they could greatly expand their market by extending credit to prospective buyers. GM led the way with its GMAC financing arm, followed by Ford and, finally, Chrysler. Henry Ford was a late convert, initially believing it was morally wrong to encourage Americans to take on debt to buy a car. GMAC, Ford Motor Credit, and Chrysler Credit (which became Chrysler Financial in 1984) not only made it possible for individuals to secure loans through a dealership but also gave the dealers a new source of income.

Two Americans, Zollie Frank and Armund Schoen, set up what is acknowledged to be the first vehicle **fleet leasing** businesses in the United States in 1939. Four Wheels (eventually changed to just Wheels) put cars being used by businesses on long-term (12-month) leases, based on their business strategy of "supplying cars to businesses and providing the support services required for their effective operation."[12] The idea of fleet leasing was rooted in the same concept as equipment leasing, namely, that motor vehicles were necessary equipment that many businesses required for operation. Three men—Duane Peterson, Harley Howell, and Dick Heather—who called their company PHH, set the stage for today's fleet leasing companies by combining maintenance and administrative support as part of the service. Peterson, Howell and Heather formed a partnership in 1946 and within the first year signed up two customers: Gibson Art Company and Johnson & Johnson.

As Mike Goddard, former senior vice-president and general manager of PHH Canada, explained, "Their concept was 'How can we take the concept beyond leasing and make it even more convenient and more productive for the driver?'"

Two years later, Stewart Holman and Frank Rice bought a Ford car dealership in New Jersey. They soon were approached by a client who needed a fleet of fifteen vehicles. The two friends created Automotive Rentals, Inc. (ARI) to provide the service. Later changed to Automotive Resources International, ARI remained a Holman family business, now in its third generation of ownership. That first client—Radio Corporation of America (RCA)—would one day be acquired by General Electric, coincidentally owner of one of the largest fleet businesses in the world.

Over the next two decades, the fleet leasing business flourished in the United States. In addition to PHH, ARI, and Wheels, others that emerged included General Leasing Co. in 1957, which would become Gelco; Service Leasing, set up by CIT (an abbreviation of an early and long since abandoned corporate name: Commercial Investment Trust[13]) in 1960; and Lend Lease, owned by Household Finance Corporation. They served the needs of companies that wanted to lease large fleets, and eventually, each moved into Canada.

In the United States, bank-owned and independent fleet lessors also served the needs of smaller companies looking to acquire a fleet of vehicles, or even businesses wanting to lease a single vehicle. The scenario was quite different in Canada. Here the dealerships drove the market, first by themselves and later with financing and administrative support from the carmakers.

General Motors' dealers, for example, had the option of financing their lease programs through a loan from GMAC, but some also enlisted bank financing to set up their leasing business. Independent dealerships that sold both Ford and GM models could seek financing from both Ford Credit and GMAC, in addition to their bank. In these instances, a dealer would have a facility for each brand; that is, in all cases, it was the dealership that took on the role of lessor. Particularly during the 1960s and early 1970s, the dealers handled the paperwork, did the billing and collections, and took back ownership of the vehicle at the end of the lease.

Although large fleet leases were still channelled through such companies as PHH and ARI, the dealerships also handled small corporate fleets (up to about ten vehicles) and almost all the consumer leases.

Competition came from acceptance companies and independent lessors that also set up vehicle leasing divisions. These companies, such as IAC, were indirect lessors. The dealer still showed the cars and negotiated the transaction directly with the customer. Before the lease was signed, the dealer confirmed with the leasing company that the latter was willing to accept assignment of the deal. If the deal was approved, the customer signed and the dealer sold the car and the lease contract to the leasing company. The dealer remained the principal point of contact for the customer, but the customer made payments to the leasing company. This legal model has remained largely unchanged.

The attraction of leasing was not lost on the carmakers, eager as they were to boost sales. They did not offer leasing directly to consumers in the 1960s and 1970s, nor did they compete with the large fleet management companies. Either through their financing arms or apart from them, each set up lease support programs for their dealers, such as GMAC's Retail Lease Service Plan and Ford Authorized Leasing System. Under these arrangements, the carmakers provided training, administrative tools, and wholesale discounts. They launched similar services for fleet management companies, such as GM's Fleet Distant Delivery Assistance Program.

The fleet business initially overshadowed consumer vehicle leasing in both Canada and the United States. Canadians in particular preferred to buy their cars either for cash or with the help of a loan. It was not until the 1980s, when carmakers realized that leasing could be a powerful marketing tool, that consumer leasing really took off.

Office equipment

By the early 1940s, International Business Machines (IBM) had become the world's leading office machine manufacturer. Its dominance was partly due to its enterprising decision to lease and rent typewriters, accounting machines, and other office equipment rather than only sell them, as its rivals did. During the Depression, when many companies could not afford to buy office equipment outright, IBM was willing to rent out its products for a monthly fee.[14]

It did not take long for other office equipment makers, such as Xerox, Pitney Bowes, and National Cash Register (NCR), to follow suit. They found they could boost revenues and bolster margins by charging a healthy interest rate on lease and finance deals. Leasing had a marketing benefit too. As technology evolved, the manufacturers could take obsolete machines out of circulation and replace them with newer models.

As with cars, the arrangements covered more than just the equipment. IBM and Xerox, for example, also offered insurance and maintenance packages, bundling the various charges into one monthly amount.

Conversely, many mid-sized and small businesses were attracted to leasing, not so much as a tax shelter or because they could not afford to buy the equipment but because it enabled them to keep abreast of the latest technology with a minimum of inconvenience. For customers, then as now, a key determinant was the monthly financing payment compared with the cost of buying. The 1960s and 1970s were a time, after all, of rapid evolution in office equipment, with the introduction of such labour-saving devices as computers, fax machines, photocopiers, and private branch exchange (PBX) telephone systems. No sooner had the first model come onto the market than an improved one became available. The stage was set for the later explosion in computer leasing.

Asset-based financing was also starting to catch on beyond the office, in factories, in mines, and even on farms. Farm equipment maker John Deere and construction machinery giant Caterpillar were among those that set up credit programs that evolved into flourishing leasing businesses. Like the office equipment makers and acceptance corporations, they understood the rich potential of offering customers financial services that banks were unable or unwilling to provide. By 1943, General Electric had set up General Electric Capital Corporation (commonly known as GE Capital), a natural evolution from its development of consumer financing eleven years earlier, when it unveiled the first electric dishwasher. It would not be until the late 1970s, however, that GE would start to take full advantage of the leasing market by offering tax shelters on equipment developed by GE and then leased by its financing subsidiary, GE Capital.[15]

Post-war transformation

The post-war baby boom brought a massive transformation in the way North Americans lived and worked—and the way office and industrial equipment was made and financed. Demand surged for the exploding range of consumer goods and services, from new cars and air travel to washing machines and vacuum cleaners. Manufacturers had to overhaul outdated operations, invest in new plants and equipment, and adapt to keep up with fast-changing tastes. The service sector grew rapidly, as did the emphasis on technology and intellectual property.

Financial markets were also in the throes of far-reaching upheaval. Prior to the Second World War, investment in business was generally confined to wealthy individuals and their families. Gradually, however, pension funds, insurance companies, and other pools of capital became more active and aggressive participants in financial markets. Mutual funds turned individuals' savings into a powerful collective force. America was soon "awash in post-war investment capital looking for returns."[16]

In Canada, foreign investors also became increasingly important players. Their money was often channelled through so-called "suitcase banks," that is, small branch or representative offices of foreign banks that may have been tucked away in an office building but still funnelled large amounts of money into the Canadian economy. Most of the "suitcase" operations were subsidiaries of such giant U.S. institutions as Wells Fargo, Citibank, Bank of America, Manufacturers Hanover, and Wachovia. Some of these banks, as well as some British banks, invested in established financial service companies, including some in the leasing sector. The capital they infused often provided the foundation for a spurt in the big ticket leasing business of the 1960s and 1970s, especially in the up-and-coming computer market.

Moving ahead in Canada

As in the United States, leasing in Canada was initially confined to a limited range of items, mostly transport and other heavy equipment, office machines, and motor vehicles. But the role of Canada's big banks, changes in tax laws, plus new macroeconomic and investment trends played key roles in the evolution of a distinct asset-based finance industry north of the 49th parallel.

At the beginning of the 1960s, Canadians witnessed the rise of a new group of entrepreneurs—independent leasing companies. During that period, businesses, even small ones, realized that there was an alternative to going cap-in-hand to a bank to finance the acquisition of essential equipment. And the emerging independents responded energetically to the demand.

chapter 2

The 1960s: Entrepreneurship, Leadership, and Vision

Neal Webster was a young dentist in the early 1960s, ready to set up his first practice in Hamilton, Ontario. But he was struggling to find a way to finance the chair, lights, and other specialized equipment needed for a dental office. He could not afford to pay cash, and his bank would offer only a high-interest personal loan.

Neal's brother, Max, who owned the nearby Queenston Motors car dealership, saw an opportunity to not only help the budding dentist but also make some money for himself. "If you can lease cars, why can't you lease dental equipment?" he asked. Within a year, Max and some friends had formed a partnership and set up Mutual Equipment Leasing Ltd., specializing in dental equipment.

When the partners ran out of money, they approached the Young family—Bill and his two sons, David and Ben—who owned The Hamilton Cotton Company, a local textile mill. At one time, textiles had been Hamilton's most successful industry; in the 1950s more people were employed there in textiles than in steel. But with Ontario mills coming under pressure from lower-cost factories offshore, the Youngs were looking to diversify.

As it happened, one of Ben Young's childhood friends, Ned Mundell, had spent the previous few years with United States Leasing International, Inc., North America's first independent leasing company, based in California. Mundell was setting up U.S. Leasing's new Canadian unit, Canadian Dominion Leasing, at the same time as the Youngs were looking for greener pastures than cotton. Ben Young talked to Mundell about "what this leasing business was all about," and the family decided to take the plunge.

Hamilton Cotton bought Max Webster's struggling company and renamed it Medi-Dent Services. Within two years, Medi-Dent was leasing equipment to dentists and doctors from coast to coast. And by the mid-1960s, the Young family was exporting its new-found leasing expertise to the United Kingdom and throughout Europe.

Although a move from cotton to financial services raised some eyebrows, it turned out to make sound business sense. The Youngs were experienced at securing funding for their business. They had built solid relationships with various banks and with two of the largest acceptance companies, IAC and Traders Group Ltd.

They also became masters in the art of credit—after all, the cotton business depended on it. The Hamilton Cotton customers transformed basic cotton textiles into retail products—curtains, underwear, bathrobes, and shirts, to mention a few—and they often needed credit from the manufacturers to finance their business until those finished products were sold into the marketplace.

A new generation of independents

The 1960s were marked by the emergence of a string of independent leasing companies.[17] Like Medi-Dent, many were built by entrepreneurs who brought together lessors, lessees, and third-party funders. They provided a package that also included maintenance, repair, and other value-added services. Profits came from the spread between the credit they arranged (often through funders like banks and acceptance companies) and the lease rate they charged. Like the acceptance companies, they reaped the tax benefits of big-ticket leases. These companies negotiated deals for equipment on behalf of their commercial clients. But they also found that the best way to get in front of a potential customer was to join forces with manufacturers, dealers, and distributors (known as vendors).

The model is akin to the three sides of a triangle: (1) the vendor, who could be a manufacturer or distributor, (2) the customer, and (3) the financing company. Each plays a key role. A salesperson from a vendor visits a potential customer who wants to buy a piece of equipment but is concerned about the upfront cost. The salesperson has learned the benefit of financing—often by attending a sales conference held by an independent—and knows how to use it as a sales tool. Typically, the vendor will have a standing commitment from the financing company, or the vendor will confirm acceptance by the financing company of the deal in advance. Then the salesperson offers the customer financing in the form of a loan or lease and the customer signs the deal.

The vendor ships the equipment directly to the customer, and on confirmation of delivery, the independent financing company buys the equipment from the vendor. The financing company retains legal ownership of the goods until the customer has satisfied all its obligations under the agreement. The vendor maintains a direct relationship with the customer even as the customer makes periodic—usually monthly—payments to the financing company.

Medi-Dent Services

The Medi-Dent pioneers were a fine example of the independent model at work. Dentists, especially new ones, need up-to-date equipment to open a practice. Medi-Dent realized from the outset that the path to success lay in persuading newly qualified graduates that the best way to start was to lease equipment rather than taking on the financial burden of buying it. In any case, banks have always been hesitant to lend to small start-up businesses. Medi-Dent salespeople made a habit of visiting dental schools close to graduation time, explaining to students that they could have all the equipment they needed right from the start and recover the cost gradually as their income grew.

"The two main distributors for the two main brands would be there as well," Ben Young recalled. "Even though they were competitors, it wasn't an issue and no one really worried about us favouring one over the other. We worked closely with the American and European manufacturers and distributors to help facilitate their sales in Canada."

The essence of Medi-Dent's presentation was to explain to the soon-to-be dentists that they could write off the cost of their equipment each year as an expense. "We got the accountants on our side because we could show on a cash flow basis that the dentist was better off with the arrangement," Young added.

Medi-Dent bundled other services, such as maintenance and repairs, into the leasing deals. It also became one of the first independents to include insurance. If the dentist had to take time off from the practice, lease payments could be suspended.

"What we provided was a worry-free arrangement," explained Young. "Apart from giving young dentists a set payment each month, Medi-Dent offered a six-month delay when they first set up. If they had a problem, we'd say, 'Let's work that out and see what we can do so you can get on with your practice.'"

The formula was so successful that Medi-Dent opened branches in every major city in Canada and leased equipment to 95 percent of new dental graduates. Although dental equipment was its main business, Medi-Dent also leased items to doctors who set up practices once they had completed school and established their specialty. "Surgeons didn't need a lot of equipment," explained Young. "But an ophthalmologist or general practitioner would, and we'd be the ones to get them set up with what they needed."

North America's first independent leasing company

Around the time that Medi-Dent began to woo dentists and doctors, the founders of U.S. Leasing in San Francisco and its Canadian subsidiary, Toronto-based Canadian Dominion Leasing (CDL), realized that that they could profit by putting together lease deals through their networks of equipment manufacturers and wealthy financiers.

U.S. Leasing, considered the first independent leasing company in North America, was the brainchild of Henry Schoenfeld and his two business partners. A forceful entrepreneur who reportedly seldom took no for an answer, Schoenfeld negotiated a pioneering deal in 1952 to lease equipment to a large food processor. U.S. Leasing grew out of that single deal, he told a newspaper reporter in 1975.

"We thought the company would have one deal and then would die," he explained. But after the transaction was completed, "someone heard about it and called.... That was the early history of the company. The telephone just kept ringing."

No one was more surprised than Schoenfeld himself. More than two decades later, he commented, "I'm still bewildered by the way leasing has caught on all over the world."[18]

Heading north: Canadian Dominion Leasing

One of U.S. Leasing's first employees was Brooks Walker, a classmate of Ned Mundell at Harvard. Walker enlisted Mundell, a Montrealer, to spearhead the company's expansion into Canada. Mundell opened Canadian Dominion Leasing's first office at 320 Bay Street in Toronto on June 1, 1959. Like its parent, CDL initially focused on office equipment. It began with addressographs and then moved on to accounting machines, described by Mundell as "the early iteration of mainframe computers."

Mundell and his bosses at U.S. Leasing initially found it difficult to drum up business from potential customers accustomed to buying equipment directly from the manufacturer.

"We came to the conclusion," Mundell explained, "that you could spend a lot of time explaining the advantages of leasing, but if the company wasn't acquiring equipment, the idea wasn't of much interest. So we decided that you would be much better off if you could put yourself in front of a customer actually looking to make a purchase. We started aligning with people that manufactured and/or distributed the equipment and already had a sales force. We then taught them to use leasing as a tool to sell more equipment.

"By 1961, we had picked up the business model that became prevalent in the United States and Canada going forward. It was called vendor leasing."

By 1963, CDL had opened branches in Montreal, Toronto, and Vancouver. One of the company's new hires was a young salesperson called Bob Graham, who had worked at one time for IAC. Graham was "discovered" selling typewriters for Remington Rand.

"One day, I did a presentation on leasing to a business school and landed three to four lease deals in one month," Graham recalled. "When CDL found out, they said, 'We better have a look at this guy,' and they hired me."

Graham encouraged his new colleagues at CDL to look on leasing primarily as a way of helping office equipment retailers boost sales. They began training the retailers' sales teams to explain the advantages of leasing and to promote a single monthly payment for the entire package.

"We emphasized the fact that customers would thank us for teaching them about the benefits of leasing," recalled Graham.

"Our advertising slogan was 'Don't put your money into equipment that depreciates. Put it into a sales effort that appreciates.'"

Graham went on to become CDL's longest-serving president. Under his leadership, CDL expanded across Canada, opening more branches, in Winnipeg, and then Halifax and St. John's. Graham remembers CDL as "a very respected company and very well liked because people were treated well." Succeeded by Jim Davidson, according to one contemporary, Ginter Baca, the two men developed one of strongest sales and marketing teams in the industry.

Meanwhile, Mundell returned to U.S. Leasing's head office in California in 1965, where he became chairman and chief executive. He remained there until the company was sold to the Ford Motor Company in 1987. Under his stewardship, U.S. Leasing was listed on the New York Stock Exchange and became the largest independent leasing company in the United States and among the largest in the world.

Vendor leasing was clearly here to stay. The strategy of joining forces with manufacturers and distributors to offer a valuable service to their customers would remain a key element of the asset-based finance business, especially for the independent companies.

Early leasing consulting

In 1959, a young accounting student at McGill University wrote a term paper for his chartered accountant final extension course. The topic was sale-leasebacks, and the student—Hamish Smith—earned an A on the paper. Smith was one of the very few who deliberately planned to enter the asset-based finance and leasing industry. After graduating, Smith worked as a lease consultant at Corporate Plan Leasing, a subsidiary of Banque de Paris et des Pays-Bas in Montreal. He then helped to set up the Canadian leasing division of Citibank in 1970. Smith was very interested in big-ticket leasing and played an important role in the evolution of the industry—particularly in big-ticket structured transactions. "My style," he wrote in his unpublished memoirs, "was constantly chasing high-quality big-ticket opportunities—elephant hunting." Among his accomplishments, Smith claims that he was the first to develop the Canadian leveraged investor lease, a form of capital (or finance) lease particularly suited to such big-ticket items as aircraft because the tax benefit of a well-structured leveraged lease reduced the lease rate significantly below what it would cost the customer to buy the asset in the first place.[19]

NABEL and The Hamilton Group of Companies

By the end of the 1960s, the fast-growing Hamilton Group included Medi-Dent, as well as Direct Leasing (which leased directly to businesses) and North American Business Equipment Ltd. (NABEL). Like Medi-Dent, NABEL started off as an independent leasing company in 1962 but with a focus on small office equipment.

Bill Bell, another young entrepreneur from Hamilton, was recruited to run the new company, with seven employees. NABEL started off leasing typewriters to business customers, then expanded into adding machines, punch card machines, and postage meters. Like Medi-Dent and CDL, NABEL forged relationships with specific vendors. It first aligned with IBM, but later Pitney Bowes would become its most important partner. Other giants of the office equipment industry, such as Gestetner, NCR, Burroughs, and 3M, soon signed up.

"Leasing was very new then," Bell explained. "A lot of legal firms were switching over to IBM Selectrics [electric typewriters] at the time, so we got a lot of big leases out of that. A $500 lease was a pretty good deal for us back then. Our people would call on IBM branches across the country and talk with sales people to get them to use leasing as a sales tool. Then we'd set up a lease for them."

Apart from arranging the lease, NABEL put together packages that included repairs, maintenance, and training for one all-in fee. Most businesses quickly adapted to the new model. There were few risks in short-term leases. On the contrary, customers could be sure of having access to the most modern technology when a lease came up for renewal, and they were covered for unforeseen repairs. Best of all, equipment costs were a predictable expense that could be written off against taxes.

"No one cared about the interest rate," Bell recalled. "They just concerned themselves with whether or not they could carry the monthly charge."

The essential customer calculation was straightforward and easily grasped: will the monthly increase in revenue generated by the new equipment exceed its monthly cost?

Eugene Basolini, president and chief operating officer at RCAP Leasing, was a young credit analyst at NABEL during this time. Basolini adjudicated such transactions and recalled, "Selectric IIIs were $1,265 for a five-year term. By financing such assets, we were helping companies adapt to new products and technology."

The independents grow and prosper

NABEL's expansion reflected the accelerating automation of offices—big and small—across Canada, starting with postage machines, typewriters, photocopiers, fax and telex machines, and later moving on to computers and software.

By the 1970s, Pitney Bowes had replaced IBM as NABEL's largest client. Bill Bell recalled, "We started with the leasing of mail machines at $250 per month, and it grew from there." At its peak, he estimated, leased equipment made up 85 to 90 percent of Pitney Bowes' total revenues in Canada, and 98 percent of its leases were arranged through NABEL. Bell remained at NABEL for nineteen years, spearheading its growth into one of the most successful independent equipment lessors in Canada.

The Young family's original textile business, Hamilton Cotton, faded in the 1960s and 1970s, like many other North American textile mills. But its leasing business flourished, becoming one of the largest in Canada and leaving a sizeable footprint abroad. By the mid-1960s, Bill and his two sons had set up Hamilton Leasing Ltd. in London, United Kingdom, followed by branches in Europe. IBM approached David Young to help it introduce vendor leasing to the United Kingdom in the mid-1970s, then asked him to do the same in France, Germany, Spain, and the Netherlands.

Big-ticket leasing expands and flourishes

Big-ticket leasing,[20] or large financing deals valued at many millions of dollars (typically the leasing of large assets such as aircraft, construction equipment or rail cars), was driven by the attraction of accelerated tax write-offs, made possible through the capital cost allowance deduction. With an expanding economy, the established acceptance companies started to add big-ticket leasing to their services and promote this type of financing to their clients.

Roman Oryschuk explained the modus operandi: "Leasing was for big-ticket, tax-driven, substantial transactions, where both finance companies and non-finance companies would purchase assets to lease to companies that didn't have the capacity to write off the cost of equipment for tax purposes. This was either because they had already maximized their allowed amount or because they didn't generate enough taxable income to make it worthwhile.

"So big-ticket transactions were either conducted by the finance companies that needed the tax shelter for themselves, or they'd find other industrial companies that were able to use the capital cost allowance and then lease the equipment to the companies that required that CCA."

Thanks to the tax benefits, the acceptance companies were able to offer leases at much lower rates than private investors and on par with or below those quoted by the banks.

"Leasing rates at this time appeared to be the same as borrowing rates from the bank because the tax advantage was so substantial," Oryschuk added. "People would finance those assets at a rate that would sometimes be 2 to 3 percent lower than the equivalent bank borrowing cost."

Industrial Acceptance Corporation (IAC), formed in the 1920s to provide credit for new car purchases, moved into leasing in the early 1960s. Bob Hunkin, who was IAC's assistant general manager of capital funds, recalled that the company's first leasing deal in 1962 involved a vessel to carry grain on the Great Lakes and the St. Lawrence River. The transaction was set up specifically to lower IAC's taxable income. Two or three other deals followed in quick succession for ferries in British Columbia.

In order to arrange the most tax-efficient leases, IAC employed tax specialists such as Owen Moher. Moher started his career at IAC in the 1950s, where he first met his mentor, Jack Otto. Moher remembered that "the leases we arranged were mostly long-term, for twenty years or so. They involved Canadian Steamship Lines and the elevator at Sept-Îles for the Iron Ore Company of Canada. Since all these pricing calculations were done on an after tax-basis, they were very complicated. Jack often asked to help him in checking the results."

Even so, as Ned Mundell had found at CDL, the acceptance companies initially encountered resistance to this new concept of equipment financing. Tom Hopkirk, who began his career at IAC and was later general manager of Barclays Bank's Canadian leasing operation, recalled, "If you phoned Canadian National Railway, they'd ask, 'Why would I want to lease?'" This hesitancy encouraged the acceptance companies to become more assertive in pointing out the advantages of leasing as a way of strengthening cash flow and as a tax write-off. Eventually, a substantial number of railcars were leased by the Canadian National Railway and a large proportion of major Canadian companies came to use leasing.

By 1964, an IAC advertisement boasted that the once slow-moving acceptance company offered "leasing, including leasing financing, equipment leasing and sale-and-lease back transactions.... Your business may be able to make profitable use of one or more of our services to augment working or fixed capital." Besides "business loans" and "capital equipment financing," the ad trumpeted, "Fleet financing for truck, trailer, bus and automobile fleets and other transportation equipment."

Traders: A touch of Canadian greatness

Traders Financial Corporation (Traders Group) became one of Canada's most important acceptance companies, owing its early growth largely to one of Canada's prime ministers, Arthur Meighen.

After losing the 1926 election, Meighen resigned as prime minister and subsequently retired as leader of the Conservative party. He received many invitations to join law partnerships and business firms, but the one that intrigued him most was from Watson Evans, founder and president of Canadian General Securities Limited, a Winnipeg-based investment company. Although born in Ontario, Meighen had worked in Portage la Prairie as a lawyer and later served as MP from Manitoba. He therefore knew the company directors and most of the shareholders.

Founded in 1920, CGS owned several subsidiaries including Traders Financial Corporation, which financed mostly trucks and automobiles. Although Evans saw great potential in the CGS, in the fall of 1926 he considered it "semi-developed" and "languishing for leadership with courage, ability and integrity."[21] In order to expand the company, including the important Traders' subsidiary, he looked to the intelligent, hard-working, and analytical Meighen. Not only was Meighen knowledgeable about public business, he also was known to command an audience with his powerful speaking skills.

Meighen accepted the appointment as general counsel and, as directed by Evans, the position was extended to "full participation in the management of the company." At the end of one year, or sooner by mutual consent, it was agreed that a sister company to CGS would be formed with its headquarters in Toronto (the office building erected in the fifties at 625 Church Street, with Traders Group etched in stone above the entrance, remains today).

Although Meighen's biographer acknowledged that the now 53-year-old former prime minister initially missed public life, he noted that Meighen "found himself genuinely absorbed in his duties ... of the rapidly expanding CGS. He became much engrossed in managing the investments of these enterprises, in studying the barometers of business activity and the fluctuations of the stock and bond market."

Meighen would also take the company through the 1929 stock-market crash, which nearly bankrupted it. The responsibility caused Meighen much anxiety, burdened with the knowledge that many modest investors had entrusted their funds to the company out of regard for him. His prudent management and long hours navigating CGS through the crisis paid off, and the worst was over within two years.

Upon the sudden death of Watson Evans in 1932, Meighen took on full management of both CGS and Traders. The same year he was appointed to the Canadian Senate, where, by all accounts, he balanced both responsibilities, accepting the position on the condition that he would only be in Ottawa when the Senate was sitting.

A recognizable figure, many Torontonians, including his young grandson Michael,[22] recall Meighen walking to work each day from his home on Castle Frank Circle to his office on Bay Street.

IAC's lasting heritage

Considered by many as a training ground for the industry, IAC also was responsible for the formal development of various lease documents and processes. The contribution included a library of leasing guidebooks, which the company placed in every IAC branch across the country.

Owen Moher recalled working on the project with lawyer Kevin Smyth, lead outside counsel to IAC. The various legal, indemnity, and amending agreements they developed included a master lease agreement for aircraft and heavy equipment and a motor vehicle lease agreement. The motor vehicle lease agreement provided car dealerships with their own lease plan, which put IAC in a better position to compete with independent fleet lessors, such as ARI and PHH. Once complete, each document was vetted by several legal firms.

Most of these documents would become the standard in the Canadian leasing industry—so standard, in fact, that, as Moher recalled, lawyers using them for their clients sometimes by mistake left IAC's name in the default clause.

Growing pains and stumbles

By the mid-1960s, Atlantic Acceptance Corporation had become one of the country's largest finance and consumer loan companies. Several employees had even left IAC to seek a more lucrative career at Atlantic. But on June 14, 1965, the mighty Atlantic Acceptance collapsed, unable to meet its obligations to its investors. As the story goes, the company had made loans to a flamboyant U.S. stock speculator, Louis Chesler, for the construction of a beach hotel and resort complex in the Bahamas. Much of that investment went sour, and Atlantic defaulted on $104 million to creditors, mostly Americans. The incident caused an international financial scandal and gave rise to a Royal Commission Report into its unsound lending practices.[23]

The commission would later reveal that the scandal represented a loss of between $70 million and $75 million. The incident shook the financial world. Loan and finance companies, including the acceptance companies, witnessed investors withdrawing funds and returning to banks to meet their borrowing needs. The finance and loan industry, led by the Investment Dealers Association of Canada, took action. By March 1967, minimum standards had been put in place for reporting for all finance and consumer loan companies doing business in Canada.

The fall of Atlantic Acceptance is a less-than-stellar moment in the history of acceptance companies. But its fall would influence the evolution of the asset-based finance and leasing industry, specifically the structure of liabilities and the quality of reporting on the activities of finance and consumer loan companies in Canada.[24] Over time, such evolutions in regulatory and accounting practices, led by "professional" pioneers in leasing and accounting, would serve to strengthen the industry's credibility.

Professional pioneers

The groundbreaking nature of asset-based financing, particularly in its early days, required innovative professionals who could structure these new transactions to pass the legal, accounting, and tax tests.

No commercial transaction could succeed without the blessing of the lawyers and accountants. They had to be equally as inventive at their jobs as their clients were. Lawyers such as Jim Bradeen, Don Bunker, John Penhale, and Kevin Smyth from Montreal and Vern Kakoshke and David Sharpless from Toronto paved the way as "Deal Counsels," as early industry swashbuckler Hamish Smith referred to them. Smyth was also a leader in the efforts of the International Institute for the Unification of Private Law (UNIDROIT) to harmonize aircraft leasing laws around the world.

Among the pioneering accountants was Ralph F. Selby, FCA, who literally wrote the book on leasing (*Leasing in Canada: A Business Guide*, Butterworths, March 1999). As one wag put it, "When God signed His first lease, Ralph Selby was holding His other hand." Tricia O'Malley, FCA, was an early specialist in leasing. She went on to serve twice as the chair of the Canadian Accounting Standards Board (from 1999 to 2001, and again from 2009 to 2010) and was a founding member of the International Accounting Standards Board in London, United Kingdom, from 2001 to 2007. John Jakolev, a former executive vice-president at Newcourt Credit, was a key part of the imaginative team there.

On the IT side, Jack Otto used one of the first computer programs on a Wang computer at IAC to speed up lease calculations. Described as brilliant but somewhat stubborn, Otto developed an early lease-pricing model, but would not revise the program when CCA rules changed, simply because he did not agree with them. "In discussions with various employees," noted one colleague, "Jack was brilliant, but he was never allowed to be involved with clients."

Both at IAC and then through Finance Technologies Incorporated, Owen Moher was involved in the migration of leasing processes to computer-based systems. Included among his achievements is the lease/buy/finance-decision system RUBICON.

Alan Bird and Mike Collins brought the first credit portal to Canadian auto dealerships. Nelson Lin built Newcourt's—and the market's—first online credit submission software.

Before the industry settled into more of a market mainstream, these professionals had to figure out how to get the early deals done, creating much of the framework for those to follow.

Leasing takes hold at car dealerships

Vehicle leasing in Canada also began in the 1960s, following the lead of U.S. companies in both fleet (also known as commercial) and consumer leasing. Before long, a flock of players had entered the field, including such U.S.–based giants as PHH, Lend Lease, and Gelco (which specialized in fleet management), as well as Canadian Vehicle Leasing (owned by CDL), CIT Service Leasing, and various dealerships such as Dueck General Motors in Vancouver and Elgin Motors in Toronto.

One of the first Canadian companies was City National Leasing, set up in 1957 by Jack Carmichael, a Toronto entrepreneur who had bought a small Buick dealership two years earlier. Carmichael saw U.S. fleet leasing companies in the Canadian market and was determined to compete with them. It was typical of the way the early fleet lessors evolved that there were no specific rules for setting up this kind of business. Carmichael also carried Frigidaire appliances, so, in addition to vehicles, the shop displayed refrigerators and stoves for lease. Al Clarke, hired as City National's president in 1968, recalled that the company focused especially on PHH and Service Leasing as its main rivals. City National Leasing would become one of Canada's largest independent dealer-owned fleet lessors, and Carmichael himself emerged as a leader of the fledgling industry. "Our success,"

Clarke said, "was related to the fact that we were well financed and that we were automotive people who understood our customers at the ground level."

Across the country in Vancouver, Jim Pattison also showed how an entrepreneurial businessman could make a mark in leasing. Pattison came to know the car business when he worked as a young man at Bowell McLean, known as BowMac, then one of British Columbia's oldest and largest car dealerships. BowMac's services included leasing. Pattison went on to buy a General Motors Pontiac-Buick dealership in Vancouver, and within a few months he was leasing cars to commercial accounts and individuals. GMAC provided financing for the dealership operation as well as wholesale lines of credit called "lease financing." In a manner that was typical of how the manufacturer–dealer relationship worked, Jim Pattison Lease had its own structure for setting rates and residual values, billing, and collections. As lessor, the dealership retained ownership of the car when it came back off lease and accepted the entire risk. This ensured a steady stream of inventory for future used-car sales.

"It was May 8, 1961," Pattison recalled. "On that first day of business, I leased one car—it was a Cadillac convertible to Vancouver alderman Frank Baker. Our lease statement when I went home that week said: 'One Car.'"

His business model was simple: use leasing to make money. By offering customers two- to three-year leases, a dealership could ensure that it had a continuous flow of used cars returning to the lot, which could then be resold. "All we were doing in the vehicle leasing business was manufacturing used cars," Pattison explained.

The key to a successful leasing operation was to know the customer and be able to calculate a car's resale value at the end of the lease. "You didn't make any money selling the new car," Pattison explained. "You made all your money, hopefully, on the used car when it came off lease.

"Everything depended on the resale value of the used car, based on where the car was going to be driven and how many miles were going to be put on it. It then gets back to how much you charge and what the car is worth when it's used and comes off the lease. It's that simple."

Pattison, a self-made billionaire, certainly made it seem simple. The Jim Pattison Group became one of Canada's largest privately held companies, having diversified far beyond car dealerships.

Pattison offered **closed-end, or "walk-away," leases**, which allowed a customer to return a car to the dealer at the end of the term with a right to buy it at a pre-arranged price but with no obligation to do so. Because cars were less reliable then than they are now, the leases typically included a full maintenance option over the entire term. These were known as wet leases because the maintenance included oil changes. Closed-end leases with a full maintenance program were most popular in the early days, although not all dealers offered them. They remain the dominant form of consumer vehicle lease to this day.

A typical lease in the 1960s included a base monthly payment plus a full maintenance option, as well as a per-kilometre charge if the driver exceeded an agreed mileage. Steve Akazawa, current president of Jim Pattison Lease, emphasized the simplicity: "All you needed to do was buy gas, insurance, and windshield wiper fluid. Cars broke down a lot in those days, so it was a very attractive deal. At the end of the term, you'd turn in the car and the dealership would get a used car to sell. The business model not only sold a lot of new cars, but it provided ongoing work for the repair shop, all paid for through the monthly premium."

Others set up similar operations in the mid-1960s. In Ontario, entrepreneur Roy Foss, another GM dealer, saw how the leasing model had succeeded in the United States and figured that it was a great way to sell more cars. Foss started leasing to his retail customers, using financing from both GMAC and his own bank.

He expanded into fleet leasing in 1972. Today, Foss National Leasing is Canada's largest privately owned fleet management and leasing company. It is also one of the few dealerships in the country that still arranges its own financing.

Auto manufacturers squeeze into growing leasing business

The Detroit carmakers' financing arms actively supported their dealers' leasing operations. Their programs were designed to help dealers enter the vehicle leasing business and compete against the large independent fleet-management companies. The carmakers also worked with fleet-management companies.

"We provided cars to clients like PHH, which then leased them to their customers," explained Tom Simmons, currently vice-president, eastern region, at Jim Pattison Lease and formerly Chrysler Leasing's controller and treasurer. "We also would network with dealers to try and get them to lease 100 percent Chrysler products. We did a lot of educating dealers about leasing back then."

The manufacturers did not initially lease directly to fleet owners. Their role was to educate dealers about the benefits of fleet leasing and to help them secure a credit line from the bank or the carmaker's own financing arm. GMAC, Ford Credit, and Chrysler Credit could all offer dealers access to wholesale (discounted) lease lines and wholesale financing to support the cost of vehicles on the lot, awaiting sale. It was a critical role because although banks also offered financing, many dealers knew, often from first-hand experience, that the banks could be fair-weather friends. When times became tough, the banks saw a greater risk that vehicle sales would drop, thus endangering the dealers' creditworthiness, and financing would be withdrawn. Seeing an opportunity, the manufacturers smartly moved into dealer financing.

The carmakers stayed out of direct competition with their dealers. For the most part, they also did not compete directly with the independent fleet leasing companies. Their own programs for direct leasing to consumers would not become a factor for another decade. There was one exception. In 1965, Chrysler Leasing decided to move into direct fleet leasing, selling full-service and maintenance leases directly to business customers. According to Simmons, Chrysler was the only carmaker in Canada at the time to attempt this, but the plan backfired. Its major fleet-management account, PHH, complained that the carmaker was setting itself up as a competitor. A year later, Chrysler retreated from direct leasing.

As more dealers entered the leasing field, tensions mounted between them and the Detroit carmakers. Many, like Roy Foss and Elgin Motors in Toronto had built up their own finance portfolios and valued their independence. Signs were also growing that the manufacturers were preparing to enter the consumer leasing market with their own rates and schedules. The dealers would no longer own the vehicles that they leased.

While many dealers saw the carmakers' entry as an encroachment on their turf, there was a silver lining. The move helped build a greater awareness of leasing and its benefits. Over the next twenty years, auto leasing ballooned in Canada through car dealerships, specialized vehicle leasing companies, and general leasing companies that added a vehicle component to their business.

Leasing at the end of the 1960s: Surviving … and thriving

The formation of Canada's first independent leasing companies, CDL and The Hamilton Group, and the emergence of vehicle leasing through dealers such as Jim Pattison and Roy Foss marked huge steps forward for the fledgling leasing business.

The model used by these pioneers was an early indication of the industry's muscle as it joined forces with suppliers of household-name goods and gained expertise in a widening range of office, industrial, consumer, and professional equipment. NABEL and CDL had demonstrated from the start that leasing office equipment could bring tremendous benefits to individual businesses and, by extension, to the economy as a whole. The advantages would be underlined as the typewriters, photocopying machines, and other 1960s-era office equipment began to make way for sophisticated and highly productive computer and telecom technology. As Medi-Dent and its U.K. subsidiary prospered, the leaders of the fledgling Canadian industry were also exporting their expertise and gaining international recognition.

On another front, Jim Pattison and others had the foresight to realize that leasing was a powerful incentive for prospective car buyers. Besides spurring demand for new models, it could guarantee a flow of used-car inventory and ensure a steady cash flow through a sustained maintenance and repair business.

The acceptance companies made a valuable contribution to asset-based financing. They added credibility; became a training ground for many future industry leaders; and in many instances were now a key source of capital for entrepreneurs, independent leasing companies, and brokers seeking to negotiate leasing deals.

Tom Hopkirk, who worked as a financial analyst at IAC, credits an astute IAC branch manager in Sudbury, Ontario, for taking a chance on a young businessman who needed financing for two new buses. Paul Desmarais went on from the bus business to build Power Corporation, one of Canada's most powerful and internationally respected companies.

The pioneers' ability to forge lasting relationships with their customers had set the stage for sustained, long-term growth. Leasing was clearly here to stay.

Turning used assets into cash and data

By 1954, tractors outnumbered horses and mules on North American farms. It was a sign of the times. In addition to the mechanization of agriculture, manufacturers—including automakers—were modernizing their processes, installing new equipment and machinery in response to increased spending on consumer goods and a steady rise in car ownership.

A natural by-product was a growing inventory of used equipment and vehicles, particularly as leasing emerged as a means to acquire more, different, or newer equipment and vehicles. The assets were still valuable, but in most instances they were surplus or had come "off lease"; occasionally, they had been repossessed.

One solution started in a modest, Canadian way. In 1958, three brothers from Kelowna, British Columbia, held an auction at their father's furniture store to pay back a bank debt. That day, Ken, John, and Dave Ritchie turned surplus inventory into $2,000 of cash. The Ritchie brothers soon expanded beyond furniture. Their first major industrial auction in 1963 brought in $600,000. Before the end of the decade, the Kelowna three had expanded into the United States; by the late 1980s, Ritchie Bros. Auctioneers was a global company. By 2012, with 44 auction locations in 13 countries, Ritchie Bros. sold U.S. $3.9 billion of equipment at 328 auctions.

From the beginning, Ritchie Bros. offered unreserved auctions—meaning there are no minimum bids and no reserve prices. Each item is sold to the highest bidder at the auction location the day it is held. This "real-time aspect" continues today—online. A typical auction features millions of dollars of equipment and trucks and thousands of bidders from around the world—many participating at their computers. The process was made even more seamless in 2011, when a joint venture between Ritchie Bros. and Travelers Group, Ritchie Bros. Financial Services, provided customers with a way to be pre-approved for leasing or financing before placing their bids globally.

From that first auction at the furniture store, Ritchie Bros. became the world's largest industrial auctioneer as well as a valuable contributor to the Canadian asset-based finance and leasing industry.

Long-standing industrial auction houses such as Ritchie provided companies in the industry with a valuable and efficient process for end-of-term and repossessed asset disposition. But their value goes even deeper. Historic values from auctions around the world establish current mark values, historic values, and historic depreciation. Such information is critical for carrying out asset valuations when determining credit, estimating residual value, or assessing risk.

Innovation in finance

Although leasing may not yet have been widely entrenched in Canada at the end of the 1960s, its influence was gradually spreading. The drivers for future growth were in place, including a cadre of far-sighted entrepreneurs—Bill Bell, David and Ben Young, Jim Pattison, Jack Carmichael, Roy Foss, and others—who were eager to thrust into the unknown and willing to take risks. The industry was also spawning new ideas for meeting the needs of a modern nation. This was demonstrated by the success of the Ritchie brothers, who saw an opportunity in used assets coming into the market and began to accumulate valuable data that the industry would come to rely on for decades to come.

Ned Mundell summed up the freewheeling spirit that infused the industry: "In the early days of the leasing business there were no rules. You were free to try anything because you weren't tied down with traditional patterns or rules.... This meant you were free to innovate."

The mantra, as Mundell saw it, was "What do we need to create now?" as opposed to "Business as usual." Ben Young added: "The guys in the leasing business were always very entrepreneurial."

The spirit that imbued the industry's early years would also be a hallmark of its future growth. Entrepreneurship, vision, and leadership would enable the three pillars of the new industry—independent leasing companies, the evolving acceptance companies, and far-sighted car dealers—to seize the opportunities that lay ahead. As observed by Roman Oryschuk, "As Canada has innovated, the leasing industry has followed that innovation very quickly and adapted to the needs of Canadian business."

These qualities would also help the industry confront two looming challenges: revisions to the *Income Tax Act* that would threaten one of the main underpinnings of leasing and demands from Canada's big banks to enter the leasing business through their own subsidiaries.

chapter 3

The 1970s: Resilience, Determination, and Optimism

After twenty years at IAC, Bob Hunkin decided to follow his entrepreneurial instincts. He accepted an offer in 1972 to run a start-up leasing company, Canadian Pacific Leasing Ltd. Known as CanPac. The fledgling company was a subsidiary of Canadian Pacific, the railroad-turned-conglomerate, which had decided that a leasing arm would make a useful adjunct to its forestry and airline interests. Hunkin was soon joined by two other IAC employees, Dave Blunt and Ron Dinsdale.

The CanPac team, as well as their bosses at CP, were delighted with their success during their first four years in business. But their growth strategy was abruptly derailed at the end of 1976, when Royal Bank of Canada and Canadian Imperial Bank of Commerce (CIBC) rocked the leasing industry with competing takeover bids for CanPac.

The bids were triggered by an imminent change in the Bank Act that would allow banks to enter the leasing business through their own wholly-owned subsidiaries. "With banks preparing to get into the leasing business, we knew CanPac couldn't compete," Hunkin explained.

Hunkin wrote a long letter to his boss, explaining why he didn't believe CanPac could maintain the growth he and his colleagues had targeted. His unhappy boss passed the message on to Ian Sinclair, Canadian Pacific's chief executive.

"You're right on the nose there, Bob," Sinclair replied. "There is no damn way we can compete with the Royal."

A deal was struck soon after. Royal Bank took over CanPac Leasing, merged it with a 10 percent share it already had in Royal Marine Leasing, and renamed the combined company RoyLease Ltd. Hunkin recalls the day, February 1, 1977, when the deal closed: "That date always stands out in my mind."

Leasing draws attention

By the start of the 1970s, leasing was firmly entrenched in corporate Canada as an effective way to reduce taxes as well as extend market reach and boost sales. For the acceptance companies, the promotion of big-ticket "tax leases" meant coming up with more and more of what Tom Hopkirk described as "neat leasing deals, with creative ways of putting them together."

The market was becoming increasingly competitive for the independent leasing companies and smaller equipment suppliers. Players involved in vendor leasing, large and small, expanded aggressively by providing additional services and leasing packages to keep ahead of the competition. Many added new specialties. For example, CDL set up two new companies: Canadian Vehicle Leasing, to give it a foothold in the fast-growing car-leasing business, and Canadian Medical Leasing, led by Murray Sutherland, which would become a rival to Medi-Dent.

Another new entrant came on the scene in the form of First City Financial Corp, controlled by Vancouver's Belzberg brothers—Samuel, William, and Hyman. The family holding company set up Pacific Leasing Corporation in the early 1970s for equipment leasing. In a 1972 article in the *Montreal Gazette*, Sam Belzberg boasted how well the leasing division was doing, with income in the first six months totalling $407,701.[25] Two years later, the company was renamed First City Capital and took advantage of the next evolution in office technology. With the introduction of magnetic cards and then floppy disks, Selectric typewriters could now save data to print later. First City Capital was one of the first small-ticket leasing companies to embrace the financing of early word-processing equipment and computers. Such niche expertise fuelled its growth into the next decade. The company expanded in 1986, adding the financing of transportation and construction equipment to become a mostly mid-ticket lessor. Gary Thompson, executive vice-president of Travelers Financial, started his career at IAC and then joined First City in 1981. "First City had a very good corporate culture," he said. "And it was a ton of fun working there."

The Big Three carmakers also took notice as more of their dealers used leases to drum up sales and create a steady supply of used vehicle inventory. Likewise, as offices moved into the age of computers, photocopiers, and automated phone systems, business equipment vendors such as IBM and Pitney Bowes were eager to get a bigger slice of the leasing action for themselves.

With the growth in leasing also came a burgeoning demand for talent. People with leasing expertise—or the potential to acquire it quickly—were hot commodities. One of Bob Hunkin's first hires at CanPac was Roman Oryschuk, a bright, young official in the City of Montreal's treasury department. Oryschuk would go on to run GE Capital Canada Equipment Financing, later GE Capital Solutions Europe, and eventually become a vice-president of General Electric. Similarly, an up-and-coming Montreal entrepreneur, Serge Mâsse, joined the Canadian Acceptance Company in 1973 as a credit analyst. Mâsse would remain in the leasing business for almost thirty years, and then form his own specialty company, FinTaxi, which helped Montreal cab drivers finance their taxi permits. On the West Coast, Jim Case joined Citibank Leasing in 1979, where he put together third-party leasing deals for one of the country's largest office equipment vendors. Committed to the industry and what it offered Canadian businesses, Case founded Lease West in 1987, which became Travelers Financial Corporation. As president and CEO, he grew the business to become one of Canada's largest privately owned asset lease and finance companies. (In April 2014, the equipment and vehicle finance assets of TFC became part of the Coast Capital Savings Group of Companies.)

Some leasing company employees, eager to be their own bosses, set up shop as brokers, spawning another branch of the business. The brokers brought together financial institutions and equipment users on a commission basis. Many brokers started off by using the leasing documents of their former employers, functioning in practice as an outsourced sales department. Before long, however, they had beefed up their backroom expertise so that they could negotiate with various lessors for the best terms.

Leasing was also catching the attention of policymakers and regulators. By the early 1970s, Canadian banks were eager to use the regular ten-year review of the *Bank Act* to gain entry to the leasing business. Separately, the federal department of finance was about to review the entire capital cost allowance system, one of the drivers of leasing's fast-growing popularity.

Five trends in particular were strengthening the industry:

1. the emergence of leasing companies as equipment experts,
2. the creation of "captive" finance and leasing operations to help move their parent companies' products,
3. the proliferation of leased products and leasing services,
4. the growth of vehicle fleet leasing, and
5. new business models.

The industry increasingly realized that it needed to make its voice heard in a more organized and effective way. The result was the formation, in 1973, of the Equipment Leasing

Association of Canada (ELAC) to speak on behalf of equipment lessors. ELAC was followed six years later by the Canadian Automotive Leasing Association (CALA) as an advocate for lessors specializing in the auto market.

The emergence of leasing companies as equipment specialists

Lessors needed to have confidence in the products they were financing. After all, those products were their primary security. Therefore, the successful ones made a point of learning as much as they could about the items they financed—which brands and models were reliable, which ones to avoid, and so on. They also needed to maintain close contact with manufacturers so that they could gain the expertise needed to properly assess sale prices and re-marketing or "residual" values.

"Leasing companies became very good at knowing how to lend," explained Tom Hopkirk. "They knew the industry, they knew all the vendors, and they knew the equipment because that was their collateral.

"Sure, banks knew about receivables and inventory, but a leasing company knew that Caterpillar equipment, for example, had a life of a certain number of years. It meant that lessors were aware of exactly what they were getting into, the good brands and the unreliable ones."

A leasing company's specialized knowledge of equipment was equally valuable to banks and other funders that provided credit to the smaller, independent lessors. Such expertise provided comfort to a funder that a lessor would not be stuck with unwanted equipment. If the lessor had to repossess that equipment, it would at least have some value.

"You could lend water to Canadian Pacific and know that you'd get your money back because CP had a good corporate credit rating," Hopkirk observed. "But if you were financing equipment for a small company, you really cared about what they were acquiring. It had to be integral to their needs because you got paid on the basis of that equipment generating cash flow."

The three-way relationship between lessor, vendor–manufacturer, and customer was clearly a smart way to do business. It gave end-users access to a knowledgeable sales team as well as a way to finance equipment predictably and—usually—affordably. At the same time, leasing gave vendors a valuable marketing tool because they could offer financing to their customers packaged with useful extras, such as insurance and maintenance. Independent leasing companies had an extra advantage, as they saw it: they were able to finance equipment on the merits of the item being leased and the business strength of the lessee, without being tied to one vendor or credit source.

The creation of captive finance and leasing companies

It was not long before manufacturers saw the advantages of leasing and wanted a bigger piece of the pie. They realized that they could boost sales and gain more face-to-face contact with customers by arranging the financing themselves. Their "captive" finance arms typically confined their business to customers of the parent company's authorized dealers. At the same time, the captive finance companies drew strength from their intimate knowledge of the equipment and its capabilities, as well as their close relationship with the manufacturer. Over time, the captives would become more heavily involved in product planning and marketing. These arrangements also gave the manufacturer a measure of protection over its proprietary technology.

Vendor equipment finance programs

The top priority of a vendor (whether a manufacturer, distributor, or dealer) is to sell, sell, sell. But pushing up sales can become more complicated if customers want to acquire equipment immediately, but pay for it over an extended period. Where will the credit come from to support such transaction? And who is willing to take on the risk?

Some well-capitalized manufacturing and service companies may provide such financing by leveraging their own equity base and core competencies rather than turning to third parties. As a result, some vendors established their own financing arms or partnered with others to manage this side of their business. In the latter case, the vendor joins forces with one or more finance companies to offer financing to its customers. The finance company makes it clear what level of customer creditworthiness it requires to accept the risk of not being paid.

The vendor agrees to make the equipment available to the customer, offers a finance option, and then submits a customer credit application to the finance company. If the credit application is accepted by the finance company, a purchase order is issued and the vendor delivers the equipment to the customer and obtains payment from the finance company once the customer confirms delivery. At the end of the lease term, the customer either buys the equipment, returns it, or refinances it.

If the vendor controls the entity making the financing arrangements, that company is known as a captive. Captive finance companies range from mid-sized entities to giant firms. Their range of services varies widely, from basic card services to full-scale banking.

In the automotive sector, Ford Motor Credit, GMAC, and Chrysler Credit (which became Chrysler Financial) were all set up as captive finance companies. Large manufacturing captives in other sectors include IBM Global Financing, Xerox Finance, John Deere Credit, GE Capital, and Caterpillar Financial.

Typically, captives limit their business to customers of their parents' authorized dealers, and they only finance sales of their parents' own products. But some have broadened their horizons. GE Capital, one of the world's biggest industrial finance providers, for years did not primarily finance GE products, even though it is a wholly-owned GE subsidiary.

White label programs

If a manufacturer, dealer, or distributor chooses not to set up its own financing operation, it may partner with an independent financing company in a "white label" program. Unless they read the fine print on a sale or lease contract, end-users would typically have no idea that the finance was being provided by anyone but the vendor. Trexar, for example, was set up by Citibank in the 1980s to provide financing plans for foreign carmakers, such as Honda Canada.

The business of vehicle leasing

Vehicle leasing was becoming an increasingly attractive business not only to carmakers but also to major financial institutions. In its early days, the market was mostly commercial, involving corporate and government fleets of all sizes, from one vehicle to hundreds or even thousands of cars and delivery trucks.

About a dozen independent leasing companies each had fleets of 5,000 vehicles or more on their books. Some were offshoots of a U.S. parent, such as PHH, Gelco, or Service Leasing. Others were controlled by car dealerships, including City Buick Pontiac Cadillac (City Buick), Humbertown, Cross Canada, and Roy Foss in Ontario; Jim Pattison Lease, Dueck, and BowMac in Vancouver; Wheaton Group in Edmonton;

Birchmount Pontiac Buick in Winnipeg; and Hartford Chieftain in Calgary. These "dealer-based" lessors competed successfully in the Canadian market, and several grew into large and diversified enterprises.

The independent fleet lessors and large leasing companies dealt mostly with government, utilities, and large corporations. These big customers were usually able to negotiate favourable pricing. They also expected a level of sophistication in putting together lease contracts and arranging delivery and servicing.

Leasing at the smaller dealer level was in those days confined mainly to one or two company vehicles, and seldom more than ten. This type of leasing became very popular with dealerships across Canada because, as Jim Pattison noted, "it was a great way to manufacture used cars." Consumer leasing was not common because banks at that time provided the necessary credit for individuals to buy new vehicles and consumer tastes were still more modest than they were to become.

Leading Canadian fleet lessors in the mid-1980s, with estimated fleet sizes:[26]

CIT Service Leasing	30,000
PHH	22,000
City National Leasing	13,000–15,000
Gelco	7,500
Lend Lease	7,000
Foss National Leasing	5,500
Jim Pattison Lease	5,500

Almost all the dealer-based lessors provided closed-end leases, which allowed the lessee to return a vehicle at the end of the lease and either walk away or buy the vehicle for a pre-arranged sum. By contrast, the larger U.S.–owned companies, such as PHH, typically offered only **open-end leases**. In open-end leasing, the customer is responsible for covering any shortfall between the pre-arranged residual value and the price at which the lessor sells the vehicle to someone else.

Direct and indirect lessors

The vehicle business was divided from the start into direct and indirect leasing. In a direct lease, a car dealership negotiates the lease directly with the customer. The dealership typically buys the vehicle with the help of financing from the manufacturer's captive finance arm. As the lessor, the dealer retains title to the asset and assumes all financial risk and related liabilities. At the end of the lease term, the customer either buys the vehicle or returns it to the dealership, in which case the used vehicle is resold to another customer or to another dealer directly or through an auction house.

Independent fleet leasing companies could also operate as direct lessors. They obtain funding from a finance company or bank and then buy vehicles from a dealership. They own the vehicles, directly administer the lease, and deal face-to-face with the fleet operator customer.

In an indirect lease, a business customer looking to lease a fleet of vehicles would choose its preferred models, perhaps following a visit to a dealership, but the paperwork was handled by the independent leasing company. If a customer required vehicles across the country, the leasing company made arrangements to buy vehicles from dealers located where they were needed. As the indirect lessor, the leasing company retained title to the vehicles and took responsibility for them when the lease expired. The indirect lessor also set up and administered the lease and collected payments.

Indirect leasing enabled financing companies and carmakers with captive finance arms to share in the burgeoning leasing business. Although consumer retail leasing was not common in the late 1970s, Industrial Acceptance Corporation added it to its offerings to compete with Ford Motor's retail leasing program, known as Red Carpet. As explained by Tom Simmons, who worked in vehicle leasing most of his career, "IAC set the formula for lease rates so that the dealership could quote the deal to the customer. IAC purchased the vehicle and the lease contract from the dealer and took over all the billing and collecting.... All the dealership had to do was sell the deal on the floor and, after the sale, provide customer support."

According to Owen Moher, who helped develop the competitive motor vehicle lease agreement, the arrangement allowed the dealerships to keep control of their customers. It also pre-emptively counteracted expected changes in the *Bank Act*. Once in place, the innovative idea turned IAC into one of the fastest growing vehicle leasing companies in Canada.

Growing pains as industry expands

Car dealerships faced a couple of challenges as the 1970s unfolded. Smaller dealerships that offered leasing on a modest scale found themselves in tough competition against the fleet management companies. Because of their size, the fleet specialists could negotiate directly with the carmakers for generous discounts and incentives. Many had developed sophisticated processes for their corporate clients, investing early in mainframe computer systems. Al Clarke, president of City National Leasing, recalled the company's first computer—a Wang similar to the one Jack Otto was using—which was advertised in the mid-1970s as a "Statistics and Number Crunching Computer."

The paperwork involved in setting lease rates, drawing up lease contracts, collecting payments, and so on was an administrative burden that took valuable time away from what dealers did best—selling cars. Most were not trained in the intricacies of lease financing or marketing.

The dealers were also constantly exposed to the risk of calculating residual values to ensure that they were not out of pocket at the expiry of a lease. Jim Pattison put the challenge bluntly: "Credit is a big deal. Let's say you're leasing to a smaller company like Jimmy's Paint Shop. The shop has been in business six months, has no capital, and wants a bunch of cars. So Jimmy goes with a small deposit and leases the cars, but then goes out and damages some of the cars. Then he can't make his payments. As the dealer, I then have to seize the cars, but now I will lose a lot of money.... I've seen all of this happen."

The Big Three step in

The captive finance companies, GMAC, Ford Motor Credit, and Chrysler Credit, played a key role in providing financing for dealerships. Their support was especially valuable to smaller dealerships, those unable to obtain bank loans, or those unwilling to risk dealing with a bank that could call in a loan if market conditions changed.

Through these captive financing arms, the carmakers set up various support and marketing programs to help dealers promote their vehicles and use leasing as a forceful—and highly effective—sales tool.

One of the earliest such programs was the Ford Authorized Leasing System (FALS), launched by Ford Motor Credit shortly after it moved into leasing in 1958.[27] Ford's entry into the leasing business was spearheaded by the carmaker's then-president Robert McNamara, who later became U.S. secretary of defence under presidents John F. Kennedy and Lyndon B. Johnson. McNamara agreed that the potential benefits of leasing far outweighed the drawbacks.

Not surprisingly, the main purpose of the FALS program was to help Ford dealers move cars off their lots. FALS-affiliated dealers were trained in all aspects of leasing, with particular emphasis on marketing. As a FALS member, a Ford dealer had access to a leasing system certified by the parent company, a valuable marketing tool.

Ginter Baca, president and CEO of Lease Administration Corporation, recalled FALS because it was in use at Elgin Motors, the Ford dealership where Baca landed his first job out of university.

"Someone at Ford in the United States saw movement by individuals towards leasing and took the initiative to support their dealer network and internal sales objectives by creating FALS," surmised Baca. "FALS helped dealers move product because it was always about moving product. The value Ford brought to the table aside from its own resources and knowledge was a template that included documents and processes to facilitate dealer leasing. I believe dealers arranged their own financing but were required to report their progress to the FALS system."

Dealers such as Elgin, however, held their own lease portfolios, which meant they did not have to depend solely on the captive, Ford Motor Credit. According to Baca, it was quite common to use FMC only for the contracts they didn't want.

"Ford Motor Credit dealers, being as smart as they were, began using the Ford system to credit review contracts. But they kept the best ones for their own book," he added. "That's one of the reasons successful dealer principals were known as horse traders!"

Although carmakers were content to stay out of direct leasing for fleets, they were eager to take on this business on the retail side. Ford's Red Carpet program was designed to help consumers lease a car from a dealership but forcing the deal through its own captive. Dealerships still marketed the lease, but all the paperwork, billing, and collections went through Ford Motor Credit, which was also the contractual lessor.

GMAC also realized that most GM dealerships were not set up to handle the paperwork and administration involved in retail leasing. But it recognized the potential of a "one-stop" service and came up with its own variation, the Retail Lease Service Plan (RLSP), to provide loans or leases to business and retail customers.

Peter Andrew, GMAC Canada's former general director of operations and now national operating officer at Royal Bank of Canada's RBC Automotive Finance, explained, "GMAC saw a need at this time for GM lease products because dealers usually didn't have the facility to fund the lease, bill it, and collect the money.

"As part of its sales strategy, GMAC decided to make it easier for dealerships to offer GM products. The RSLP program gave dealers a formula for setting the residual value and quote for customer payments. The dealer could price a lease more easily and then assign it to GMAC and we'd bill the customer. The dealer got the money up front and remained the lessor under the agreement."

Retail leasing—dealerships move over

Although GMAC's RSLP program was slow to take off, it eventually became very popular. The name was later changed to Direct Lease and then SmartLease. Under SmartLease, GMAC took over ownership of the vehicle during the lease term and dealer liability was eliminated. Such retail lease programs moved dealers away from financing and back to their core business of selling cars. Instead, they received a percentage of the deal from the captive or independent leasing company. This evolution was a critical step in the vehicle leasing business and would be emulated by many others.

These new arrangements received a mixed reaction from dealers. Smaller ones were content to give up a direct role in leasing. But others saw the manufacturers as rivals and started to push back, building their own lease portfolios and promoting their own dealer-based programs.

The dealers' skepticism turned out to be justified. The carmakers' fleet sales and leasing departments were indeed direct competition to independent fleet lessors and dealers with commercial accounts. On the retail side, the carmakers' involvement was so pervasive that U.S. and foreign car companies would come to dominate this segment of the market.

An array of vehicle leasing options

Among the relatively small vehicle leasing operations that remained independent of the carmakers were Foss National Leasing and Lease-Win. Based in Ontario and set up in the 1960s, both leased any and all models. They not only survived but thrived through thick and thin over the following decades.

Foss National Leasing was an offshoot of Roy Foss, a family-owned GM dealership. According to Jeff Hartley, current president of Foss Leasing, Roy Foss arranged all the financing himself. Foss Leasing specialized in closed-end, full-maintenance fleet leases, focusing on companies with 100 or more vehicles.

Lease-Win, owned and operated by Ron Rubinoff, was formed as an independent vehicle lessor with no link to any dealership. It used bank funding to help it grow. It worked with Ford Motor Credit for deals on Ford vehicles, with GMAC for GM models, and so on.

Lease-Win offered the newer open-end option, where the customer is responsible for covering any shortfall between the pre-arranged residual value and the price at which the lessor sells the vehicle to someone else at lease end. The advantage for the lessee was that it could choose to raise or lower the amount of its monthly payments knowing that the difference would be made up one way or the other at lease end. The advantage for the lessor was that the residual value risk was transferred to the lessee. A lower exposure to this risk made it easier for the finance company to secure third-party funding to support the cost of the transaction.

Lease-Win

Ron Rubinoff recalled that when he entered the leasing business in 1974, his office "was about the size of my desk." He had joined a new company, Lease-Win, and two years later was a partner, running the business.

Lease-Win's offices were on Caledonia Avenue in Toronto's west end, not far from the gas station owned by Rubinoff's father. Ron had worked the pumps as a kid and knew the car industry inside out. Lease-Win had been set up by Motorcade, an automotive parts supplier, giving it access to auto repair and maintenance shops—a valuable connection for a car leasing operation.

"It meant that our first accounts were those related to the car business, like the major brake companies and transmission businesses that needed cars for their salespeople," Rubinoff said. "Our biggest customer was Midas, a national operation, so we registered Lease-Win in every province.

"We'd stock a dozen or so vehicles, and when we ran out of cars to lease, I'd drive down to Dean Meyers [a larger dealership in the city] to pick up cars. Oldsmobile Cutlasses, Cadillacs, Corvettes, whatever.... Putting together maintenance packages for the vehicles was a natural for us because we were a parts company. The arrangements were open-end leases, where the customer had to guarantee the residual or buy the car at the end.

"At the end of the term, most customers at least broke even, or had made money to put toward their next car," Rubinoff explained. "This was particularly the case when inflation rates started to rise in the '80s. Coming off lease, cars would often be worth more than we had originally paid, especially luxury cars. We could lease a Corvette or a Mercedes convertible, and sell it three years later for what we had initially paid. Those were some of the good old days."

Rubinoff bought Lease-Win in 1987. The company would enjoy thirty-eight years of success under his ownership. It acquired two dealerships in 1987 and became a public company in 1998 under the name Chesswood Group Ltd. With Barry Shafran as president and chief executive, Chesswood went on to own several U.S. financial services companies as well as the Acura Sherway dealership in Toronto's west end.

Foss National Leasing

Roy Foss set up Foss National Leasing in 1972 as an adjunct to Roy Foss, his General Motors dealership, offering typical open-end, full-maintenance leases. Like others in the trade, he assumed that the leasing operation would funnel a steady stream of reliable used-car inventory to the dealership, enabling the latter to make money on a resale at the end of the lease.

Part of Foss's success was his focus on customer relationships. "Our company signed its first commercial customer, Wimpey Construction, in 1972," said Jeff Hartley, Foss Leasing's current president. "They are still one of our largest accounts. Not many companies can say that their first account is still with them forty-one years later."

Besides Wimpey, Foss Leasing's early clients included Continental Can and Canada Trust. With Foss's help, each built up a fleet of more than 100 vehicles.

Foss National Leasing expanded steadily, eventually becoming Canada's largest privately owned, dealer-based fleet management and leasing company. From the start, Foss built its own leasing portfolio, and it has remained independent. "We provide any kind of vehicle that is licensed to travel on the road," Hartley explained. "In fact, today we have a lower market share of GM products than any of the other major fleet management companies in Canada."

New business models

It did not take long for leasing's entrepreneurial pioneers to explore different business models. The founders of National Leasing, started in Winnipeg in 1976, soon realized that a few large companies were all competing for the same business in a limited number of sectors. In response, they charted a strategy that would turn National Leasing into one of Canada's most successful commercial equipment leasing operations.

"The leasing companies at the time were all focused on the large-equipment distribution lines out of Toronto; which meant they all kept price-cutting each other," said Nick Logan, National Leasing's president since its inception. "So we made the decision right from the beginning to be a generalist equipment leasing company. We would be like Heinz 57, with plenty of vendors in each city."

The vendors encompassed manufacturers, distributors, and other suppliers that broadened National's reach. For example, one of National's first vendors was Stevenson Equipment, a distributor for Hunter Automotive equipment in the United States.

National did not confine itself to just a few product categories. It built a large base of vendors to meet the varied needs of its small- and mid-sized business customers. The equipment available for lease expanded from hoists, brake, and alignment systems to photocopiers; office telephone systems; the new cordless "bag" phones that were just hitting the market; medical equipment; and, finally, farm equipment. By building such an extensive and varied network of customers and vendors, National Leasing became a stable, profitable company with a national presence.

From National Leasing's standpoint, transactions almost always start with the vendor. This is where the end-user goes first; then the financing company is brought into the transaction. "We worked across the country, helping the vendors sell equipment by providing some training and financing to help them close their transactions," said Logan. "It meant that we went to all the small distributors in every city across Canada. While the other guys fought over the top 50, we just kept adding smaller ones across the country."

National Leasing also worked with brokers, who received incentives in return for referring customers with high-quality credit ratings. The brokers had to meet strict performance standards.

The original fifty vendors have grown, by Logan's last count, to 12,000, serving about 70,000 end-users of leased equipment. National Leasing prides itself on the strength of its vendor network, which Logan believes lies at the heart of its success.

"We have earned them through being a value-added partner, supplying fast turnaround, sales training, consistency of service, and personalized attention," said Logan. "Our model was tougher to build, but now is sounder in that we do not rely on any one source for business."

National Leasing was also unusually nimble in the way it marketed its services. As the leasing business evolved, deals were becoming more complex, with various tax angles and incentives. For smaller businesses, this often slowed the transaction and delayed the delivery of what they most wanted: the equipment.

"In the '70s, we looked at the companies in Toronto and were mystified," Logan explained. "They were always making things more complicated, creating different kinds of leases and adding tax twists.

"We said to ourselves, 'This is pretty basic stuff.' Our key to success from the beginning was to make things simple, be right there at the point of decision making and get the deal done. We had sales people who'd meet a farmer right in his field beside his tractor. That meant we could always beat the banks because we could get the deal done before the banks even found out about it."

National Leasing did not waver from this approach. It embraced technology whenever that helped move a deal along. It was the first leasing company in Canada to go paperless, with all documents available online. It was an early adopter of online credit applications submitted through a local National Leasing account manager or through an array of affiliated equipment dealers across Canada.

Lenders of last resort

The leasing industry gained something of a reputation during this time as "lender of last resort," a sign of its value to businesses that could not easily borrow from a bank or other financial intermediary.

Certainly, leasing companies competed with conventional sources of financing, such as bank loans. In some cases, banks may have discouraged their customers from using more "risky" financing options, feeding the notion that for some, a lease was the only type of financing available. The real issue, however, was that for many businesses, there was no other way to finance equipment over a long period of time. Even companies with seemingly strong potential often had difficulty securing the necessary debt or equity. Banks were typically short-term lenders, and businesses were often unable to tie up their assets as collateral for traditional bank loans.

The gap was filled by acceptance companies and independent lessors such as CDI, which, unlike the banks, were willing to finance an asset for periods as long as seven years.

"Leasing was the extension of intermediary credit, which, in Canada in the '60s, '70s and '80s, was very hard to come by," Ned Mundell explained. "Banks just did not lend on a long-term basis. If you went into a bank and asked for a five-year term loan, the bank would tell you to get lost."

Revenue Canada steps in

In May 1976, Revenue Canada unveiled the first in a series of moves aimed at halting what it viewed as a growing abuse of lease financing by wealthy individuals and businesses using the capital cost allowance (CCA) solely as a tax shelter.

Although some in the industry questioned whether the practice was as widespread as critics maintained, the changes came after an extensive review by the then-Liberal government. The CCA system had been introduced in 1949 as a way of simplifying depreciation of capital goods and encouraging investment in capital equipment. But by the 1970s, it was clear there was a need for a wide-ranging review. The finance minister at the time, Donald Macdonald, announced in his 1973 budget that there would be "a thorough examination of the capital cost allowance system." He expressed concern that "the system for business depreciation be fair and reasonable, and not a hidden method for avoiding taxation."[28]

The government conducted a survey of 230,000 businesses to gain a better understanding of depreciation practices and to assess the strengths and weaknesses of the CCA system. Macdonald presented the findings in his budget speech on May 25, 1976, along with a proposal to clamp down on the use of the capital cost allowance to shelter income from tax.

Among other things, the new rules aimed to put a stop to lease arrangements under which a lessor could claim the CCA in return for passing on lower financing costs to the lessee.[29]

In future, the CCA would be available only to companies that made leasing their core or principal business. To qualify under the new rules, a company needed to show that it earned "at least 90 percent of its gross revenue for the year from renting or leasing property, or from leasing property combined with selling and servicing equipment of the same kinds as it leases."[30]

For most of the small, independent leasing companies, business would continue as usual. But the new edict was a clear sign that Revenue Canada was watching the use—and perceived abuse—of leasing as a tax shelter.

Tom Hopkirk, who at the time was working as a financial analyst at IAC, wondered if the change was designed specifically to prevent Imperial Oil, Canada's biggest energy group, from going ahead with a rumoured entry into the leasing business. The government would have been denied millions of dollars in tax revenues if Imperial Oil had started to lease assets to other oil companies and then claim generous tax deductions.

In any case, many high-income taxpayers, such as lawyers and doctors, were sheltering a big part of their professional income using the CCA. "There were so many of these that Revenue Canada decided to act," recalled Ralph Selby, then a chartered accountant at Price Waterhouse.

Selby remembered a sharp backlash against the new rules, especially from one of his clients, Traders Group. As an acceptance company, Traders was concerned that the part of its business that set up tax leases for non-leasing entities would be hit. Like other lessors, it was also worried that an even tighter clampdown might follow, with more severe repercussions. "The tax rules around capital cost allowances were about to change in order to stop perceived abuses," Selby noted. "Revenue Canada had stepped in and said, 'Thou shalt no longer claim a loss from leasing.' ... There was a fear that what was being proposed would eventually alter the industry."

Selby's fears were well founded. The changes announced in 1976 were a foretaste of what was to come—in 1981, 1987, 1989, and 1995. The ever-tighter restrictions would make the CCA system more complex and erode many of its benefits for the leasing business.

Bank Act revisions that changed everything

As things turned out, the biggest shake-up in the fledgling leasing industry was to come from the Finance Department, not Revenue Canada.

Until the late 1970s, Canadian banks could only set up a leasing arm as a joint venture with limited ownership.[31] This meant that although some of the big banks had an exposure to leasing, they could not compete as direct lessors. Banks were then not seen as a significant threat to the independents. For example, Royal Bank of Canada owned a 10 percent stake in Royal Marine Leasing in Buffalo, New York. Toronto Dominion Bank and Bank of Nova Scotia joined forces to form Scotia-Toronto Dominion Leasing Ltd. CIBC and Bank of Montreal had no leasing interests at that time.

As U.S. banks plunged into the leasing business, their Canadian counterparts began lobbying to follow suit. The government accepted the banks' argument in a White Paper tabled in August 1976. The White Paper's recommendations were incorporated three years later into Bill C-14, the scheduled ten-year review of the *Bank Act.*

Even before the new law was tabled, the banks were on the prowl for acquisitions that would expand their stake in the leasing business. Although they had to wait for parliamentary approval before closing any leasing deals, they were eager to lay the groundwork so that they could hit the ground running. The Provincial Bank of Canada acquired the acceptance company Laurentide Financial in 1976 to serve Western Canada and set up ProCan Leasing based in Montreal. In 1976, New York–based Citicorp hired Tom Simmons to set up a fleet leasing business in Canada. Bank of Montreal closed a deal in 1980 to take over Canadian Dominion Leasing.

In the biggest deal of all, Royal Bank made its move on CanPac Leasing in 1976 to gain a foothold in the general leasing business. Although the bank could not yet operate as a leasing company, CanPac was renamed RoyLease Ltd. so it would be ready to jump into the market when the law changed.

Roman Oryschuk, who had moved to Royal Bank in 1979 via CanPac, felt that some of the banks were a bit presumptuous as they drew up plans to expand their leasing interests even before Ottawa had made any final decisions. "When the department of finance said that revisions would be made to allow banks into direct leasing, even though the changes to the *Bank Act* had not passed yet, the banks started to think about how to get into it. They could do so by either purchasing an existing operation in the leasing business or by expanding their own structures."

Not content to confine itself to equipment leasing, Royal Bank wasted no time trying to figure out a way to get into the lucrative vehicle leasing market. One of its first moves was to hire staff from PHH, the well-established leader in fleet management.

"The move was too aggressive, too visible, and perhaps foolish," Oryschuk recalled. "It drew attention to how the banks were preparing to compete against an industry sector firmly entrenched in fleet leasing."

Although Royal eventually backed off its plan to enter the fleet financing business, the mere threat caused a commotion. Dealerships that had set up fleet leasing operations, as well as independent fleet lessors, quaked at the thought of the powerful banks moving into their territory. They wasted no time rolling out a vigorous lobbying drive to keep the banks out of all vehicle leasing.

A no-holds-barred lobbying effort

The prospect of unfettered competition from the banks mobilized the leasing industry. Equipment and vehicle lessors united in their newly formed industry associations in an effort to sway lawmakers to their side before the changes were cast in stone.

Bob Hunkin, a charter member of the Equipment Leasing Association of Canada (ELAC) and its volunteer president during this critical period, recalled the mood around the table after the *Bank Act* revisions were announced: "The members of ELAC were pretty shaken up at the prospect of having to compete against the banks, given their size and relatively lower cost of capital, amongst other market advantages."

ELAC arranged various meetings with government officials in the hope of having the proposal reversed, but to no avail.

The vehicle leasing side unleashed an even more vigorous lobbying campaign. Independent fleet lessors were convinced that the banks' main interest was fleet leasing, and they were determined not to back off without a fight.

The banks maintained that the dominance of the carmakers' captive finance arms amounted to a foreign stranglehold on the Canadian vehicle leasing market. The auto industry countered that the banks had a clear conflict of interest because the fleet leasing companies and dealerships would be both their customers and competitors.

The fleet lessors contended that the banks would use their deep pockets and alleged oligopolistic power to drive the lease specialists out of business. With access to customer lists and cheaper finance, the banks would have a competitive edge; they would put the squeeze on them by withholding credit. Once the banks gained control of the vehicle leasing market, so the argument went, consumers would face higher lease rates and less choice.[32]

On the other hand, smaller dealerships that did minimal fleet leasing did not see the proposed changes as a huge threat. "They didn't see it as their fight," explained John Carmichael, whose father, Jack, owner of City National Leasing, was in the thick of the fight.

After much discussion and strong lobbying by carmakers, the Federation of Automobile Dealers Associations, and the newly formed Canadian Automotive Leasing Association, the government backed down on one crucial issue and reached a compromise on another.

As recorded in a research paper prepared for the federal Task Force on the Future of the Financial Services Sector, "The final version of the 1980 Bank Act contained a compromise solution, arrived at after closed negotiations with opposition parties. Banks were to be allowed to engage in (equipment) leasing but only indirectly, through wholly-owned subsidiaries."[33] They were allowed to lease heavy trucks and equipment weighing more than twenty-one tonnes, but the act also specifically stated that banks would be barred from leasing light vehicles—in other words, cars, SUVs, and light pickup trucks. As for owning a vehicle company, banks were reduced to a minority position, which virtually excluded them from this industry sector. They could own up to 2 percent of the shares but had only 10 percent of the voting rights.[34]

Some opposition members remained skeptical. Bob Rae, in his first term as federal member of parliament for the Toronto riding of Broadview-Greenwood, commented, "When you allow the banks to get into indirect leasing, the extent of their market power is such that we could well be giving over large aspects of that business, which is not the intention of the committee to give. The only people in favour of the wording on indirect leasing are the government, the government's bureaucratic advisers and the Canadian Bankers Association."[35]

Even so, the vehicle leasing lobby had achieved a major victory. The ban on Canadian banks leasing passenger cars and other vehicles weighing up to twenty-one tonnes remains in place today. But the *Bank Act* amendments did represent a partial victory for the banks. Though they were barred from leasing vehicles, they could still provide funding to vehicle leasing companies. They could also set up their own equipment leasing subsidiaries and, as indirect lessors, offer credit through finance leases, also known as capital leases.

Under a **capital or finance lease**, a bank can buy equipment on behalf of a customer who is considered to be the owner of the asset.

These changes had ramifications for the entire gamut of leasing companies because of their dependence on the banks as a crucial source of funding. Overnight, companies like The Hamilton Group found they were dealing not only with a bank but with a competitor. "We had to find other ways of funding and ways to compete on service and products," said Ben Young, vice-president.

Small lessors and large acceptance companies alike would feel the pinch in the decade to come.

"When the tax act changed, there was no real panic because the smaller lessors weren't that affected," Young observed. "But the *Bank Act* change—that was pretty big because it hurt all our funding. In leasing, our raw material was capital. None of us was sure exactly how the banks were going to compete. Not on service, but now they would certainly have the edge on rates and ready access to that raw material."

Speaking with one voice (1): The Equipment Leasing Association of Canada (ELAC)

After a few informal meetings, representatives from a couple of dozen equipment leasing companies gathered at the Skyline Hotel in Ottawa in April 1973 for the first annual meeting of the Equipment Lessors Association of Canada. Glen Langdon, from a small leasing company, was named the association's first president, succeeded by The Hamilton Group's Ben Young. Russ Neal was hired as part-time manager.

"Equipment leasing companies at the time acted very independent of each other," Tom Hopkirk recalled. "But because the industry was small, we all knew each other. For example, some of us at IAC would get together with the competition and play golf. But there was no mandate to do any lobbying. It was just an informal network."

Priorities changed, however, when word filtered out from Ottawa that big changes were in the offing, first the 1976 revisions to the income tax regulations, and then lobbying by the big banks to enter the industry. The challenges hammered home an important message to players in the leasing industry: despite being rivals in business, they needed to speak with a single voice when their mutual interests were under threat. An industry association seemed an obvious solution.

A precedent had already been set south of the border. In response to regulatory changes that allowed U.S. banks to enter the vehicle leasing market, U.S. players had come together to form the American Association of Equipment Lessors (now the Equipment Leasing and Finance Association) in 1962 to promote leasing and monitor federal and state regulations.

"We were conscious that the regulators were suddenly paying us more attention," NABEL's Bill Bell said. "We [in the Canadian leasing industry] were also getting pushed around a little by the banks. So we thought: Why don't we get together as a single voice and then maybe we can approach the government?"

From that first meeting in Ottawa, ELAC had a national reach. It held its annual meeting in a different place each year—Montreal, Vancouver, Ottawa, Calgary, Montebello. Apart from the advantages of networking and the pleasure of socializing, members recognized that a trade association was more than the sum of its parts. The association gave lessors an opportunity to explain the intricacies of their business—not to mention its benefits—to outsiders. "We all had the same issues," Ben Young said. "And they were industry-related, not competition-related."

ELAC also provided a vehicle for newcomers to the industry to learn from the seasoned pioneers. Serge Mâsse, for example, was at the start of his career in leasing, working at the Canadian Acceptance Corporation in Montreal. Mâsse would remain committed to ELAC (and later the Canadian Finance & Leasing Association [CFLA]) throughout his career.

"When I was first getting involved with ELAC," Mâsse recalled, "I was sitting with about ten members around the table and we were getting ready to lead a delegation to Ottawa to meet with the department of finance. I said to myself, 'Here I am, sitting with the heads of all these companies. This is the group of people I want to be part of because of the learning and because their ideas will sustain me.' So I stayed involved for thirty-five years."

Speaking with one voice (2): The Canadian Automotive Leasing Association

In the early 1970s, Jack Carmichael, owner of City National Leasing in Toronto, called two friends, Don Cooke of Gelco Leasing and PHH's Ed Gibson, to chat about the upcoming *Bank Act* amendments. The three agreed that they should get together with like-minded vehicle leasing executives to see what could be done to keep the banks at bay. Jack's son John was volunteered by his dad to put out feelers to others in the industry.

"Everyone was on board from the beginning," recalled John Carmichael. "Roy Foss in Toronto, Ross McLaughlin at Canadian Vehicle Leasing, Peter Burk from Duek, Jim Pattison in Vancouver."

The Canadian Automotive Leasing Association was born in 1979, following a similar trajectory to ELAC. For the first few years, CALA operated from City National Leasing's offices. Although the body was created primarily to respond to the proposed changes in the *Bank Act*, members soon discovered that speaking with a single voice brought numerous other benefits.

PHH's Ed Gibson was the first chairman. Tom Simmons, who at the time was setting up Citicorp's fleet leasing business in Canada, recalled some of the others who attended those first meetings. Apart from Jack Carmichael and Don Cooke, early members included John Jackson, also from PHH; Fred Booth (Lend Lease); Ross McKenzie and Hugo Sørensen (Triathlon Leasing); Doug Fulford (Gorries National Leasing); Bill Gow (Cross Canada Leasing); John Samuelson (Hertz); Doug Leith (Black & McDonald Leasing); John Turback (Service Leasing); and Tiff Trimble (Jim Pattison Lease).

The new body's first priority was to try to block the banks from moving onto its members' turf. CALA members also wanted to distinguish themselves from the carmakers' captive finance arms, which had their own agenda.

Jack Carmichael, Ed Gibson, and Don Cooke travelled to Ottawa to represent the vehicle-leasing industry before the House of Commons finance committee. Their mission was to convince the committee that, as lenders, the banks were privy to the leasing companies' confidential information and should not be allowed to compete against them.

After winning the fight over the banks, CALA continued to provide a common voice to lobby against what was seen as unfair government interference and legislation. CALA also became an important voice for smaller lessors, including dealerships.

Rob Rubinoff, Lease-Win's founder and one of CALA's charter members, recalled, "I joined the association at the time as a small leasing company to have a voice to represent our concerns in the industry. CALA provided the strength in numbers to deal with the manufacturers, giving voice to the little guys."

Nothing is going to stop us now

By 1978, the London Financial Group's World Leasing Handbook estimated the global value of the asset-based finance business at US$40 billion, excluding vehicle leasing. The market continued to grow, topping US$460 billion by 2002 and reaching US$868 billion in 2013.[36]

The Canadian market was no exception. The challenges posed by changes in the tax rules and revisions to the *Bank Act* did not discourage the fledgling industry from forging ahead. Instead, these events fed its determination to survive, innovate, and demonstrate the benefits of dealing with a leasing partner rather than a traditional bank. Now excluded from any kind of meaningful participation in vehicle leasing, the Bank of Montreal would be forced to divest 90 percent of its interest in Canadian Vehicle Leasing (part of its CDL acquisition), leaving the door open for a new independent to seize the opportunity. Leasing would steam ahead in the 1980s to enjoy one of its most lucrative and expansive periods of growth.

chapter 4

1980–89: Growth, Creativity—and Risks

Hugo Sørensen started work at Canadian Vehicle Leasing in the early 1980s. Following its divestment from the Bank of Montreal, the former CDL subsidiary had been bought by four Canadian entrepreneurs: Ross McKenzie from Toronto, Vancouver's Ian McFarlane, Don Wheaton from Edmonton, and Winnipeg's Bob Chipman. But within months of Sørensen's arrival, the four owners sold out to Trilon Financial, one of the holding companies in the sprawling industrial and financial group controlled by Peter and Edward Bronfman, nephews of Sam Bronfman, founder of the Seagram liquor empire.

Canadian Vehicle Leasing was renamed Triathlon, with fleet leasing the focus. The Trilon acquisition made Triathlon Canada's largest fleet leasing company, with clients such as John Labatt, Dome Petroleum, and Rothmans. Triathlon's services included arranging pink Cadillacs for Mary Kay Cosmetics.

Buoyed by the end of the recession in the mid-1980s, Triathlon decided to grow by acquisition, adding a computer leasing company, a fleet leasing arm (City National Leasing), and a dealer finance specialist (Trexar). It created PayPlan, a program that made it easy for customers' employees to lease a car, with monthly payments conveniently deducted from their pay. It also moved into heavy equipment leasing.

But Triathlon lost sight of one of the fundamental tenets of the leasing business: pay attention to asset quality. "Bad assets lead to bad losses," Sørensen noted. "And like all leasing companies, Triathlon was highly leveraged."

By the end of the 1980s, Triathlon was drowning in red ink. Investors, mostly banks, demanded their money back, and its business shrank.

In 1994, the company was acquired by GE Capital. Triathlon had once been the largest company of its kind in Canada. When the GE deal was announced,[37] *it had more than 47,000 vehicles under lease or management and served more than 1,600 corporate clients.*

The wild eighties

Triathlon's story epitomizes both the wide-eyed optimism and the substantial risks that pervaded the leasing business in the 1980s.

As the decade began, the Canadian leasing industry entered a golden age. Independent companies were still able to offer competitive rates. Funding was readily available because many investors wanted to take advantage of fast-rising interest rates. Because their core business was leasing, not structuring "tax deals," the independents were largely unaffected by the new capital cost allowance restrictions. In fact, the 1976 changes in the *Income Tax Act* had—at least for a time—removed some of the competition from the market and helped solidify leasing's reputation as more than just tax-driven.

Ironically, given initial industry opposition, the big banks' entry in 1980 brought fresh credibility to the leasing business. Leasing was finally being accepted as a legitimate source of financing, on a par with term loans and project finance. After all, if the usually conservative banks were comfortable with the risks, then leasing had surely come of age as a credible option for financing business assets. Companies of all sizes started to adopt—or at least consider—leasing as part of their overall financing strategy.

Tom Hopkirk, by now assistant general manager at IAC, remembered preparing a speech on leasing for the University of Western Ontario's business school. "It was around 1981," he recalled. "In order to make my point, I had to search through Fortune 500 companies. I found that 60 percent of the top 100 companies in Canada at the time had leased assets."

Even so, dark shadows were creeping across the leasing landscape. The 1980s would be marked by some of the industry's most serious challenges to date, as well as its greatest opportunities. Among the trends that shaped the decade were:

- the economy: good times and bad,
- powerful competitors: banks and large manufacturers,
- the rise of structured financing,
- consolidation and sophistication in fleet leasing, and
- an intensified drive by carmakers into retail leasing.

The industry notched up a major achievement by developing a securitization model that opened a new way for lessors to structure their funding. On the other hand, Revenue Canada stepped in again and withdrew an important tax benefit. Two new—but very different—entrants stole much of the limelight: GE Capital Equipment Finance, the financing arm of the giant U.S. conglomerate General Electric, and Newcourt Credit Group, the brainchild of a young Toronto accountant called Steve Hudson.

The economy: Good times and bad

Canada's economy was in trouble at the beginning of the 1980s. In August 1981, the Bank of Canada's bank rate hit 21 percent. Inflation peaked in that year at 12.5 percent. The country also faced rising unemployment and tax increases because of soaring government debt. The Toronto Stock Exchange's main index tumbled from 2,400 in late 1980 to little more than 1,400 in July 1982, a decline of more than 40 percent. Canada fell into a recession, and many businesses, particularly in the manufacturing sector, were in deep trouble. Long-term financing was increasingly difficult to obtain as banks and other lenders recoiled at the instability faced by their clients.

The leasing business was by no means immune to this tougher, more risky environment. A lessor's stability is inextricably tied to the success of its customers, and when business slows, lessors need to consider more carefully than ever whether the assets they are financing will retain value if they are returned or repossessed. During the early 1980s, many lessors, anxious to clinch a deal, fell into the trap of financing assets of dubious quality.

Sørensen, who had become Triathlon's chief operating officer, recalled coming across one leasing company that found out too late that the asset it had financed was wooden scaffolding. To no one's surprise, pieces of used wood had little value, especially at a time when the construction industry was stagnating.

Sørensen also remembered a desperate attempt to recover salmon cages from a company that owed Triathlon more than $250,000. Alas, the cages were at the bottom of the Pacific Ocean. Sørensen's chagrin at his naïveté for financing such an asset was tempered only by the knowledge that a big bank had made an equally foolish mistake—it had backed the purchase of the fish. "Our losses were phenomenal," Sørensen acknowledged, "because we were leasing crummy assets."

Many other lessors made the mistake of straying from the business they knew best. Like Triathlon, they were propelled by a quest for rapid growth and outmanoeuvring their rivals rather than laying a foundation for long-term growth.

Triathlon survived a few more years through consolidation and restructuring. But many others were not so lucky. Some had difficulty sustaining momentum when funding became tight and their own customers were struggling. Others fell into the trap of borrowing short (for a few days or weeks) to fund long-term leases stretching over several years.

Borrowing short and lending long, also known as mismatched funding, at times gave lessors an advantage over those who matched their funding to the terms of the leases they wrote. The practice could be extremely profitable, but during turbulent economic times it came with considerable risk. Lessors could get stuck paying back the loan at a much higher rate, or being unable to meet their own financial obligations if their customers ran into financial trouble and defaulted on payments.

Powerful competitors: Banks and manufacturers

The leasing industry not only struggled to navigate the recession, but it also faced mounting competition from the big banks in the wake of the 1980 amendments to the *Bank Act*. With the banks setting up their own equipment leasing divisions (often by acquiring leasing companies), the independent lessors suddenly found themselves competing against the banks for the same customers. The banks were usually able to offer more attractive terms, putting the squeeze on lessors that could not offer their customers added value.

Barbara Hannesson, now senior business development officer at RCAP Leasing, was working in the 1980s at an independent lessor in Calgary. She referred to the period as "the rate wars." "We'd be competing against a company that had been recently acquired by the CIBC," she noted. "We couldn't beat them on rates, but we could offer more personalized services and faster turnaround."

Acceptance companies, once the giants of the leasing industry, were especially vulnerable. They depended on funding from the banks, which meant that they, too, could no longer compete on rates. Banks now could also arrange big-ticket leases, which meant that from the customer's point of view, they offered much the same service as acceptance companies. The well-respected IAC was among those that fell into the dangerous practice of borrowing short and lending long to finance its operations.

Before long, the venerable acceptance companies had all but disappeared. Laurentide had already been acquired by the Provincial Bank (which by 1979 had merged with the Banque canadienne nationale to form National Bank of Canada). IAC obtained a bank charter in 1981 and was renamed Continental Bank.[38] A year later, Royal Bank of Canada acquired the struggling Canada Acceptance Corporation and merged it with RoyLease. By 1983, Traders Group had been dissolved.

The good news was that the economy picked up in the mid-1980s. Indeed, from 1984 to 1986, Canada's growth rate was among the highest of the major industrialized countries. The improved business climate meant that leasing once again became an attractive option for companies that needed equipment and vehicles to expand their operations. Conversely, these investments could significantly boost profits of not only the leasing specialists but also the leasing arms of banks and manufacturers.

Big manufacturers spotted an opportunity to follow the carmakers' example by expanding into leasing through their own captive finance companies. Daimler Truck Financial in Canada was founded in 1984 as the captive finance arm of German-owned Daimler Trucks North America. This large captive financed purchases and leases of vehicles from Daimler's sizeable truck and bus business, including Freightliner, Western Star Trucks, Mitsubishi Fuso Truck and Bus Corporation, SelecTruck Centres, Thomas Bus, and the Freightliner Custom Chassis Corporation.

Long-time lessor Caterpillar Leasing was renamed Caterpillar Financial Services to underline the breadth of its services.

Office equipment

Similar forces were at work in the office equipment sector. Companies such as Pitney Bowes, Xerox, and IBM no longer wanted to hand over their customers' financing deals to outside companies.

With mainframe systems giving way to personal computers, IBM needed a new business model to generate more cash for investment in research and technology. Its answer was to set up its own captive finance unit. The U.S. parent set up IBM Credit Corporation in 1981 so that monthly payments from end-users could be funnelled to IBM rather than to an outside leasing or vendor finance company.

According to Eugene Basolini, by this time at Citibank Leasing, IBM outsourced some of its origination support and credit adjudication processes until IBM Leasing Canada was set up in the late 1980s.[39] A decade later, IBM Leasing adopted the name IBM Global Financing.[40] Today, IBM Global Financing is one of the largest captive IT financiers in the world.

The transition was different with Xerox but had the same result. Xerox paid Citibank Leasing for certain intelligence in order to set up their own finance division, called Xerox Finance, or XFD.

The Connecticut-based office equipment maker Pitney Bowes moved into Canada in 1980 through its financing subsidiary, Pitney Bowes Credit, followed by Pitney Bowes Leasing a year later. Pitney Bowes hired a leader in the business equipment sector—Bill Bell, formerly of NABEL—to head its new Canadian leasing arm. "It allowed me to finally run my own show," Bell said.

In a way typical of how the industry continued to reinvent itself, it was the former NABEL (now owned by Citibank Leasing) and a transition team that included Basolini that helped Bill Bell set up the new company. "It was inevitable that Pitney Bowes, and others, would want its own captive," explained Basolini, noting that Citibank Leasing was the dominant player at the time as a vendor finance provider. "We helped transition Pitney Bowes, department by department, over to their own company."

During Bell's sixteen years at Pitney Bowes, the leasing operation ballooned to the point where, in his words, "Pitney Bowes Leasing was making more money than the manufacturer's side of the business." Under Bell's leadership, the company would become the fifth-largest lessor in Canada. Its reach would expand beyond the office into construction and large transport equipment, including aircraft, buses, and tractor-trailers. Pitney Bowes Leasing would eventually be sold to Newcourt Credit Group in 1996, the year that Bell retired.

Like Pitney Bowes, captives typically started off financing only their parents' products, but once they understood the business, many expanded into similar products made by other manufacturers and even into completely different product lines.

U.S., European, and Asian manufacturers and distributors in Canada, such as Pitney Bowes and IBM, also opened doors for foreign-owned financial institutions, in particular U.S. banks. The banks could support these companies' Canadian subsidiaries with international banking services, including vendor financing. One example was Cleveland-based KeyBank, which first set up in Toronto in the mid-1980s.

"Key's market strategy was to have programs where we could help vendors finance their customers, and those customers are all over the world," said Richard McAuliffe, now senior vice-president and chief operating officer of Key Equipment Finance Canada Ltd.

U.S. manufacturers set up their own credit divisions in Canada separate from leasing. Pitney Bowes Leasing and Pitney Bowes Credit, for example, had little to do with each other in Canada. Pitney Bowes Credit dealt in U.S. funds and served U.S. clients doing business in Canada. Pitney Bowes Leasing arranged its own funding and served the leasing needs of its own clients.

Canada's first dealer (broker) captive

Jim Case, chief executive of Travelers Financial Corporation, began his career in the asset-based finance industry at Citibank Leasing, where he managed outsourced leasing deals for a Canon equipment dealer, Benndorf Verster. The Burnaby-based company had become the second-largest office equipment dealer in the country. Case soon joined the company to set up its own captive leasing and finance division. But with the influx of Japanese copiers, fax machines, and computers at the time, businesses across the country were keen to take advantage of the growing number of choices in new technology and equipment besides just Canon products. Benndorf Verster turned to Case once more, who set up Lease West, Canada's first dealer (independent third party) captive for office equipment. In 1990, Case bought out the partners, and Lease West became the genesis of Travelers Financial Corporation.

Leasing proves itself in turbulent times

The banks and the captives garnered a sizeable chunk of Canada's leasing market during the 1980s, partly by acquiring some of the independents. Bank of Montreal bought Canadian Dominion Leasing in 1980, naming Hamish Smith as its first president. Across the border, Ford Motor Company swallowed venerable U.S. Leasing, North America's first independent leasing company. In many instances, banks were forced to compete for the most successful companies. Citibank acquired the U.K. arm of

The Hamilton Group and its pioneering subsidiaries, NABEL and Medi-Dent. The ownership was short-lived. In 1987, the majority of Citibank Leasing's assets were acquired by Onex Corporation.[41] Renamed Norex Leasing, the company became Canada's largest small-equipment leasing company. Three years later, Norex was sold back to a bank—CIBC—and the name was changed to Commcorp Financial Services.

Banks would also jostle for position in the industry with an eye to making sure their client base was protected from other bank competition. Whatever Royal offered its customers, Scotiabank or TD would not be far behind. When Lease Administration Corporation's Ginter Baca asked one of his industry colleagues at the newly established Commcorp why its rates were so low, the response he received was: "We're not in this business to make money, we're in this business to protect our client base."

Some leasing companies were able to use the tough economic climate to their advantage. As banks tightened credit, the strongest and most nimble among them were able to secure longer-term funding from other deep-pocketed financial institutions, notably the big life insurers. The leasing companies generally remained less risk-averse than the banks, compensating for the extra risk with higher interest charges. As a result, prospective customers sought them out as the best way of acquiring equipment after being turned down by a bank for a loan or lease.

Lessors trumpeted leasing as a stable alternative to conventional financing techniques in uncertain times. The remaining CCA tax benefits still offered a way of quite legally deferring tax. Even as interest rates soared in the early part of the decade, a company could acquire a valuable piece of equipment in a package that combined financing, service, and maintenance in a single, predictable fee for a predetermined term. Leasing was thus able to offer a measure of certainty and convenience unmatched by bank finance.

To be sure, prudent lessors did tighten their risk standards as the economy weakened. But they were able to be more selective than their bank rivals because of their close relationship with customers and their specialized knowledge of the assets being financed. A tighter "credit box" did not mean cutting off leases to all and sundry, but selectively limiting exposure to an amount that both the customer and the lessor could tolerate and still survive.

The leasing companies made many careful judgment calls in financing sound customers and curtailing business with riskier ones. But a few decisions turned out to be based on less-than-wise assessments of the customers' long-term creditworthiness. At one point IAC advised its sales team not to call on two Canadian companies—Bombardier because some thought it was going to go "belly-up at any moment" and Pattison Enterprises in Vancouver because it was seen as over-leveraged with a "hot dog" businessman as its leader.

The flurry of acquisitions and mergers that occurred as banks expanded their leasing business in the 1970s reads like a genealogical "begat" list from the Old Testament.

- Toronto Dominion Bank formed Scotia-Toronto Dominion Leasing Limited in 1973, in partnership with the Bank of Nova Scotia.
- Royal Bank of Canada acquired CanPac Leasing, which became Royal Bank Leasing.
- Scotiabank created the Scotiabank Leasing Group, which included Roynat Lease Finance.
- Bank of Montreal bought Canadian Dominion Leasing and renamed it Bank of Montreal Leasing

- National Bank of Canada started Pro Can Leasing.
- Citibank acquired The Hamilton Group Ltd.
- Following the sale of Canadian Dominion Leasing, a group of former employees set up Pacific National Leasing.

GE Capital

No industrial company has made more waves in the leasing business than General Electric, through its financing arm, GE Capital.

Originally named General Electric Credit Corporation,[42] GE Capital was set up in the United States in 1932 as a subsidiary of General Electric Company to help Americans buy washing machines. It never looked back.

According to Peter Ringler, GE Capital Canada's chief commercial officer, by the early 1980s GE was on the lookout "fairly aggressively" for leasing opportunities across a wide spectrum of the economy. It was especially attracted by the "hard, asset-backed nature" of leasing.

GE Capital moved into Canada in 1984 through a finance partnership with Navistar, a well-established U.S.–based maker of commercial trucks, buses, military vehicles, and engines. Navistar had a strong presence in Canada, notably in Alberta and Ontario, where it had built its first plant in 1938. Navistar was looking for a respected finance provider to help serve its Canadian customers. GE wanted a strong physical presence in one of its preferred sectors: transport and construction. The two made an excellent match.

GE brought a new level of competition to the Canadian market and raised the bar for the entire industry.

"It was the Jack Welch era," Ringler recalled, referring to GE's former chairman and chief executive, one of the most respected business leaders of the late twentieth century. "Our mantra was to be number one and number two in every business, and that applied to leasing as readily as anything else."

GE Capital's business grew rapidly each year until the 2008 market crisis. Acquisitions made up about half of its expansion through the 1980s and 1990s, notably the purchase of Gelco in 1987. Leveraged buyouts contributed nearly one-fifth of GE Capital's $600 million profit that year. Its leasing business—which included truck trailers, shipping containers, railcars, and much else—produced a meagre $25 million in earnings.[43] But that contribution would soon climb sharply.

Leasing sets itself apart

Angela Armstrong, newly graduated from university in the mid-1980s, landed her first job as part of National Leasing's sales team in Winnipeg. One of eight new hires across the country, she said that her boss, Nick Logan, told the group in no uncertain terms to go out and expand the business. "There was a growing enthusiasm for leasing as a financing source," she recalled.

"The message was that companies needed more consistency in their financial tool belt. Usually run by entrepreneurs, these companies—auto parts suppliers and makers of light industrial equipment, among others—were always pushing to see what was available to them. Although they may have been aligned with a bank, most needed another financing source so they could buy the stuff they needed to make money. Leasing offered them a way to get to the next level of growth and still keep their relationship with a bank."

In other words, leasing was coming into its own as a mature financing technique that could complement rather than replace conventional bank lending.

Logan underscored the point, emphasizing that expert leasing companies increasingly formed part of a company's cadre of outside professional advisers. Leasing specialists understood the nitty-gritty of running a business in a way that few bankers did, including the need to get a deal done rather than tying it up in paperwork for weeks at a time.

Others recall moving deals forward by meeting customers around a kitchen table or even in a truck cab. "Can you imagine a banker doing that?" asked Bill Bell, reminiscing on his years at Pitney Bowes Leasing.

For her part, Armstrong went on to make her own mark as a successful entrepreneur. In 2000, she founded her own independent leasing brokerage in Edmonton, Prime Capital Consulting. With a small bank loan a year later, she evolved it into an equipment finance operation that also manages captive vendor portfolios. In 2003, she founded Forest Leasing, adding a lease funding operation to her business.

The rise of structured financing

At around the same time as General Electric entered the Canadian leasing market, Toronto venture capitalist and entrepreneur Steve Hudson set up a business that would demonstrate the power of leasing far beyond the dreams of the industry's pioneers. Within a few years, Hudson's creation, Newcourt Credit Group, would be vying with GE Capital for the title of the world's largest asset-based finance company.

Newcourt Credit

Hudson was working as a financial manager at Toronto General Hospital when inspiration hit in 1983. He had noticed that cash-squeezed health administrators were struggling to find money to buy costly MRI machines and that the banks were reluctant to help. Hudson, then twenty-four years old, wondered why public sector institutions could not take advantage of the same tax-driven lease deals that industrial corporations had been using for the previous two decades to acquire badly needed equipment.

"The hospital equipment was originally called NMRI, Nuclear Magnetic Resonance Imaging, and no bank wanted to touch it," Hudson recalled. "So I put together a group of doctors as investors to provide the financing."

Hudson quit his hospital job and formed Newcourt Credit Group in 1984. "As a contrarian entrepreneur, I was looking for holes and under-serviced components in the marketplace," he explained. "So I mortgaged my house and went for it."

Michael O'Keefe, chief executive of a suburban Toronto hospital, described his reaction when Hudson first approached him with his idea. "This was completely new," O'Keefe told *Maclean's* magazine. "It was a window that had never been opened."[44]

Steven Small, one of the doctors who invested in Newcourt Credit early on, was similarly impressed: "He [Steve Hudson] had a brilliant idea, seemingly simple but extraordinarily sophisticated. He was thinking big right from the beginning."[45]

Newcourt Credit began with $400,000 in start-up funds, raised from the initial doctor-investors plus Hudson's own contribution. Hudson saw these partners as "a perfect match for the leasing industry" because they usually looked for a five-year return, the same term as an average truck lease.

Newcourt's first target was the healthcare sector. Within the first year, it had notched up leases valued at half a billion dollars. Funding came entirely from Canadian and U.S. life insurance companies. Newcourt's lease business quickly expanded to construction, transportation, and aircraft, with clients such as Yamaha Motor Canada.

Hudson then set his sights on becoming North America's biggest non-bank corporate lender, with ambitions to overtake even GE Capital. Newcourt added such blue-chip clients as Dell Computer and the big telecom equipment maker Lucent Technologies. It vaulted to the number-two slot among the world's non-bank lenders in early 1998 when it absorbed AT&T Capital Corp. in a $2.3-billion deal.

But like what had happened to some other ambitious leasing entrepreneurs before him, Hudson's meteoric rise was followed by an equally spectacular fall. A year after the ambitious AT&T transaction, Newcourt was forced to succumb to a rescue by the American financial conglomerate CIT Group Inc., based in New Jersey. The deal was initially valued at $4.1 billion, but just before it was finalized, Newcourt took a write-down of $1 billion and CIT's share price dropped by 50 percent. The sale, completed in November 1999, eventually valued Newcourt at about $2.4 billion.[46]

"Newcourt went from having $400,000 in capital to a company that was worth $6 billion dollars on the New York stock exchange," Hudson recalled. "We ended up selling for $4 billion and gave $2 billion back."

In 2001, Hudson moved to the United States, where he refused to sit idly on the sidelines. Hudson invested in the Hair Club for Men and put his talents to work expanding the business from hair replacement to hairstyling. Within four years, he and his partners sold the company for an estimated nine times what they paid for it. Next Hudson set out on a chain of diet centres called Herbal Magic. Nine years later, he returned to lead another independent finance company, Element Financial.

Hooked on other people's money

Hudson is candid about what went wrong at Newcourt. "If I had stayed with the medical/life insurance company model, we probably wouldn't have had to sell."

Newcourt made the mistake in 1998 of abandoning its early practice of relying on stable funding from investors such as life insurers in favour of short-term borrowing in the more volatile commercial paper market. Hudson later compared the switch to becoming hooked on heroin—a short-term high, followed by a devastating letdown.

The lure of that strategy was the ability to lend for longer periods at higher rates, with the hopes of reaping a handsome profit from the spread. But it was also much more risky. Newcourt's cash flow came to depend on its ability to constantly roll over short-term loans at low interest rates. When markets seized up during the Asian financial crisis in 1998, Newcourt quickly found itself in trouble. "We were in a credit crunch with not enough money to pay our creditors," recalled Hudson. "Our borrowing costs tripled overnight."

Moe Danis, a leasing veteran who is now vice-president with Pacific & Western Bank of Canada, watched Newcourt's rise and fall. "I have a lot of respect for Steve," he said. "But the lesson he learned is that leasing companies can get hooked on OPM—Other People's Money. Lessors don't have a ton of their own money, so they have to borrow everything. If you're a public company, you're pushing your quarterly results to push the stock price instead of having a long-term view in the market. It means you can get really caught up in the short-term view, which can be to your detriment if you're not careful."

Others share Danis's view. On the one hand, they have great respect for Hudson's innovative ideas, his forceful personality and energy, and his success in building Newcourt into a powerful multinational company; on the other, a keen awareness of where Newcourt and its founder went wrong.

"In this business," said Jeff Hartley, president of Foss National Leasing, "you need multiple sources of funding and you also need to focus on what's known as match funding. If you're going to fund for four years, you'd better borrow money for four years, not thirty days. Otherwise, when the banks come and ask you to pay it back, if there's any kind of market crisis, there's suddenly no money to borrow to fill the gap."

Darling or rogue of Bay Street?

The October 1996 cover story of *The Globe and Mail Report on Business* magazine vividly mirrors the great excitement in the business community that greeted the ascendency of Steven Hudson and the Newcourt Credit Group. The charismatic Hudson sincerely believed in a positive future for Newcourt. In order to get everyone in the company on board with the dream of success, the company designed an employee wealth-creation strategy. The strategy included an employee share loan program, a long-term incentive program, deferred profit sharing plan, and employee share purchase plan. Programs were aimed at four levels in the organization, and by 1998, almost all employees were share owners. Executives and senior management made up the greatest proportion.

According to many who worked at Newcourt, Steve Hudson's energy and optimism were infectious. Staff were encouraged to participate in the company by speaking up on how the company could be run better. Hudson himself would stroll through the office to answer questions. Employees were also encouraged by their superiors to participate in the share plans.

The Deferred Profit Sharing Plan, for instance, gave managers and employees some portion of stock ownership. Although no one was forced to sign up for these programs, there was a built-in expectation that everyone would want to participate. When Newcourt's share price fell, many employees lost thousands of dollars. The impact was particularly severe for those who had not profited—unlike the original investors—from the company's early gains. The original shareholders of Newcourt were reported to have made 120 times their money. But those who bought closer to the peak before the company was sold lost substantial sums."[47] One source recalled, "Many managers bought shares in the company, worked hard but never saw the fruits of their labor."[48]

Bitterness over losses remained for those who felt they had misplaced their confidence in Newcourt. For them, Hudson took risk too far, and the fallout impacted the credibility of the asset-based finance and leasing industry.

"Newcourt ... at one time was the darling of Bay Street," writes William Rankin, former vice-president, human resources at Newcourt. "Yet at another point in its history, Newcourt was the devil incarnate as viewed by investors who either bought stock too late in the game or held on for the long run."[49]

Demise of the entrepreneurs

Less than two years after taking on the banks and winning, the fleet leasing industry received two more welcome—though not immediately obvious—boosts.

The first was the 1981 federal budget doubling the taxable benefit that accrued to individuals lucky enough to drive a company-owned car. While the change imposed a new penalty on a popular fringe benefit, it unleashed a stampede from ownership to leasing.

The second development was the so-called "half-year rule convention." Up to 1981, companies could write off 100 percent of the value of a vehicle or piece of capital equipment within a year of purchase. They typically bought the item at the end of the year, depending on the state of their business and what tax write-off was required. But the government decreed that, starting in 1982, it would allow only half a year's worth of depreciation, thereby reducing the write-off to a maximum of 50 percent.

The new half-year rule gave fleet lessors a big advantage in that the benefit of writing off a bought vehicle as a capital cost had been cut in half. Companies looking to assemble or expand a fleet could now save much more in taxes by writing off lease payments as a business expense. In other words, leasing had indisputably become a better option than buying.

Despite these two helpful developments, the fleet leasing business was becoming more challenging. A rush toward consolidation had started in the United States after reforms in 1986 that removed the tax benefit for vehicle fleet lessors. The writing was on the wall for many smaller fleet management companies.

North of the border, life also became tougher for independent, family-owned leasing businesses that had grown through hard work, building relationships, and figuring out the next steps as they went along. Survival became a constant struggle as they scrambled to hold down costs and keep their highly leveraged businesses afloat. Their bigger, often U.S.–based competitors had easier access to credit. The U.S. companies also typically had deeper pockets, giving them the resources to keep abreast of the latest technology that made their systems more efficient—and thus more competitive. Many of the small fry were squeezed out, speeding up the industry's transformation.

Even some successful family-run businesses grew weary of the constant pressures of searching for funding and managing risk. One was City National Leasing, one of Canada's most successful independent fleet lessors. With offices in Vancouver, Edmonton, Calgary, Toronto, and Montreal, it leased thousands of vehicles a year to customers such as Consumers Gas, Warner-Lambert, Honeywell, and Air Canada. Al Clarke, who served as president from 1968 to 1985, recalled that, by 1985, the Canadian company was one of the top three in Canada, along with PHH and CIT Service Leasing. But in 1986, the Carmichael family sold City National's leasing business to Triathlon to focus on its dealership network.

"We reached the point where the company needed to be in the hands of a bigger entity," explained John Carmichael, whose father owned City Buick and City National Leasing. "It was a wonderful time, but my father was tired of the worry and the risk." Carmichael added, "Up until 1985, fleet leasing was in its earlier, 'wild west' era, with strong, independent entrepreneurs like my father at the helm. But then the captive leasing arms of the manufacturers became a factor, as well as tough competition from the large U.S.–owned fleet lessors. Tax reform also made the rules more defined and more complex."

Apart from GE, the big banks and holding companies such as Trilon Financial (later Triathlon) were actively looking for acquisitions in the early 1980s. The large independents—led by PHH, Gelco, CIT Service Leasing, Lend Lease, Don Bodkin Leasing, Birchcliff National, BML (Black & McDonald Leasing), Foss National Leasing, and Jim Pattison Lease—were also in expansion mode. By the end of the 1980s, a recurring talking point in leasing circles was how to prosper—and even survive—without falling into the arms of a bigger, stronger rival.

Jack Carmichael continued to run the dealership that he had started in the 1950s until his death in 1992. Today City Buick continues as a family-owned business under the name City Buick Chevrolet Cadillac GMC, led by Jack's grandson Michael. Following a successful career in the family business, Michael's father John was elected as the Conservative member of parliament for the Toronto riding of Don Valley West in 2011.

Vehicle leasing reinvents itself

Buffeted by shifting rules and stiffening competition, fleet leasing players set to work yet again in the late 1980s to reinvent themselves.

They continued adding new services, not only in providing cars to their customers but in managing them too. Although many had already installed computerized systems, the expansion into fleet management opened even more doors. The arrival of personal computers and online data systems facilitated this process. A customer could tap into the mainframe computer of the fleet-management company, submit electronic orders for the vehicles it wished to lease, and manage and track vehicles and drivers. Other improvements included more accessible billing information, shorter delivery times, and improved accuracy.

"When I joined PHH Canada in 1982," said Mike Goddard, now retired, "information was captured by ticking off boxes." PHH, an early adapter of technology, moved quickly to develop ways of producing reports; of analyzing the data; and, eventually, of sharing the information with customers. "The magnitude of the fleet business model demanded such technology in order to survive," Goddard noted.

Paul Hilder, retired vice-president of fleet management services at U.S.–owned Donlen Corporation (now part of Hertz), also recalled how computerized services revolutionized fleet leasing.[50] Referring to Donlen founder Don Rappaport, Hilder wrote in a 1990 article in *Automotive Fleet* magazine, "It didn't matter that other lessors weren't doing it. Don felt that an online system would reduce paperwork, make order processing more efficient, and provide our customers with access to a wide variety of information."

First introduced by Donlen in 1981, the online capability ushered in a new era of high-tech communication between auto leasing customer and vendor. As Hilder described, access to a sophisticated computer network was a milestone that marked the switch from "just doing business" to "fleet management."

The entry of Asian carmakers into Canada created more fleet leasing and management opportunities. The newcomers, notably Toyota, Honda, Nissan, Hyundai, Mitsubishi, and Isuzu, set up leasing operations, though none of them initially went so far as to form captive finance subsidiaries along the lines of GMAC or Ford Credit.

"The acceptance companies, like IAC, used to provide this service to the foreign car dealerships," explained Tom Simmons, who joined Citicorp (now Citigroup) in the late 1970s. Simmons's job was to set up Citi's fleet leasing operation, but when banks lost their fight to enter vehicle leasing, he was reassigned. His next job was to help fund Trexar, an operation dedicated to the import brands' lease business. Set up in 1984, Trexar came to fill much of the gap left by the demise of the acceptance companies.

"Trexar was the lessor for any dealership leasing an imported vehicle," said Simmons. "We funded Trexar in a similar way to GMAC, one lease at a time."

Trexar bought leases from Toyota and Nissan and some Chrysler dealers. It also managed Honda's private, white label lease program. Trexar remained in place until the foreign carmakers set up their own captive finance companies—Toyota Motor Credit Corporation in 1982, Honda Canada Finance in 1987, and Hyundai Motor Finance in 1989.

Carmaker captives eye retail leasing

The stage was set for one of the most significant developments in vehicle leasing—a no-holds-barred assault by the carmaker captives on the retail market.

As car prices rose during the 1980s, consumers increasingly balked at buying a new vehicle outright. But carmakers soon realized that they could move many more cars off dealer lots by offering leases at more attractive rates than loans, and by promoting a lease as a way for a "regular guy" to drive even a luxury car.

Ford set the ball rolling with its Red Carpet Lease program in the early 1970s, with promotions targeted at the individual car buyer. Dealers trumpeted the scheme with messages like this one: "We can arrange through Ford Credit's Red Carpet Lease to provide qualified leases for a 1984 Topaz or Lynx for a lot less than you think. For as long as 48 months!" This ad promised a monthly lease payment on a Topaz of $143.61, with a down payment of $706.39. Potential customers were directed to participating Lincoln-Mercury dealerships.[51]

GMAC's Retail Service Lease Plan evolved into SmartLease in 1988. Like Red Carpet, SmartLease was directed at the retail market through GM dealerships. Chrysler's Gold Key program followed in the 1990s.

Many dealers preferred to leave leasing to the captives because it simplified their own business. Thus, if lease payments were overdue, the captives handled collection procedures and—if necessary—repossession. For a fee, dealers could sign up for a "release of liability" option that relieved them of any residual responsibility for the vehicle. "That's when retail leasing really took off," said Peter Andrew, former general director of operations at GMAC Canada and now national operating officer at RBC Automotive Finance. "It was driven by the desire of the market to have more leasing and by the desire of the dealers to have less responsibility."

Two other developments during the 1980s had lasting ramifications for the leasing business. One was a groundbreaking innovation to expand the financial resources available to support leasing deals. The other had its origins in a new tax rule that dealt a serious and transformative blow to the industry.

Securitization

Moe Danis worked at Toronto-Dominion Bank until 1987. He then moved to the insurance industry, joining Mutual Life, where he put together funding deals for leasing companies. "One day," said Danis, "I stumbled across a leasing company that was selling on deals one at a time for small pieces of office equipment like computers and copiers to blue-chip investors."

Having expertise in both banking and actuarial science, Danis was comfortable with the concept of spreading a sizeable risk among many smaller transactions. "I thought to myself, I should look up other leasing companies that are doing these kinds of small deals for large, stable customers. What I found was that there were many such deals, about $5,000 each on average, and they were doing hundreds of them every year."

Danis had spotted an opportunity with far-reaching ramifications. He proposed that Mutual Life[52] buy small lease deals from lessors and bundle them into packages of securities, a process known as securitization. The packages could be traded like bonds. The beauty of this arrangement was that it lowered the risk for investors and the funder because the packages were backed by a variety of assets, all with tangible value. The risk was also spread across various industries, equipment types, and locations.

Danis did not invent securitization. But many give him the credit for bringing the model to Canada and making it work.

It did not take long for the industry to embrace the securitization model. Leasing companies liked it because they could easily move customer financing transactions off their books. At the same time, by putting together packages of securities to spread the risk, they could raise more money from investors and thus generate more leases. The technique gave them access to cash, or what Tom Pundyk, president of National Leasing, described as "reasonable funding." It was a godsend to small- and mid-sized lessors that had struggled to fund themselves, as well as to large companies putting together multimillion-dollar deals.

Lessees or end-users were usually unaware of the securitization transaction. They continued to make their contractual lease payments to the leasing company, but the money flowed to buyers of the packaged securities, rather than to the leasing company.

As Angela Armstrong put it, "Money is our most important resource along with people. Without the securitization model, the leasing industry would not have grown. Securitization played a pretty significant role in how the industry could expand the way it did."

Leasing pushes the envelope

During the 1980s, another leasing structure was developed to offset the high cost of borrowing funds. Sale-leasebacks are an arrangement where equipment is purchased by a lessor from the company owning and using it. The lessor then becomes the owner and leases the goods back to the original owner, who continues to use them. **Sale-leasebacks** were particularly attractive to non-profit taxpayers because the CCA depreciation was of no use to them. By structuring transactions as a sale-leaseback, such arrangements could be profitable for both the sellers and the tax-paying financial institution that bought them—and that could use the CCA.

Sale-leasebacks were developed earlier in the industry by individuals such as Hamish Smith. Smith first came up with the idea of "de-bundling of assets" when he worked at Lomcan Leasing (which became MedCan and, eventually, Confederation Leasing). By de-bundling assets into component parts, each component achieves a greater CCA depreciation rate separately than they would as a single piece of equipment. Confederation Leasing then applied the concept of de-bundling to create sale-leasebacks for hospitals and universities. These institutions would sell assets—anything from window frames to surgical equipment and beds—to a large financial institution. As taxpayers, that institution then would take the CCA benefits and lease the assets back to the hospitals through an annuity.

Confederation put the idea to work. The company bought equipment from institutions such as hospitals and university libraries in order to lease it back to them and gain the CCA benefit. Of course, these transactions had the potential to reduce federal tax revenues by tens of millions of dollars—and the tax department took notice.

The Finance Department strikes again

Little more than a decade after the federal government first clipped the wings of the capital cost allowance as a leasing benefit, it stepped in again to tighten the rules, specifically as these applied to sale-leasebacks.

The amendments, unveiled in the 1989 budget, addressed the issue of leases set up for income tax purposes, such as sale-leaseback arrangements. The most significant change in 1989 was the introduction of "specified leasing property rules," which made various items ineligible for the CCA deduction.

Lessors of so-called "exempt assets" continued to be entitled to a full CCA deduction. These assets included office furniture and equipment, such as computers; household items, such as furnaces and appliances; cars, delivery vans, and small trucks; and railcars.

But deductions were tightened on a new category of "non-exempt assets," primarily "big-ticket" items such as industrial machinery, ships, energy-generation equipment, oil and gas equipment, flight simulators, and telephone switches, among others. It meant that a lease was now treated in the same way as a loan for tax purposes. The bottom line was that the advantage of sheltering another entity's income through a capital cost allowance had disappeared.[53]

Some saw the move as part of a drive to clamp down on lessors that had claimed CCA benefits for themselves by arranging sale-leasebacks for public institutions. Confederation Leasing was often mentioned as a prime culprit. The deal that many believed caused the government to change the *Income Tax Act* was the company's library books sale-leaseback agreement with the University of Ottawa. Confederation Life (a taxpaying company) purchased the books in the university libraries for $1 million and leased them back to the university. The CCA on the books was 100 percent. Confederation Life used the tax benefits to lower the lease payments to the university.

As Roman Oryschuk saw it, "The Feds, to say the least, became upset and changed the rules around capital cost allowance for all of the leasing industries. It curtailed the tax advantage and created a more complex mechanism for calculating the tax advantages for lessors and lessees."

Like many others, Oryschuk was not happy about the change. "It was an over-reaction by the government, which took a cannon approach. Instead of just limiting the sale-leaseback, they got emotional about it."

Tom Hopkirk, who had just completed a big ship leasing deal for Saint John Shipbuilding and Dry Dock Company, realized that the industry would have to take a different tack in future. "You no longer could go into the large corporations like CNR, Air Canada, or Voyageur Bus and offer very attractive monthly rates because of the ability of your company to defer taxes. From then on, the leasing business would become 100 percent about financing, not about creating tax deals. It forced companies to get very clever about doing vendor finance programs."

Equipment lessors push back; Vehicle lessors protect their turf

Not everyone raised their voices in protest. The banks, as newcomers to the leasing business, were reluctant to rock the boat and antagonize the Finance Department. Vehicle lessors were relieved that the new rules did not affect their business. But ELAC members, protecting their interests in equipment leasing, lobbied vigorously against the clampdown. ELAC sent delegations to Ottawa and held numerous consultations with finance officials in an attempt to soften the blow.

One such meeting was held in the basement of the Traders Group building on Church Street in Toronto. "What was being proposed would alter the industry," said Ralph Selby, a partner at the time with accounting firm Price Waterhouse. "While ELAC members were all fierce competitors, that night the group was united in being both anxious and angry, and asking what we were going to do."

The lobbying drive bore some fruit. The Finance Department restored a provision that gave companies a little wiggle room to claim a tax benefit. They could, for example, accumulate a CCA benefit if they had not claimed one in previous years. They could also claim a loss at the end of a lease if they no longer owned the relevant piece of equipment.

"We thought the changes from the original federal proposals were great," said Selby. "And Revenue Canada was content because it got what the government wanted—to treat a lease as a loan for tax calculations."

The downside was that the 1989 rules added complexity. Dividing leases into exempt and non-exempt categories made extra work for accountants and auditors. The tax benefit for most items was still there, if structured correctly, but companies had to do an in-depth analysis over a four- to five-year period to figure out whether a lease or a loan was the better option.

Even so, the message many companies took away was that a CCA deduction was no longer a good reason to lease a piece of equipment. "It really put the kibosh on major growth in leasing in Canada," said Bob Hunkin.

Serge Mâsse worked at Canada Acceptance Corporation, which depended on tax-driven leases. He remembered an even darker interpretation: "The doomsayers immediately said that this would be the end of the leasing industry."

Certainly, the new restrictions forced big changes. New marketing programs had to be created to drive home the message that there was more to leasing than a tax deduction. The clampdown also pushed many hitherto-successful leasing companies out of business or into the arms of stronger rivals.

Meanwhile, vehicle lessors had a separate fight on their hands. The big banks were still upset from their defeat less than a decade earlier. Through the Canadian Bankers Association (CBA), they again began pressing the government to lift the remaining curbs on their involvement in vehicle leasing. A CBA position paper, prepared in 1991, made the argument that consumers would benefit from dealing with the banks. But the Federation of Automobile Dealers' Associations (now the Canadian Automobile Dealers' Association [CADA]) and the Canadian Vehicle Manufacturers' Association strongly opposed giving the banks free rein.

The government once again took the auto industry's side. Although amendments to the *Bank Act* that were passed in 1992 enabled banks to set up new lines of business through subsidiaries—for example, trust companies—they continued to be barred from car leasing or from owning a car-leasing company.

Apart from the debate over unfair competition, members of parliament faced the argument that allowing the banks to muscle into car leasing would cost jobs in the auto sector. This was an issue that the Conservative government at the time preferred not to confront as it entered an election year.

Lessons learned

"Never, ever compromise on credit standards," Tom Pundyk advised. "When things get tough in the marketplace, companies want to make their numbers, so they drop their standards to get more business. But when things get bad, losses increase. You can only control your losses if you set your credit standards and stick with them."

Not everyone heard that message during the 1980s, a time marked by a heightened awareness of risk and the importance of enforcing solid credit standards. The leasing industry was forced to face up to the hard reality that outside capital was its lifeblood. During tough economic times when capital dried up, all but the strongest players faced a funding squeeze and liquidity crunch, leaving them unable to finance new business or, worse, pay their own creditors.

But the decade also opened up exciting new horizons for the industry. Although the term *asset-based financing* was not in general use at the time, it was clear that leasing had become a major element in financing deals based on the securitization of assets such as machinery, office equipment, and vehicles—and later, credit card receivables and mortgages.

"Leasing was becoming fairly big business in Canada, going from plain-vanilla financing to structured financing," noted Roman Oryschuk. "With consolidation, tighter credit, and powerful competitors, the 1980s were a fractious time in the leasing industry, but an exciting one."

The upshot of the upheavals was that leasing shed some of its Wild West reputation and matured into a more disciplined, rules-bound business. The industry's tolerance for risk ebbed, helping to turn leasing into a more sophisticated and respected force in Canadian financial markets.

Similarly, survival and resilience took on new meaning during the 1980s as companies merged, were sold, and shifted from one type of business to another. "The late 1980s was a pretty active period for everyone," said Bob Hunkin, who knew a thing or two about resilience, having first left IAC to set up CanPac, only to see it acquired five years later by Royal Bank.

"Leasing survived," Hunkin said, "because it had a degree of magic to it."

Tom Hopkirk, another industry leader who switched horses during the turbulent 1980s, added with the wisdom that comes from experience, "If leasing could overcome the 1989 changes in the *Income Tax Act*, it should be able to overcome anything."

Modern growth: Four global catalysts

In June 1998, David Powell, president of the Canadian Finance & Leasing Association, addressed the Financial and Business Research Group of The Conference Board of Canada. In a speech titled "Changes in the Financial Services Sector—The Last Ten Years in Perspective," he looked back to identify the key trends that contributed most in transforming the asset-based financing and leasing industry.[54]

Newcomers unbundling financing services

Over the 1980s and 1990s, the modern industry grew dramatically through the combined effect of four global catalysts, propelling the asset-based financing and leasing industry forward to become a significant provider of innovative financial services and products to business customers and consumers—both in Canada and worldwide.

During this period, the classic banking model was challenged by non-traditional bank financing products and the rise of a broader array of non-bank financial providers.

In the traditional model, financing was a seamless process comprising five functions—origination, credit adjudication, funding, administration, and collection—all performed through one institution. This model shaped the regulatory framework and regulatory culture.

In financial services, this was no longer the only model, as a growing number of specialized providers dedicated themselves to only one or two of these functions. This "thin-slicing," unbundling, or separation of financial functions worked when it is more cost-efficient to share responsibilities.

New as well as existing financial institutions chose to concentrate on just a few of the traditional components of financing by joint venturing, outsourcing, partnering other services out, or creating alliances of service companies. It was this combination of non-traditional bank financing and the unbundling of financial functions that opened the door to new financial providers.

Globalization: Proliferation of funding sources

The unprecedented availability of huge pools of private capital seeking global investment opportunities was merely a subset of the trend toward globalization of the marketplace. These pools of capital have caused a proliferation in the number of potential providers of funding who actively pursued global investment opportunities. This, in turn, engendered a dramatic increase in competition in a sector that, for the past fifty to one hundred years, had been limited to a small number of participants. This dramatic increase in competition generated a growing choice of new financial products and services and spawned new organizational models for the delivery of those products and services.

Without these pools of available capital, the newer, non-traditional providers of financial services would have had great difficulty in funding themselves to compete against traditional bank lenders.

Diversification of funding techniques

The third catalyst—diversification of funding techniques—flowed from the proliferation of funding sources. Two of these techniques were of particular importance: "securitization" and the growth in "captive" financing companies.

For an asset-based finance company, securitization was an alternative, generally lower-cost source of funding to that available from a bank. The combination of investors with large pools of capital seeking to invest in pools of cash-generating assets transformed the ability of non-bank financing companies to raise cost-competitive funds.

While not new, the second funding technique was another phenomenon generating capital growth of significance. Well-capitalized manufacturing and servicing companies with substantial earnings decided to leverage their own equity base and core competencies rather than those of third parties. This led to many manufacturers establishing their own financing arms or partnering with those who could do it for them.

Financial historian Ron Chernow argued that, historically,

> ... banking was a mere by-product of the world of trade [hence the origin of the term merchant bank] and it took a long time to evolve into a discrete profession, consecrated by legal authorities with protective charters. Commodity merchants often advanced farmers money against crop deliveries or extended loans against the security of merchandise for safekeeping.... The natural progression from commerce to finance is worth mentioning, for it left open the possibility that clients of merchant banks with surplus lendable funds might someday become rival banks themselves. As we have seen repeatedly in our own day, any successful business that engenders a large surplus is, potentially, an embryonic bank. In the absence of special regulatory restrictions, banking seems to grow spontaneously from other forms of economic activity.[55]

The last part of Chernow's comment deserved some emphasis: "In the absence of special regulatory restrictions, banking seems to grow spontaneously from other forms of economic activity." This phenomenon, a natural outgrowth of economic activity, was nothing new. It has happened before. If the traditional banking and financial institutions of today had been created a century or two ago in this same way, then this simply reflects a continually evolving process.

New technologies

The fourth catalyst is the introduction of new communications and information technologies.

Increasingly in financial services, any enterprise is only as good as its technology. Communications technologies created new distribution channels for financial services that allowed newcomers to leapfrog the traditional, more cumbersome distribution systems at a fraction of the set-up and operating costs.

The speed and reach of new technology to capture information and to rapidly analyze that information made possible, on an unprecedented scale, the identification and exploitation of many different markets in several time zones at once. New technology revolutionized the capacity of a much broader range of professionals to manage risk.

· *chapter 5* ·

1990–2007: Disruption, Innovation, and Consolidation

Angela Armstrong's first cool toy was a cellphone that weighed in at almost a kilogram. The Motorola "bag phone" cost almost $4,000 and came with its own carrying case and a shoulder strap. She was given it when she moved to Edmonton in 1990 to manage National Leasing's branch office there.

Besides making a personal statement, the phone said something about Armstrong's job. Leasing bag phones made up 40 percent of her branch's business. "Bag phones were expensive, but they were regarded as a great business tool," she recalled. "Everyone wanted one."

Within a year, word came from National Leasing's head office in Winnipeg that the branch should stick to financing products with more promising technology. "The writing was on the wall," said Armstrong. "The company had looked down the road and realized that bag phones were on their way out."

"It was a big shock to have to find new accounts and still make your targets for the year," Armstrong remembered. "But strategically, it was the right decision. The expensive part of owning a cellphone had become airtime. We had a hard time with this because, for us, financing the equipment was what we did."

It was not only in the world of cellphones that one technology was rapidly giving way to another, with far-reaching consequences for the leasing industry. In offices and homes across North America, tumbling computer prices helped put a PC on every desk.

"By mid-decade, things shifted again," Armstrong observed. "Computers were considered important hardware, but software was becoming the critical—and more expensive—tool that made it possible to run a business."

Armstrong's team once again scrambled to keep pace, this time moving gingerly into software leasing. "There were tight restraints—each lease transaction could not be more than 25 percent based on software."

Armstrong took these lessons with her when she set up as an independent leasing broker in 2000.

As she recalled, "I learned that it's only by looking ahead down the road that you stay sustainable and profitable. If you kept looking at yesterday and not constantly updating your strategy and mandate, you got caught in no-man's land behind the fast-moving technology curve."

Bountiful and challenging decades

Following a bumpy start to the 1990s, leasing enjoyed almost two decades of bountiful growth. Funding was plentiful and cheap. Fast-changing technology and expanding international trade paved the way for expansion into new asset categories and a host of new customers.

But nimble footwork was needed to stay ahead of the fast-moving game. Companies were bought, sold, trimmed, and realigned, making some careers and breaking others. Newcourt, GE Capital, and various life insurers—among others—continued to expand into businesses once considered the preserve of the banks. The banks pushed back with products of their own that enabled them to circumvent the curbs that barred them from direct participation in vehicle leasing.

A hallmark of the 1990s was the revolution in business and consumer technology. The emergence of the digital age had a massive impact on virtually every Canadian home and business. Armstrong's experience at National Leasing was typical. Lessors not only had to incorporate new technology into the way they ran their businesses; they also had to keep a sharp eye on the equipment they financed to be sure that it would not soon become obsolete and thus have little residual value. Bag phones, fax machines, dedicated file servers, dot-matrix printers, floppy disks, and videotape—to name just a few—were all headed the way of the dinosaur.

The Canadian economy entered a period of readjustment as it made the transition from the borrow-and-spend fiscal climate of the 1980s to the more disciplined era of the 1990s and early 2000s. Yawning government budget deficits gradually turned into surpluses. Likewise, after a serious downturn in 1990 and 1991, businesses focused on cutting costs and improved productivity to bolster profits. Expenses were carefully tracked to make sure capital was being directed at activities that led to profitable growth.

Richard McAuliffe at Key Equipment Finance compared the discipline of the new decade to the frontier mentality of the 1980s: "The growth model was that you had to grow by a specific percentage a year, not just in leasing, but in every industry."

The high-tech revolution, as it was then called, aided the new emphasis on prudence and productivity. Advanced software systems made it possible for line managers to identify activities that were not profitable. Advances in communication curtailed the need for face-to-face meetings. Services such as email, tele- and video-conferencing, and customer portals on websites emerged as novel ways to interact across continents and oceans, enabling companies to slash travel and even bricks-and-mortar office expenses.

Sensing the need to serve an increasingly sophisticated industry with a unified voice, Canada's top leasing players pushed for a merger of their two trade associations, ELAC and CALA. The result was the Canadian Finance & Leasing Association (CFLA).

Adding to the upheavals, the asset-based finance industry was forced to confront some serious errors in judgment as some players once again turned their backs on the fundamental principles of sound financing practice, namely:

- Never compromise on credit standards, even when market conditions get tough.
- Pay attention to the bottom line and not just sales numbers.
- Never compromise on residual values. The calculation needs to determine a realistic market price at the end of the lease term.

As things turned out, the industry came through the following series of tumultuous events with resolve and innovation:

- Canada's 1990–91 recession and a new economic order,
- a revolution in technology and communications,
- a new generation of resilient leaders,
- the rise of the broker,
- a transition from fleet buying to fleet management,
- rewards and risks in consumer vehicle leasing, and
- a single voice for the industry.

A new economic order and the struggle to adjust

The 1990s did not start well for Canada's business community. Inflation had picked up again in the late 1980s. Many lessors misguidedly took that as a signal to step up their borrowing and use much of their extra leverage to speculate on real estate and other volatile assets. When the Bank of Canada tightened monetary policy to curb inflation, the economy went into a spin. Companies suddenly faced a sharp drop in asset values and, to make things worse, higher interest rates on their swollen debt.

Another, much broader problem was also starting to take a toll on companies from coast to coast. Canadian business had not prepared well for the new era of rapid technological change and intensified global competition. In a 2001 speech to the Canadian Club in Toronto, the Bank of Canada's then-governor, Gordon Thiessen, noted, "The effects of technological change, including a decline in communications costs, meant that, through the 1980s, national markets had become much more susceptible to international competition. In Canada, however, the relatively high inflation of the 1970s and 1980s had distracted Canadian firms: rather than focusing on product design and innovation, cost control, and productivity improvement, many of them had been looking for ways to take advantage of inflation. Thus, they had tended to postpone the adjustments needed to respond to a changing world economy."[56]

These skewed priorities ended up taking a heavy toll. "By the early 1990s, the realities of the new world economic order were becoming clearer to Canadian companies too," Thiessen noted. "Only at that time, they were also coping with the fallout from the high-inflation years, especially the sharp drop in the prices of speculative investments and the burden of servicing large debts, as well as with declining world commodity prices. Working their way out of these difficulties was disruptive and painful for Canadian businesses. Defaults, restructurings, and downsizings became the order of the day."

The casualties included highly leveraged leasing companies. Many took heavy losses as banks called in their loans.

Refinancings and corporate rescues took place, many dressed up as mergers and acquisitions.

Hugo Sørensen had a front seat during this turbulent period as the president of Triathlon Leasing. Although Triathlon's assets had ballooned from $80 million to $1.2 billion during the course of the previous decade, the company needed money to make money. But the taps began to run dry as concern grew that Triathlon had overextended itself.

"Margins were getting thinner, equity requirements were getting more, banks were getting fussy because the economic times were challenging," recalled Sørensen. "You began to see a lot of consolidation of portfolios." Triathlon eventually ran out of options and fell into the arms of GE Capital Fleet Services on January 31, 1994.

Vancouver's First City Capital, which had expanded during the 1980s, also faltered by 1991. The successful lessor had bought Industrial Funding Corporation, a small-ticket lessor based in Portland, but the new arrangement put a former office equipment executive in charge who did not know the business. AT&T took over the company, renaming it AT&T Capital Canada, a subsidiary of the U.S. parent's leasing business. Led by Tim Hammill, president, and Joe LaLeggia, CFO, the business regained its mojo and began turning a profit once more. "They hit the ground running," said Gary Thompson, one of the team members who stayed on a couple more years. "It was a testament to what First City had built."

Smaller companies were even more vulnerable, especially when faced with rapid technological change. One example was Québec-based Crédit-Bail Clé, which had made a name for itself in furniture and office equipment leasing during the 1980s. Founded by René Bronsard in Trois-Rivières in 1979, Crédit-Bail Clé was an unusual animal in the leasing business. It was financed by some of Québec's most prominent financial institutions, including Caisses Desjardins (now the Desjardins

Group). But what really made Crédit-Bail Clé different was that its shareholders were also partner vendors who helped sell its leasing services. This relationship created a loyalty and built-in ownership that served the company well in its early years.

But like Triathlon, Crédit-Bail Clé could not resist the temptation of easy credit. "The company invested too much in IT systems and had to face increased losses," said current president, Luc Robitaille. "It went through very difficult times, dropping from thirty employees in 1989 to three by 1995."

Robitaille, a former banker, entrepreneur, and university professor, joined the board in 1995 as part of a drive to inject new life into Crédit-Bail Clé. "The loyalty, patience, and trust of some employees, shareholders, and lenders saved the company," he recalled. "Growth restarted slowly from 1997 and accelerated after the acquisition by new shareholders at the end of 1998." As one of the new shareholders, Robitaille bought the feisty Québec company a year later. Crédit-Bail Clé rebuilt its business and its reputation to the point where today it is once again regarded as a Québec success story. With forty-three employees, it specialized in such areas as transport (including motor vehicles), restaurant supplies, chairs for health and beauty salons, and heavy construction equipment. A wholly-owned subsidiary, CLE Leasing, with twenty-eight employees, served English-speaking Canada from its base in Burlington, Ontario. Twenty years later, the company demonstrated the strength of its client base and stability. In March 2014, it was acquired by Hitachi Capital Canada Corp. Robitaille commented that "the acquisition gives CLE many new opportunities for growth and improved performance."

Recovery with a shift in mood and culture

Canada started pulling out of recession in 1992. The economy stabilized as the private and public sectors adjusted to the new realities. Business was not alone in feeling pressure to run leaner operations and adapt to new technology. The federal and provincial governments of the day belatedly began to tackle their towering budget deficits through spending restraint. By 1996, investment in new machinery, equipment, and technology was picking up. Economic output, measured by gross domestic product (GDP), rose steadily into the 2000s.

"Low and stable inflation, together with a declining public sector debt, now provided a stronger base for the Canadian economy than it had experienced in three decades," Thiessen would remark at Toronto's Canadian Club as he looked back in 2001. "In addition, there is the shift in business attitudes toward a greater focus on cost control, productivity, and international competitiveness."[57]

The mood after 1992 was decidedly different from the carefree days of the mid-1980s. Companies were more prudent in how they structured their operations and spent money. Many sold or closed unprofitable divisions, especially those considered not to be part of their core business or not to offer the most prudent use of capital.

Manufacturers with captive finance arms also came under pressure from the investment community. Even though the financing business was in some cases making more money than the core manufacturing operations, "investors couldn't analyze a company and break it down if they didn't know the industry," said Bill Bell, who worked for Pitney Bowes Leasing at the time.

"Brokerage houses demanded to know if a company was a financier or manufacturer. You couldn't be both. It was too confusing. A company had to decide whether or not it was a manufacturer or a finance company, and then divest accordingly."

Xerox and Clark Equipment, a maker of heavy machinery, were among those that succumbed to the pressure, spinning off their captive finance units to specialists in financial services. Similarly, Pitney Bowes sold its Canadian subsidiary Pitney

Bowes Credit to Newcourt Credit in 1996. The U.S. parent had pulled the plug three years earlier on Pitney Bowes Leasing, also sold to Newcourt Credit. Although the leasing business was profitable and Pitney Bowes had been extremely successful in Canada, it was no longer considered an integral part of the parent's global operations. "We were a division of a U.S. parent, and no one got a say in the matter," Debbie Sands, who managed the Calgary branch noted. "It was the old story that when America sneezes, Canada catches a cold."

Pitney Bowes Leasing disappeared in name, but its staff remained intact and its operations added a substantial new dimension to Newcourt's transport and construction equipment business. When Bill Bell knew that the Canadian division was about to be sold, he approached Steve Hudson and said he would sell part of the company's external portfolio as long as he took the people.

Many mid-size lessors were also falling prey to large institutions, such as banks that wanted to fill out their portfolios with regional or niche players. The most aggressive consolidators of the period were GE Capital and Newcourt Credit, both of which served broad segments of the economy and had access to multiple funding sources. By the late 1990s, GE had tucked several equipment finance businesses and at least two auto finance specialists under its wing in Canada.[58] And it did not stop there. It went on to acquire part of transport equipment giant Bombardier's financial services division in 2005.

In the race to catch up with its bigger rival, Newcourt made eighteen acquisitions in the six years between 1992 and 1998, including several businesses spun off by banks. Among its targets: Bank of Montreal's leasing division (1992); Commcorp Financial Services, which gave it a minority sale in CIBC Equipment Finance Ltd. (1997); Business Technology Finance, a division of U.K.–based Lloyds Bank PLC (1997); and AT&T Capital (1998).

On the West Coast, Lease West made its first acquisition, Travelers Acceptance Corp., a consumer finance business being sold off by its U.S. parent. Lease West continued its acquisition spree, adding Custom Lease for prime auto financing and Essex Financial, an Alberta-based commercial finance business. By 1997, the company had rebranded itself as Travelers Group, with Travelers Financial Corporation its leasing and financing subsidiary.

The big banks also extended their thrust into leasing—especially the vehicle side of the business, even though they could participate only indirectly. By 1996, the banks were financing 57 percent of cars and trucks leased in Canada. CIBC, Bank of Montreal, and Scotiabank led the way. Each offered a varied menu of financial services to dealers. In Québec, Desjardins targeted the vehicle leasing market with a car dealership program.

In 1994, Scotia unveiled its Dealer Value Lease Plan (DVLP). Through the DVLP, the bank provided funding to auto dealers for leasing deals. It also managed the leases on the dealers' behalf. Scotiabank uses the DVLP to this day as its vehicle for dealer-based funding.

U.S. and foreign leasing interests expand in Canada

By lowering cross-border barriers to trade and investment, the 1987 Canada–United States Free Trade Agreement (FTA) encouraged more foreign leasing companies to move into Canada; in the case of those already here, it allowed them to expand their services.[59]

Volvo Commercial Finance, a division of Volvo Trucks North America, set up a Canadian subsidiary in the mid-1990s. The offshoot was based in Thornhill, north of Toronto. KeyCorp Leasing, owned by a Cleveland-based bank, expanded its interests in Canada and many other countries by acquiring Leasetec, a specialist in information technology and telecommunications equipment leasing. The name was changed to Key Equipment Finance in 2001. Key again reached across the border three years later to buy Toronto Dominion Bank's lease portfolio. "We have a great portfolio that's performed well over twenty-two years here in Canada," said Richard McAuliffe, a former TD executive who joined Key Equipment Finance.

The U.K.'s Barclays Bank was among other foreign banks that strengthened their Canadian leasing operations. Tom Hopkirk, who headed up the Canadian arm in 1993, recalled how the bank and its leasing business thrived at the time. "The bank had ten branches across Canada, and the leasing division experienced good volumes and low losses."

Leasing goes online

By 1995, business and individuals could access the Internet from desktop computers. The first Web-based email service—Hotmail—was launched the following year, and the move toward the supposedly paperless office had begun with the introduction of the soon-to-be ubiquitous PDF (portable document format) document. Almost overnight, any document could be easily stored and transmitted electronically. PDF technology was just one example of the way in which computers could capture, store, and share information.

The Internet and the digitization of data revolutionized the way in which businesses operated and communicated. The speed of the transition was unprecedented. Leasing companies—and their customers—had no choice but to adapt or, in Angela Armstrong's words, "to be caught in no-man's land."

The digital age brought immeasurable benefits to leasing. The new technologies reinforced the many advantages that lease providers had over traditional bankers—an ability to move quickly; be flexible; bundle together services; and make down-to-earth, easy-to-understand decisions.

The new online world also supported innovation. Lessors could compare prices more easily and more quickly; search vendors; and then provide customers with cost analysis, reporting, and quotes to meet specific needs. New subsectors emerged, such as software, technology consulting, and management services, which brought an extra dimension to the services that leasing companies could offer their customers.

Mike Collins was among those in the thick of the transformation. Collins began his leasing career at CDL's vehicle arm, Canadian Vehicle Leasing. By the 1980s, he was working as an account manager at Triathlon.

"When I started, I was in customer service and sales," Collins said, recalling the pre-computer era. "Every fall we had to visit all our fleet customers and approve their vehicle selection. One was Chubb Security Systems. At that time, everything was done with bail wire and Band-Aids. I'd go to my price book—literally a binder—pick the car, price it out with an adding machine, give it to a secretary to type out so I could send out the requisition to companies we dealt with—Ford, Chrysler, GM, maybe a foreign distributor. The fleet manager at Chubb would then review what was sent back, approve it, and that same secretary would then type the orders.

"Next I'd drive to Brampton with the thirteen-part requisition forms and, once signed, drive them back to my office. I kept them in milk crates in my car because if you ran out of forms, you'd lose the deal. When I got back to the office, someone would enter the data by hand into the various ordering systems at GM, et cetera. It all happened using adding machines and gasoline."

Collins was on the frontlines during the transition to online applications, software, and Web-enabled services. Now, a dealership could process a lease application simply by logging on to a website. Thanks to "credit-decisioning" software, a credit score was available within two hours. The software could perform an automated decision on simple applications without any need for human intervention. "An application that used to take several hours now took about forty seconds," said Collins. For more complex applications, the software quickly gave credit officers the information they needed to make a sound judgment call. The upshot was a surge in activity at the dealer level.

"The activity of fleet leasing remained the same," Collins observed. "But suddenly, companies differentiated themselves by their Web applications, instead of a salesperson driving around burning fossil fuel."

Collins himself moved into the technology side of leasing. In 2000, Collins joined with others to found Curomax Corporation, Canada's first online portal for vehicle financing applications at dealerships. The company was led by Alan Bird, a visionary and entrepreneur who had left AT&T Capital Canada after the Newcourt acquisition. Seven years later, Curomax was sold to DealerTrack Technologies, which had developed similar technology in the United States. The Web-based software system at DealerTrack Canada transformed and now dominates how credit is submitted to multiple funding sources from auto dealerships. It still operates in Canada, with Collins as vice-president for lender finance solutions and Canadian operations.

"We're the number-one provider in an industry that didn't exist before 2000," Collins reflected.

Another leader in online systems for fleet leasing was PHH, the U.S.–based company that had been one of the earliest to recognize the potential of vehicle leasing and fleet management.

PHH launched its online system in 1999, a move described as a game-changer by Mike Goddard, who joined the company in 1982 and headed its Canadian operations from 1994 to 2006. PHH was one of the top-six fleet management companies in Canada at the time, along with GE Capital, AT&T Capital, Black & McDonald (BML), Automotive Resources International (ARI), and Transportaction Lease Systems (TLS).

"The Internet completely altered the way we did business," Goddard recalled. "Not only did it have huge implications for efficiency and report making, but it opened up information and reports to customers in real time. Real time meant that analysis and policy change could be made right as 'stuff' was happening. Clients could perform their current financial and administrative reports with the click of a button."

Goddard also noted how the Internet helped to underpin PHH's customer service vision, set out when the company was founded way back in 1946. "PHH had always asked: 'How can we do more for companies? How can we make it easier for them to manage their fleets?' Technology supported this value proposition, providing efficiency, administrative ease, and driver productivity."

Ramping up the speed of credit decisions

In their quest to move faster than a bank, equipment leasing companies had also become early adapters of technology, initially for creating pricing models and later for assessing credit risk. In 1981, when IAC became the Continental Bank, IT pioneer Owen Moher worked with I.P. Sharp Associates to develop a computer-based pricing model for complex tax calculations. The bank then used the code to develop a PC-based system. Around the same time, NABEL put a credit-scoring technology in place that would predict, through statistics, the ability of a client to fulfill obligations on a lease through the term. Data that defined the attributes of a client was fed into the system, such as how long they had been in business, the nature of the business, and its payment history. A score was then produced to determine whether they were approved or declined.

In the early 1990s, Moher spoke about lease/buy calculations at the annual conference of ELAC in Niagara Falls, Ontario. He noted the "ridiculous results presented to clients" because of the shortcomings of doing such calculations with paper, pencil, and calculators. After his talk, he was approached by Ralph Selby of Price Waterhouse, to vet the methodologies, and by Bill Jensen, president of Scotia Leasing, who offered a test site. The result was a new credit decisioning system called RUBICON (now owned by Constellation Financing Systems).

Adapting to changing times

Software and other technology breakthroughs propelled various new business models during the 1990s and 2000s. Process engineering was touted as the hottest way to analyze and design workflows within an organization. *Core competency*, a term coined by the *Harvard Business Review* in 1990, became a buzzword in boardrooms across North America. *Strategic outsourcing* implied a more comprehensive analysis for selecting preferred vendors and tracking their performance.

Businesses around the world found myriad ways to increase speed, quality, and thus productivity as they sought to emulate Toyota's vaunted doctrine of continuous improvement and lean manufacturing. Leasing was no exception. Branch offices were closed. Video conferencing and webinars replaced face-to-face meetings and training. The Internet became an essential tool to collect and share information. Specialized software could draw up spreadsheets and compile reports in a fraction of the time that humans would take to do the job.

More products emerged to offer companies a competitive edge. In 1999, BMO and Citibank Leasing formed FinanciaLinx, an Internet-based auto lease product. FLinx, as it was known, dramatically cut down on the time it took a dealer to obtain a lease by reaching an online decision. In its first year, the alliance signed up 20 percent of Canadian new-car dealers with the e-business leasing product. Hyundai Auto Canada subsequently awarded the company their leasing business.[60] FLinx quickly became the largest independent indirect consumer automobile leasing entity in Canada, with $2 billion in average earning assets and in excess of 120,000 vehicles on lease.[61] In 2002, Lease Administration Corp (LAC), originally created to liquidate Pacific National Leasing, became the managing partner of FinanciaLinx.

National Leasing was one of numerous players roiled by internal upheaval as management took an axe to labour and other costs. "Because of centralization and technology, everything changed," said Barb Hannesson, a National veteran who managed the Calgary office. Hannesson found herself without a job after head office decided that the way of the future was a single, central operation using technology to support sales and service personnel in the field.

As Hannesson put it, "Branch offices were really just mini leasing companies and the industry didn't need them now. So companies like ours changed their model, closed branches, and centralized."

Although such decisions were a tough blow for Hannesson and many others, they also helped separate the wheat from the chaff. Some companies thrived, some just survived, and many others disappeared. As for Hannesson, she moved over to Citicorp's leasing office in Calgary. Today she is senior business development officer at RCAP Leasing in Calgary, which is wholly owned by Royal Bank.

A new generation of resilient leaders

The turmoil of the 1990s required fresh, imaginative thinking. Companies had been bought, sold, and restructured. There were gaps in the market waiting to be filled, new lines of business to pursue, and internal tensions to overcome. Clearly, a different kind of leadership was called for in Canada's asset-based finance business.

As restructured companies looked for ways to carve out their own segments in the marketplace, examples abounded of disruption, stumbles, and career-altering changes along the way. Many industry executives were forced once again to think outside the box, or at least reassess their own career paths.

Jeff Hartley was emblematic of the new breed. Hartley began his career in 1987 at Gelco, one of Canada's largest U.S.–owned vehicle lessors. Five years later, Gelco found itself owned by GE Capital. "There was lots of consolidation going on at the time," said Hartley, now president of Foss National Leasing, "and it was GE that was doing it all. All in all, it was good to be with the 'consolidator.'"

Many former Gelco employees struggled to adapt to the GE culture. One in three left. But Hartley embraced the opportunity to work for a global company and to make an impact as an up-and-coming leasing executive.

One of his first assignments was to find a home for ten repossessed buses parked in rural Québec. (There were originally eleven, but one was destroyed by fire in Vermont.) Hartley came up with the idea of leasing them, even though no such deals had been done at that time in Canada. After all, he figured, motor coach and school bus leasing were one of GE Capital's core businesses in the United States.

As the banks saw it, buses were no different to cars when it came to financing, so a loan to buy a bus would have to be amortized over sixty months. But monthly payments under such an arrangement were so high that bus operators were discouraged from even thinking about expanding their fleets. GE, on the other hand, was accustomed to ten-year amortizations with minimal to no down payment. This kind of financial arrangement significantly reduced the monthly cash flow required to finance bus fleets.

After scouring the country, Hartley was able to put the buses back on the road by leasing them to small operators. He set up an affordable plan under which the lessees' monthly payment was just half the cost of servicing a bank loan. Word soon spread that anyone with a bus to sell or lease should call Jeff Hartley at GE. Hartley launched GE Capital Fleet Services' bus business with ten vehicles; within a few years, it had hundreds of coaches and school buses on its books, valued at about $50 million.

Jack Marandola was another who found new opportunities. A seasoned financier by the 1990s, Marandola had spent twenty years running commercial accounts, including many leasing deals at Bank of Montreal. When Newcourt Credit acquired Bank of Montreal Leasing Corporation in 1992, Marandola left the bank to work at Newcourt, switching from banking to leasing and servicing Newcourt's relationship with BMO in Eastern Canada. It seemed a perfect opportunity. Newcourt was well on its way to becoming the second biggest lessor in North America. "I knew the ways of the bank, how it operated, who was in the network," explained Marandola. Yet by 1999, he found himself caught up in Newcourt's dramatic fall and its sale to CIT Group.

CIT asked him to run its commercial and industrial finance division. The upheavals continued unabated. For a time, Marandola headed up CIBC Equipment Finance, which had been part of Newcourt's 1997 Commcorp acquisition. Tired of being shuffled around in a big company, Marandola left CIT in 2001 to set up his own brokerage and consulting firm. But he later returned to the corporate world, taking a job with National City Commercial Capital until National was swallowed by PNC Financial Services Group. He then joined CLE, the new Ontario branch of Crédit-Bail Clé, in 2008, and has worked there ever since. It would not be the last change. In 2014, CLE was acquired by Hitachi Capital.

The pin-ball effect

This kind of bouncing around had become increasingly common. As one in the industry recalled, "I would come home at the end of the day and say to my wife, 'Guess what company was bought today?'"

Doug McKenzie, managing director of BAL Global Finance Canada Corporation, aptly summed up his experience: "I came to leasing the way of the pinball." McKenzie began his career in the inventory finance division of BorgWarner in 1981 but moved into equipment leasing when he joined Commercial Financial. When Montreal Trust Company of Canada acquired Commercial Financial's leasing operations, McKenzie found himself working for the bank. Ironically, when he left Montreal Trust to join Scotia Leasing in the 1990s, Scotia turned around and bought Montreal Trust. In 1995, McKenzie took a position at Commcorp Financial Services, a company acquired by Newcourt. McKenzie then moved to the Canadian leasing division of FleetBoston Financial Corporation, which was acquired by Bank of America in 2004. Since then, McKenzie has been managing the vendor finance business of BAL Global Finance Canada Corporation.

In spite of the corporate musical chairs, some leasing divisions and their leaders remained largely intact from one owner to the next. From his Mississauga office at PHH Canada, Mike Goddard watched a dizzying series of deals unfold at his New Jersey–based parent, starting with a merger in 1996 with hotel franchiser Hospitality Franchise Systems (HFS). A series of subsequent corporate marriages and divorces involved PHH and Avis Group, French-owned Arval Service Lease in Europe, and Cendant Corporation.

Despite the ever-shifting ownership, PHH was "always allowed to run its own [fleet management] business," Goddard said. "We retained all our management, and we remained unique within the structure. We carried on, trusted that we knew what we were doing. Our biggest challenge was explaining what was happening when people heard that we had been sold once again. They thought we were in trouble when, in fact, it was just the opposite. We were trading on the New York Stock Exchange and doing very well."

Goddard remained at PHH Arval until he retired in 2006.

Rise of the non-prime credit providers

In 1996, another imaginative businessman identified a market niche for meeting the needs of start-ups in their first two to three years of business. Originally from the Montreal apparel trade, Larry Mlynowski set up a desk in his basement and worked out a financing model for the non-prime credit market. His market was cash-strapped entrepreneurs who needed a piece of equipment to manage their business, help them grow, or both. Now in its eighteenth year of operation, Equirex Leasing Corp. provides equipment leases for an unending variety of assets, from sewing machines to delivery trucks. Although transactions are all under $100,000, neither the banks nor prime leasing companies are interested in taking on the risk. "Our clients are business owners with a dream, lots of desire, and a good covenant," said Mlynowski. "They are willing to work twenty-four hours a day, seven days a week, but they don't have credit history."

Mlynowski's most interesting lease arrangement was for dairy cows. When first approached about the idea by a broker in B.C., Mlynowski thought it was a joke. But he quickly learned that dairy farmers consider cows their most important asset. The lowly animals not only produce product. The residual value of cows is much better than that of most equipment assets—an important benefit for Equirex. "The difference between a cappuccino machine and a dairy cow," explained Mlynowski, "is that when the machine stops working, it goes into the garbage. When a cow stops giving milk, it enters the food chain."

Equirex arranged leases for thousands of dairy cows, always dealing with small farmers, mostly in Ontario and B.C. The practice continued until the government changed quota laws, restricting how such farms could operate profitably. There was only one occasion when Mlynowski had to repossess cows. He did, however, have to create a new clause in the lease in order to assign ownership of the calves, a by-product of lactating cows—back to the farmer.

Known as one of the first to bring non-prime credit into the market, Equirex expanded to more than eighty staff, with customers across Canada. Competitors emerged, although none have remained in business as long as Equirex. As observed by its energetic leader, the best part of business is when it "loses" clients. "It's a sign that they've reached the point where the banks will lend the money, which means they've reached their dream," boasted Mlynowski.

Around the same time, Travelers Financial Corporation set up Travelers Leasing Corporation (TLC), one of Canada's first brokers in non-prime automobile finance. TLC provided financing to customers that ranged from young buyers with no credit rating to new immigrants, the self-employed, or those with a troubled credit history. While its head office is in Burnaby, TLC built its national presence with offices in Ontario and Québec by 2000. "The whole notion of the non-prime auto finance market was just emerging," recalled CEO Jim Case, "so our timing was great."

Rise of the small broker

One side effect of the corporate upheavals of the 1990s and early 2000s was a surge in the number of leasing brokers. Travelers Financial Corporation was one such example. With its acquisitions and rapid growth, the company was destined to become one of the countries largest and most successful finance and lease brokers.

At the other end of the spectrum, a small brokerage business made good sense for experienced and skilled individuals who found themselves out of a job as their employers were bought, sold, or merged, or simply disappeared. Many had grown tired of being the "pinball" and were ready to run their own show.

For those with a network of vendors, underwriters, and customers, working as a broker could be both lucrative and satisfying. The barriers to setting up a full-fledged leasing company had become steep. Hefty financial backing was essential, and competition was intense with multinational giants such as GE in the game. By contrast, setting up as a broker was a low-risk way to stay in the industry without having to commit to costly infrastructure or taking on potentially crippling credit risks.

Debbie Sands, an equipment leasing manager out west, was among those who led the way. Sands was running the Pitney Bowes Leasing office in Calgary when the firm shut its doors in 1992. She recalled how she and her colleagues scrambled to vacate the office: "We had to sell off the desks, the curtains, everything." An industry contact offered to put Sands in touch with a group of underwriters looking to fund some small leasing deals. She agreed, and she incorporated her own brokerage firm, Priority Leasing, in 1993.

As brokers, Sands and her team shopped clients' leasing needs around to various underwriters, inviting them to come up with their best offer to finance assets as diverse as computers, telephone systems, forklifts, backhoes, light industrial gear, and construction equipment. By staying small, Priority Leasing also stayed nimble. Its staff—never more than six—prided themselves on the personal touch, always being available to take customer calls and do business with a minimum of red tape.

"Sometimes the bigger companies choke each other and the clients with more paperwork than they need," Sands noted. "They actually become like a bank. Smaller companies like us were always more flexible. And we just always seemed to be faster than larger lessors, particularly the banks."

Priority Leasing is still in business with Sands as president. Many consider her the first small-ticket lease broker in the country. "Certainly, I was one of the first," Sands agreed.

A Canadian hustle

The 1990s were not without their hiccups. The most notorious scandal in the asset-based finance and leasing industry began to unfold early in the decade when a massive fraud was discovered at Pacific National Financial Corporation and its three wholly-owned subsidiaries.[62]

A small-ticket leasing company, Pacific National Leasing (PNL) leased mostly office equipment. It had been set up by some former employees of Canadian Dominion Leasing. Typical in the industry, PNL sold the financial benefits of its leases to several large funders, which included Mutual Life, Sun Life, Great West, Investors Group, National Bank, Barclays Bank, National Trust, and Royal Trust. The company also had lines of bank credit. Although the funders owned the leases, PNL did all the administration, which at the company's peak amounted to about 44,000 leases, worth around $300 million.

Despite being a public company, the founder often treated PNL like a family operation. Several family members were on the payroll, providing questionable value, and many "corporate" assets were solely for private use, like fancy homes in Hawaii, California, and Whistler. According to Moe Danis, the company was "run like a personal ATM." Its board of directors turned a blind eye to what was going on until the company was forced into bankruptcy in 1992.

For several years, PNL used various fraudulent schemes to conceal problems and keep the company out of financial trouble. In addition to filing false financial reports, PNL "double-funded" its assets. The company bought equipment to lease through two credit sources, Royal Trust and National Bank. But when it needed to show it had enough assets to back borrowing, the same set of assets was used for each credit line. Assets were moved back and forth on paper so PNL could "honestly" say that the assets existed on the relevant margin reporting dates.

When the company filed for protection under the Companies' Creditors Arrangement Act in July 1992, the assigned commercial court judge was relatively inexperienced. As is often the case, the judge ruled to leave the management in place while a recovery plan was drafted and a further $15 million "went missing." When the company finally declared bankruptcy, hundreds of shareholders and creditors lost money. "The bankruptcy impacted everybody in the industry," said Danis. "These kinds of events are never good, negatively impacting the many small mom-and-pop lessees across the country who require this kind of financing, as well as forever changing the way the funders did business."

Six years of complex proceedings and confrontation followed, with infighting among the financial institutions as to who owned the paper.

The case was complicated by a team of auditors that was decidedly conflicted. Shoddy accounting hid what was going on to such an extent that PNL was technically bankrupt years before even the funders knew it. Chartered accountants lost their professional designations and the funders successfully settled with the audit firm.

When the case finally closed, the court ruled that Mutual Life owned their lease transactions—and eventually, it was excused from the bankruptcy. It was a landmark decision. But there were other lessons to be learned.

Danis at the time was with Mutual Life, which had $90 million of exposure. Mutual Life further tightened its own audit practices and, working with Bill Cochrane at Sun Life, put in its own lease administration service company to liquidate PNL. Its mandate was to run off the portfolio while trying to recover funders' cash advanced to PNL to acquire leases. Ginter Baca, hired to run Lease Administration Corporation, recalled the enormity of the task, trying to figure out where the leases were held and collect as much money as possible: "With all the funders concerned about their exposure," he joked, "the whole affair was a dog's breakfast."

In addition to collecting the PNL leases, LAC became engaged as backup servicer to all Mutual Life's leasing accounts. By 1998, LAC had recovered all funders' cash, as well as all of LAC's expenses during the liquidation period.

Most of the other financial institutions exited the business of funding leasing companies after the Pacific National scandal. Great West never came back. Although both Canada Life and ManuLife returned later, neither did in a major way. When Sun Life acquired Mutual Life/Clarica in 2003, it became (and remained) the largest insurance funder for lease transactions, with Danis responsible for its book of leases until 2009.

David Chaiton, the lawyer who played a prominent role in the case, called PNL "Canada's Enron." In reflecting back on the case he wrote, "If a funder lets a leasing company administer its lease without diligent oversight, the potential for fraud is about as certain as the fox having chicken for dinner if it's left to run the henhouse."[63]

Out of the ashes

One of the big winners out of the mess was the emergence of LAC as a model for other funders and lessors who required portfolio administration.

After LAC completed its role in the PNL recovery, funders agreed to surrender their shares in LAC at the point their leases were all collected. Looking to the future, LAC convinced Clarica Life, the remaining shareholder, to invest in LAC. After all, LAC had proven how helpful it was to have a standby servicer to assume control of any lease portfolio where the borrower defaulted in its obligation to the funder. In addition to acting as an insurance policy on behalf of funders, LAC began offering its services to other lessors and funders in the area of portfolio administration. LAC's first new client, TD Bank, acquired a 25 percent interest in the company and retained that position until the bank sold its leasing portfolio to Key Financial. Under Ginter Baca's leadership, from the period 1998 to present date, LAC has administered and managed in excess of $4 billion of contracts in both commercial and consumer space for both equipment and vehicles.

Fleet leasing spreads its wings

The belt-tightening of the early 1990s turned out to be both a curse and a blessing for fleet lessors. Government cost-cutting and corporate downsizing cut into business volumes. Fewer employees meant fewer vehicles, both for corporate fleets and for executive company cars. On the other hand, as companies focused on their core businesses, they increasingly turned to outside contractors for fleet management services. In the process, a fleet manager's job became far more complex than just choosing vehicles and maintaining them.

The cost-cutting mantra of the day meant that managers were under constant pressure to squeeze expenses. At the same time, the rise of environmental activism made fleet owners more conscious of the need to avoid waste, cut pollution, and promote safety. Demand was growing for performance data on such variables as gas consumption, driving habits, and route efficiency, and software programs were developed to capture and analyze this information. The "new" strategic sourcing methods of the 1990s forced fleet lessors to provide more detailed cost and performance analysis so that clients could choose vehicles best suited to their needs. The entire business of fleet management took on a level of sophistication that only large, well-financed companies could handle and afford.

Foss National Leasing was among those that rose to the challenge. For almost twenty years, Foss had viewed fleet leasing primarily as a tool to sell more cars. But the leasing business could only be expanded by hiring more sales staff, which in turn drove up costs. By the early 1990s, vigorous competition and low interest rates had squeezed Foss's leasing returns.

Keenly aware of the benefits offered by emerging digital and online technologies, Mike Collins, head of Foss National Leasing from 1995 to 2000, set out to broaden the horizons of the fleet business. After Collins moved on, his successor, Jeff Hartley, continued the drive toward a more profitable business model. Hartley had built his leasing experience at GE and Volvo Commercial Finance and felt strongly that fleet management was the right direction to take.

"Foss was in the fleet leasing business, but it didn't know how to make money at it," Hartley recalled. "Collins started to change the mentality toward fleet management, and I finished the job."

The cornerstone of the strategy was to expand services and improve efficiency without taking on more staff. Foss began offering not only a vehicle and a lease, but full maintenance, fuel management and tracking, and driver training. It handled customers' insurance claims and calculated the taxable benefit for employees who drove a company car.

"Our promotion to customers became, 'We can help you buy gas, get your cars fixed, negotiate the best maintenance package, prepare your cost-per-mile report, and do your taxable benefit reports,'" Hartley said. "The model differentiated our company and diversified its income so that eventually the income earned from fleet management far exceeded that of leasing."

The new direction enabled Foss to sell fleet management as an "outsourced business process" at a time when companies were looking for exactly that service. It even provided a white label fleet management service for the government of Alberta.

After a few years the government was renting Foss's systems and running them itself.

The shift turned out to be a smart one for Foss. Before long, the size of the fleets it managed had grown from thirty vehicles to as many as five hundred. The leasing unit's net income quadrupled in four years.

Fleet management without fleet leasing

In 1993, U.S. fleet giant ARI asked Fred Booth to join the company as president. Booth, who joked that the first word out of his mouth was car, began his career at Avis Rent a Car System in Montreal. He moved into the leasing industry when the U.S. company Lend Lease wanted to set up a Canadian operation. Booth spent ten years as president, until ARI bought Lend Lease as a means to extend its own reach into the country.

With proven experience on how to run a U.S. company north of the border, Booth was an ideal choice. Shortly after Booth's arrival, he hired Brent Ford, a sales manager determined to bid on the contract for federal fleet services. The government certainly did not require the credit assistance; it was the fleet management side that caught their interest. The bid was successful. By 2004, the federal treasury department mandated that all departments use ARI. Others followed, including the Ontario government and crown corporations that were given the same terms, Ontario's Hydro One, BC Hydro, and Nova Scotia Power.

The genius of ARI's service was its "garage program," designed to capture all the repair data on government vehicles stored and maintained in garage bays across the country. To support the program, ARI opened one of the first 24/7 customer service lines. Instead of calls being directed to a U.S. office, regional reps took the call. "When a Québec driver called for maintenance, day or night," explained Booth, "someone at ARI talked with them *in French* and directed them to the nearest repair shop. CBC was one of our biggest clients. Their technicians drove the trucks that did the NHL hockey broadcast, coast to coast, in various time zones. If these vehicles broke down, someone, somewhere, would miss the hockey game. CBC depended on ARI's regional reps and service to get them up and running again."

From New Jersey dealership to global company

A Canadian operation run by Canadians, with regional offices and bilingual service, would remain a defining feature of ARI Canada.

Now led by Melinda Holman, granddaughter of founder Joe, ARI applied the lessons it learned running a business in Canada to the way in now operates in a global marketplace. "When we set up the company for the federal government contract, everything had to be adapted to Canada, such as language, taxes, income, and sale taxes," observed Booth. "This is similar to how global companies today need to be able to meet their customer needs in the United Kingdom, or Europe, or Asia. We learned that listening to Quebecers!"

ARI has remained the top fleet management company for government vehicles in Canada.

The incentive financing debacle

The dawn of the digital era had a big impact not only on leasing companies, but also on the items they financed. The change was especially profound in motor vehicles. A proliferation of on-board electronic systems made cars more complex and also more expensive. Meanwhile, family incomes were stagnating. By one estimate, the average Canadian had to work about thirty weeks to pay for a new car, instead of only twenty weeks a decade earlier. Any prospective car buyer clearly needed to gird for "sticker shock" at the dealership.

Sales of new passenger vehicles in Canada plummeted in 1988, and they kept falling for the next seven years, twice as long as any previous decline. Close to 500 dealerships out of a total of about 4,100 went out of business. The rest were forced to find new ways of moving cars off the lot. Leasing turned out to be one of those ways, and a highly effective one too.

GM, Ford, and Chrysler set out to persuade customers that leasing a car made as much sense as buying it, and was more affordable. Ford and GM offered closed-end retail leases through their Red Carpet Lease and SmartLease programs, respectively. Primus Automotive Financial Services, a Ford Credit subsidiary, offered private-label leases to dealers of several import nameplates, including Subaru, Jaguar, Suzuki, Mazda, and Hyundai. Chrysler created its Gold Key program in 1994, offering, as one ad put it: "A Great Way to Drive a New Car More Often."[64]

Chrysler Gold Key

- Lower monthly payments
- New car more often
- Guaranteed trade-in value
- More car for the money
- Ownership option at lease end

The lure of being able to drive a new car every three or four years was just one part of leasing's appeal. An even more powerful come-on was the aggressive pricing rolled out by the three Detroit carmakers to bring down monthly lease payments. Their captive financing arms—GMAC, Ford Credit, and Chrysler Financial—began to subsidize leases out of the profit they made from selling cars to dealers. By inflating residual values or cutting interest rates, they were able to bring down monthly payments.

Monthly lease payments on a new car were often lower than loan payments on a used one. Among the most imaginative promotions were leases that stretched beyond the typical three-year period to keep monthly payments very low. Few tire-kickers realized that the longer the lease term, the higher their finance charges would be. All that mattered was that they could get a new car every few years and fork over less each month than they would with a conventional loan. There was talk of a twelve-year deal with the vehicle replaced every two years, and a weekends-only lease for city-dwellers. "Leasing a car for personal use became more of a mainstream product for anyone who wanted a new car," said Peter Andrew, then general director of operations at GMAC Canada.

The car leasing business boomed for the next decade and a half. In 1990, 13 percent of all new cars in Canada were leased; by 1997, the figure had soared to 47 percent.[65] The domestic captives dominated the market, accounting for 70 to 80 percent of all lease deals, as they piled on special deals in the hope of regaining market share from Toyota, Honda, and other import brands.[66]

The incentive addiction

At first these promotions worked well. "People got very excited about buying the cars at a low rate," recalled Steve Akazawa, president of Pattison Lease, "and they bought cars by the thousands." But the aggressive tactics of the Detroit Three eventually backfired. Industry analyst Dennis Desrosiers called these incentives "the crack cocaine of the auto industry," enabling consumers and dealers to become hooked on leasing without considering the long-term consequences.[67]

The generous residual values that held down monthly payments were based on Detroit's misguided confidence that its cars would solidly hold their value over the three- or four-year lease term. After all, cars were supposedly being built better and lasting longer.

That turned out not to be the case. Why buy a used car, many consumers figured, when they could lease a new one for a lower monthly payment? At the same time, the surge in lease volumes meant a huge increase in the number of late-model used cars coming onto the market. With supply outstripping demand, prices for second-hand Detroit models fell sharply during the early 2000s. Trade-in values for a Chevrolet, Ford, or Chrysler dropped well below those for the equivalent Toyota, Honda, or Volkswagen.

Rather than recalibrate leases to make them more profitable, GM, Ford, and Chrysler doubled down in a desperate bid to preserve market share. They flooded the market with new vehicles and offered irresistible bargains to move them off dealers' lots. The rationale was that as consumers replaced their cars every three to five years, dealers would have a steady stream of good-quality used cars to sell. But as used car values sank, the captives found themselves sitting on massive losses on their leases. From the 1990s up to the 2008 market crisis, many used domestic cars were sold at a loss, either to consumers or at auction. "The domestic manufacturers were losing $4,000 to $5,000 per car," said Akazawa.

"The customers didn't want to buy them from the dealers because the price was too high, and the dealers lost money when they sold them at auction," added Tom Simmons, also of Jim Pattison Lease. "That's what happens when you try to force a market that isn't there."

A Statistics Canada consumer trends report in 2002 confirmed the disaster that was unfolding: "Automobile manufacturers lost billions of dollars during the mid-1990s by overestimating cars' residual values in leasing contracts."[68]

Peter Andrew summed up the impracticality of Detroit's incentive strategy: "If you lease too many cars and too many cars are coming back, then prices get out of whack and this affects the residual value. And that's what happened in the mid-2000s. There were too many cars coming back. Dealers weren't able to absorb them all, which meant there was downward pressure on pricing and too many people started losing money."

Simmons remains amazed to this day by the misguided thinking behind the incentives. "The Big Three kept thinking that the retail leasing market would go higher, and they kept losing money," he said. "Losses on a Cadillac Escalade could be as high as $15,000. The manufacturers lost billions."

The botched incentives had even wider consequences. "I truly believe that this practice contributed more than the recession to the bankruptcy of GM and Chrysler and the near-collapse of Ford," Simmons added.

The practice of overstating residual values in order to lower monthly payments and pump up lease volumes was not confined to the Detroit Three captives. Some banks and independent leasing companies also fell into the trap and suffered financial losses.

Entrepreneurs like Jim Pattison and Roy Foss managed to escape the carnage by sticking to the tried-and-trusted principles of sound leasing practice. While the manufacturers pressed their captives to be very aggressive with generous front-end incentives, Pattison, Foss, and others like them exercised a more cautious approach. They calculated with cool heads what the residual values would be in three years, and then made sure they set the monthly lease payments at a rate that covered their costs, so that, at the very least, they would not lose money. Higher monthly payments made it more difficult to compete with other dealerships, but it kept them from going out of business as a result of bad debts and losses.

The foreign carmakers also did not fall into the Detroit Three trap. Their models were more popular than the much-maligned domestic vehicles and thus commanded stronger trade-in and residual values. Toyota, Honda, Hyundai, and Nissan, among others, had no need to follow the path taken by the Detroit Three.

The CFLA is born

Industry leaders such as Bill Bell at Pitney Bowes Leasing, Newcourt's Steve Hudson, GE Capital's Roman Oryschuk, and Ted Hawkin at Commcorp Financial Services came to the conclusion during the course of the early 1990s that change was overdue at ELAC, the equipment lessors' trade association.

The problem was that the group was no longer representative of the leasing and asset-backed finance industry. The association had been created in 1973 by equipment lessors to represent their interests. But with asset-based finance players now an important part of the industry, the association needed to speak for a wider group of interests.

The vehicle leasing side had similar concerns. Many members of the Canadian Automotive Leasing Association (CALA) felt that interest in the body had waned, and that by the early 1990s it was representing only the interests of smaller dealerships.

If proof was needed that the two associations were not pulling their weight, membership of both had shrivelled, even as the industry had grown.

Hudson took a lead role in pushing for change. He contacted Gord Thompson, head of the large and successful Canadian Home Builders' Association. "Hudson and others he had talked with in the industry felt the relevancy of ELAC was diminishing," Thompson said, reflecting on the two men's first conversations. "Neither ELAC or CALA had an effective voice in Ottawa or at the provincial level. And there was a feeling that if you don't have an effective voice, if you really don't represent the industry, no one is going to take you seriously."

Hudson and other like-minded industry leaders set out to convince their colleagues of the benefits of bringing the

Courtesy of Michael Collins.

An original Canadian Dominion Leasing sign from Canada's first independent leasing company, which opened in 1959 at 320 Bay Street in Toronto.

Courtesy of Jim Pattison.

Jim Pattison leases his first car to Vancouver alderman Frank Baker on May 8, 1961.

Courtesy of IBM Canada.

The popularity of "new" Selectric typewriters in the early 1960s opened the way for office equipment lessors such as North American Business Equipment Ltd. (NABEL) to package leasing deals for offices across Canada.

Courtesy of Power Corporation of Canada.

From a small bus line in Sudbury, Ontario, Paul Desmarais grew his family company into the multibillion-dollar global conglomerate Power Corporation of Canada. The initial financing for his first two buses came from Industrial Acceptance Corporation.

Courtesy of Bea Labikova.

Traders Building at 625 Church Street, Toronto, head office of Traders Group, one of the early acceptance companies. In 1989, equipment lessors met here in a basement classroom to lobby the federal Department of Finance for changes to the proposed 1989 Tax Act.

Advertising for Industrial Acceptance Corporation in the April 1964 issue of The Rotarian.

Courtesy of John Deere.

John Deere Financial was one of the first manufacturers to set up financing for its customers, usually farmers, who were considered high risk for the banks.

Corey Mihailiuk and courtesy of *The Globe and Mail.*

The October 1996 cover story of The Globe and Mail Report on Business Magazine *vividly mirrors the great excitement in the business community that greeted the ascendency of Steven Hudson and the Newcourt Credit Group.*

Courtesy of Impact Public Affairs.

At CFLA's urging, the Honourable Jim Flaherty, federal Minister of Finance, allocated up to $12 billion in his January 2009 budget to support "the financing of vehicles and equipment for consumers and businesses, large and small."

Speaking to the 2009 CFLA National Conference, the Minister said, "As global credit markets froze up, asset-based financing paid a disproportionate price. I know that the financial crisis has been very tough on your businesses. While our short-term expectations should remain modest, things are getting better." But, "we are under no illusions that our work is complete."

Courtesy of Moe Danis.

A piece of equipment financing history from the Pacific & Western Bank of Canada.

Courtesy of Toyota Financial Services Canada Inc.

Mr. Toshio Kunii, president of Toyota Canada, booking the first Toyota lease in Vancouver 1992.

Courtesy of Gary Batchelor.

Gary Batchelor represented CIT in 2004–05 in financing the largest hydraulic excavator in the world in the oil sands north of Fort McMurray, Alberta.

Courtesy of David Powell.

CFLA Accounting Committee chair Loraine McIntosh discusses proposals to overhaul lease accounting standards with International Accounting Standards Board member Darrel Scott in July 2012, with then-Canadian Accounting Standards Board chair Gord Fowler in the background.

Courtesy of GE Capital.

From the City of Montreal budget department, Roman Oryschuk moved through RoyLease to the Royal Bank, becoming president and CEO of National Bank Leasing in 1988, and then president and CEO of GE Capital Canada Commercial Equipment Financing in 1993. In 2003, he became president and CEO of GE European Equipment Finance, in 2006 president and CEO of GE Capital Solutions Europe, and later vice-president of General Electric Company.

Courtesy of National Leasing.

Tom Pundyk, then-CFLA secretary/treasurer, represented the CFLA at the Second China Financial Leasing Summit held in Tianjin, China, in May 2011. With asset-based finance and leasing now serving global markets, Pundyk spoke on the business of asset-based financing in Canada.

asset-based finance sector, equipment lessors, and vehicle lessors under a single umbrella. They quickly won the support of four key companies, AT&T Capital, Commcorp, GE Capital, and Newcourt Credit. Each promised $25,000 in annual membership fees for two years to get a new association representing the entire industry off the ground.

On October 7, 1993, ELAC changed its name to the Canadian Finance & Leasing Association—Association canadienne de financement et de location (CFLA-ACFL). CALA simultaneously transferred all its assets to the new body and was wound up.

Early CFLA leaders step up to the task

Hugo Sørensen, Triathlon Leasing's president, was elected the CFLA's first chairman, and Thompson was hired as president. A second staff member was responsible for membership. The two of them worked out of an office at Pitney Bowes Leasing in Mississauga for the first few months.

Sørensen remembered a widespread sense of caution leading up to the merger. Many members wondered whether they would still find any benefit in a group with such diverse interests. "There were members who headed up very large organizations, such as GE Capital and Newcourt Credit," he noted. "But on the vehicle leasing side, members ranged from small, family-run dealerships to PHH. Some were nervous about being swallowed up in the new, larger association. There wasn't any acrimony, but there was some caution on both sides as to how it would all shake out." It helped that Sørensen was a respected leader with wide experience. "It probably assuaged some of the nervousness to know that the first chairman was a vehicle leasing guy," he said. "I was running a company that included vehicle, equipment, and computer leasing. It meant I had exposure to all of them."

The members of CFLA's first executive committee were equally well respected. Roman Oryschuck, GE Capital Canada

Equipment Financing's chief executive, and AT&T Capital Fleet Services' Peter Kidd were the two vice-chairmen. Ralph Selby, senior leasing partner at Price Waterhouse, took the job of secretary/treasurer.

CFLA's first directors were drawn from a wide cross-section of the industry: Steve Akazawa (Jim Pattison Lease), Fred Booth (ARI Canada), Mike Goddard (PHH Canada), Bill Gow (Cross-Canada Car Leasing), Tim Hammill (AT&T Capital Canada), Ted Hawken (Commcorp), Tom Hopkirk (Barclays Bank of Canada Leasing), Steve Hudson (Newcourt Credit Group), John Jackson (Foss National Leasing), Ralph Karthein (IBM Leasing), Greg Korsos (Sako Auto Leasing), Jake McLaughlin (Canadian Automotive Fleet), Len Micallef (Greyvest Financial Services), Graham Morris (Comdisco), Tom Pundyk (National Equipment Leasing), Tom Simmons (Grant Brown National Leasing), and Jake Thun (Royal Bank of Canada Leasing). Two lawyers represented the Associate Members David Sharpless (Blake, Cassels & Graydon) and Kevin Smyth (Lavery De Billy).

Thompson spent much of the CFLA's first year recruiting new members and trying to raise the industry's profile in Ottawa and the provincial capitals. He had his work cut out for him. Two contentious government proposals required immediate attention: a move to introduce photo radar on Ontario roads, and issues stemming from the introduction of the new federal goods and services tax in 1991.

Lessors were skeptical of photo radar because, as the registered owners of leased vehicles, they might be held liable for speeding offences by lessee drivers. The problem with the GST was that anyone leasing a car would pay the tax twice—on their monthly payments and on the residual amount at the end of the lease term.

The CFLA mounted a vigorous lobbying campaign on both fronts. To plead its case on the GST, Sørensen travelled to Ottawa to meet with then–finance minister Michael Wilson and the House of Commons Standing Committee on Finance. On photo radar, the association lost no opportunity to remind both the Ontario New Democratic Party (NDP) government and, after 1995, the incoming provincial Conservatives of the impracticalities of the system.

The lobbying efforts were rewarded on both counts. Ontario scrapped photo radar as one of the new government's first orders of business, and the federal government revised the *Excise Tax Act* to ensure that vehicle leasing would not take a double tax hit. Sørensen was thrilled with the result. He recalled that of the hundreds of lobbying groups that made submissions on the GST, the CFLA was one of only a handful whose voices were heard.

These early victories enhanced the association's credibility and helped spur its drive for new members. "We got people to join by fighting these issues," recalled Thompson. "We told the members what we were doing. Next thing, they'd get out there and tell their friends. Soon they were saying: 'Hey, these guys are out there trying to protect our industry and trying to change it—not just having an annual meeting where everyone gets a free drink and a sandwich.'"

Within a year of its formation, the new association had mushroomed from 20 corporate members to almost 100.

Thompson remained for two years, leaving in the summer of 1995 to join Newcourt Credit Group as senior vice-president of corporate development. Following Thompson's departure, Bill Bell, recently retired, took over as interim president pending a search for a permanent successor. The board hired David Powell, who took over as the CFLA's second president in October 1995 and has remained in the position ever since.

The bilingual Powell hailed from Montreal and had been educated at the Sorbonne, Cambridge, and McGill. His diplomatic skills, inherited from his diplomat father, as well as his keen interest in public policy, served the association well. Powell had been associate director of the Canadian Trend Report, political assistant at the European parliament in Luxembourg, a senate lobbyist for Ralph Nader's Congress Watch in Washington, D.C., and chairman of the Board of Trade of Metropolitan Montreal. Just prior to joining the CFLA in 1995, he was a partner in the Montreal office of the national law firm Fasken Martineau. "A major milestone was when we were able to find David Powell," Moe Danis enthused. "He has done more for this industry than some may realize. In many instances, he's been our voice with the government."

From the start, the CFLA has held an annual conference, the first in early October 1994 at the Hockley Valley Resort in Orangeville, Ontario. All subsequent annual conferences took place in September. The only exception was 2001, when the event was due to start on September 12 in Banff, Alberta. As soon as word of the attacks on the World Trade Center and the Pentagon broke, the conference was cancelled, stranding some delegates en route. One of them, Mike Goddard, was due to take over as the association's chairman at the meeting, succeeding National Leasing's Nick Logan. Goddard was duly installed at a special members' meeting in Toronto in January 2002.

A CFLA snapshot: 1994

One of the most gratifying aspects of the CFLA from the start has been the diversity of its membership. Of ninety-two members in the fall of 1994, sixty-one were classified as "regular members," in other words, active in the asset-based finance and leasing business. Thirty-nine of those came from the equipment side and twenty-two from the auto industry. Most—though not all—of the auto members had been active in CALA.

The combined association also opened its doors to twenty-eight "associate members"—in other words, regular suppliers to the industry, such as law firms, consultancies, and accounting firms.

Keeping up with terminology: Asset-based and commercial equipment finance

With the 1993 merger of the Equipment Leasing Association of Canada and the Canadian Automotive Leasing Association to form the Canadian Finance & Leasing Association, there was a prescient decision to expand the name of the industry's association to include the broader term of *finance*. Although it would seem that non-lease financing (essentially different types of loans) grew slowly within the industry, the 2008–09 crisis accelerated the shift to loans. This was especially the case in consumer vehicle and equipment financing, most likely due to diminishing tolerance among members and their funders for residual risk under leases. In the fleet business, financing had assumed less importance over the first decade of the 2000s as outsourced fleet management became the more profitable offering. Today, for example, many of the equipment members in the CFLA are more apt to describe themselves as being in "commercial equipment finance" (encompassing loans and leases), rather than simply as "lessors."

Judges consider CFLA's code of ethics

One of the CFLA's first orders of business was to adopt an association code of ethics. The code was referenced—and tested—during the first half of the 2000s by two judicial inquiries. The hearings considered the dealings of MFP Financial Services Ltd., a CFLA member, with two Ontario municipalities, Waterloo and Toronto. Although the CFLA at first was concerned that these incidents would tarnish the industry and its financial products, in the end both inquiries confirmed the importance of the code. Comments from the two judges, however, highlighted differing expectations that financing companies may be expected to face in the marketplace.

The first incident was somewhat outside the mainstream asset-based finance and leasing business. It was a public–private partnership where the City of Waterloo decided to finance a large sportsplex by way of a structured financing transaction. The city then claimed that the financing cost had greatly exceeded what it thought it had agreed to pay. At several points in the nearly 500-page final report released in 2003, the judge used the CFLA code of ethics as a point of reference—and was complimentary. While recognizing that the association was an advocacy group acting in the interests of the asset-based finance sector, he viewed the code as an appropriate and positive statement by the association. He stated that the adoption of the code by the industry demonstrated recognition that a business sector without a reputation for integrity, professionalism, and trustworthiness would be unsuccessful in the marketplace.[69]

The judge did note, and without criticism, that the CFLA code of ethics was essentially "an ethical framework to be considered but not a specific solution to a problem."[70] He concluded that lessors have an ethical duty to ensure that customers understood each transaction.

In 2005, a Toronto judicial inquiry considered the leasing of IT hardware and software to the municipality. City council claimed costs were much higher than what they had approved. The far-ranging terms of reference asked the judge to generally "inquire into all aspects (of the particular) transactions, their history and their impact on the ratepayers of the City of Toronto as they relate to the good government of the municipality, or the conduct of its public business, and to make any recommendations which the Commissioner may deem appropriate and in the public interest."[71]

In her four-volume, almost 2,000-page report, the judge found no find fault with lease financing. Rather, she focused on poor municipal management and questionable activities by certain individuals inside and outside the City of Toronto. She did, however, note in passing that it was "not uncommon for customers to lack the necessary expertise to properly evaluate whether they should be leasing acquisitions or finding some other way of acquiring the equipment they need. Leasing companies ... have no legal obligation to educate prospective clients. A typical lessor would assume that an organization the size of the City [of Toronto] would know what it is doing."[72]

Although these two inquiries came to somewhat contradictory conclusions, both served as a good reminder: "know your customer" and "know your employee," especially your salespeople.

Capital lease pilot project fails to soar

There would be many victories and some lessons to be learned along the way for the newly formed association. One was the ill-fated Capital Lease Pilot Project.

Starting in 1994, the CFLA lobbied the federal government to expand the federal *Small Business Loans Act* (SBLA) to include capital leases. In most industrialized countries, governments offer guarantees to banks lending to small business; nowhere, however, do they include capital leases.

As a result of the association's effort, the federal government authorized the development of the Capital Lease Pilot Project, a first anywhere in the world. The five-year project was launched April 1, 2002.

A small technical working group composed of then CFLA board members lawyer David Chaiton and Tom Hopkirk, and accounting committee member Raja Singh volunteered many hours to craft the unique and specialized program.

Although two CFLA member companies, Wells Fargo Equipment Finance and Equirex Leasing Corp., used the program extensively, a year before its designated end date, an Industry Canada review revealed that few others had taken advantage of it. At the 2006 CFLA national conference, senior representatives of both Wells Fargo and Equirex presented how they had used the program and its value. But it was too late. On March 31, 2007, the government allowed the pilot project to expire.

CFLA president David Powell summarized it thusly: "Despite a tremendous amount of work, particularly by our volunteers, this was one of the few initiatives that that did not fly with many members. We thought that the pilot project held great promise. It was an important lesson. Don't start leading a parade unless you have plenty of people lined up behind you."

The Federal Task Force on the Future of the Financial Services Sector

The appointment of the Task Force on the Future of the Financial Services Sector, in December 1996 by Paul Martin, then the federal finance minister, offered the most significant opportunity to date for the industry, and its new association, to define itself and present a full picture of its significance to the Canadian economy.

"Up until the task force, the industry was largely in a reactive mode, responding to piecemeal proposals from governments," said David Powell. "This was the first time the industry could tell its story in its own words in a high-profile public forum."

Powell recalled, "I remember one of my first visits to Ottawa. It was at Industry Canada. After introducing myself and the CFLA, one of the officials said: 'Oh, right. You guys are like Hertz and Avis right?' It was only then that it came fully home to me how much education work we had to do."

The task force's mandate was to conduct a comprehensive review of public policies affecting the financial services sector, with a view to enhancing economic growth, competition, efficiency, and innovation.

"We had a choice," said Powell. "Like so many others, the CFLA could submit its laundry list of self-interested policy requests, or we could actually make an effort to answer the questions asked by the task force."

The association opted for the latter approach. There was significant member consultation and much debate. Two senior Newcourt Credit executives, John Sadler and past–CFLA president Gord Thompson, were particularly challenging sounding boards, always pressing for thoughtful and well-researched public policy arguments. Thompson had continued as the volunteer chairman of the association's government relations committee after serving as full-time president of CFLA.

CFLA titled its October 1997 submission "Choice: Financial Services into the 21st Century" and gave it the subtitle "Globalization is shifting the advantage from the provider of financial services to the user of financial services."

The introduction to the submission noted:

> *The title of this submission ("Choice") was selected deliberately. The CFLA vision for the financial system turns on the concept of "choice." An evaluation of user choice must consider not only the factors which enhance choice but also those factors which diminish choice. Issues such as competition, concentration, efficiency, innovation and regulation are, then, merely means to an end, and that end is user choice.*[73]

The association's "vision for the financial system" was based on the following two premises:

1. The financial services system should be designed for the user rather than the provider of financial services.
2. The priority of the financial system should be to assure users of a reliable and stable mechanism to facilitate commercial exchange and transactions, and to ensure maximum access to capital and credit.[74]

A diversity of providers of financial services is the best assurance of user choice. The CFLA believes that the users of financial services, both individuals and businesses, stand to benefit most in the future if the financial services marketplace:

- assures an expanding diversity of choice of providers,
- increases the pool of available credit and capital,
- improves access to credit and capital,
- ensures access to innovative services and products, and
- increases available specialized technical expertise.[75]

The CFLA urged that these principles should underpin the future financial system.

A federal task force looks at the future of financial services in Canada

The federal task force raised a perennial question: should the government loosen restrictions on the big banks in the retail car leasing market?

The issue was so sensitive that it risked seriously splitting the association. Members on the vehicle leasing side, especially the carmaker captives and the big fleet management companies, were adamant that restrictions on the banks should remain in place. After all, as they were quick to point out, the old Canadian Automotive Leasing Association had been set up precisely to oppose the banks' thrust into vehicle leasing.

But the CFLA's equipment-financing members took a different line. They had been competing with the banks since the 1979–80 amendments to the *Bank Act* and did not share the concerns of their auto leasing colleagues. To complicate matters, the banks were also members of the association. Indeed, Jake Thun from Royal Bank Leasing sat on the board of directors. Several equipment leasing members had banks as major customers.

The members were able to agree on a couple of major principles. The case needed to be made that the asset-based finance and leasing industry was a vital part of a robust and diverse financial services sector. The industry saw itself as an important player, and the CFLA set out to remind the task force of this fact.

There was no question about the banks' overwhelming power in the marketplace. Despite government efforts for many years to diversify financial choices for Canadians, history had shown that the sheer size and reach of the banks could make it very difficult for other players to gain a foothold.

In this context, the title of the CFLA brief—*Choice*—may appear to have been "something of a paradox," Powell explained. "In arguing to maintain legal limits on bank financing activity, it could appear that we were arguing against choice. But the underlying thesis was that those limits, at least in the short to medium term, were needed to assure choice in the long term."

Given the conflicting views, the CFLA submission needed to walk a fine line. So while the main body of the brief argued the case that asset-based finance played an invaluable role in the financial services industry, the discussion of the banks' powers was consigned to an appendix.

The CFLA board put the submission to a vote. "In the end, the key equipment members went along with the submission out of a sense of solidarity with auto members and to support the association," recalled Powell.

Thun, head of Royal Bank Leasing, was in an especially difficult position. He wanted to remain loyal to the association but also needed to respect his employer's position. He ended up voting against the submission, and asked that the final vote be recorded—the only time in CFLA history that this was done on any decision. There were also a number of abstentions. "Jake remained very loyal to the association," Powell noted, "believing that it was playing an important role for the industry and for the bank, notwithstanding this board decision."

The issue of the big banks' powers stirred up strong feelings outside the CFLA as well. In its September 1998 final report, the task force reported that "some of the submissions and interviews bordered on passionate pleas on both sides of the debate rather than putting forward economic arguments of substance."

Nonetheless, the secretary of state for international financial institutions, Jim Peterson, praised the CFLA's submission as one of few that truly attempted to address the fundamental questions raised by the task force. In a speech to CFLA members in Toronto on January 13, 1999, Peterson commented, "The CFLA made a thoughtful and useful submission when too many others had simply restated long-standing, self-interested policy 'asks.'"[76]

Even so, the tensions surrounding the task force submission left a scar on the CFLA. While Thun remained on the board, another bank member left the association and did not return for almost a decade.

"There was no doubt in my mind and in the minds of key members that this issue was the first major test for the association," recalled Powell. "We passed—somewhat bruised perhaps, but essentially united. Any early concerns that vehicle and equipment members would not work together were put to bed. This was my proudest moment in my time with CFLA."

Unique legal challenges for asset-based financing companies

One of the recurring issues for the industry arises from the ownership of the financed assets. As described earlier in this book, the unique legal nature of asset-based finance requires that the financing company retain ownership of the asset until the customer satisfies all the terms and conditions under the financing agreement.

Soon after motorized vehicles were introduced early in the previous century, road accidents followed. The courts held the owners responsible for the use of their vehicles, and this principle was enshrined in statutes in most Canadian provinces and American states. Such laws, however, failed to anticipate the leasing and rental of vehicles four decades later. While it may be obvious that a rent-a-car company owns a rental vehicle, under a lease, the finance company also remains the owner of the vehicle until the customer buys it or returns it.

The serious consequences of this "vicarious liability" for financing and rental companies as "owners" of vehicles was illustrated in a case that involved Canada's Tilden Rent-a-Car. In 1991, one of Tilden's rented autos had an accident with a gasoline tanker truck in New York City. Dozens of stores burnt, and there were explosions in nearby parked cars. Claims and pressure mounted against the company (as owner of the vehicle), including suits for wrongful death. First, Tilden sold its auto leasing operations to Newcourt Credit Group in 1995. A year later, facing seventeen lawsuits, the rental part of the company sought protection under the *Companies' Creditors Arrangement Act.* In June 1996, a U.S. judge ruled that Tilden could be held liable. Tilden sold its rental fleet to National Rental Car and went out of business.

Several American states (especially New York) were notorious for substantial vicarious liability awards. In 2005, the

U.S. congress acted to exempt all lessors and rental companies everywhere in the country from any responsibility for the use of vehicles they owned.

Canada is different. The issue had to be addressed province by province. When it came to leased vehicles, provincial policymakers could not believe that a lessor could be held liable for an accident involving a vehicle it had leased long-term. After all, the lessor had no control over how a lessee chose to use it.

In late 2004, a $24 million judgment rendered by an Ontario court against a national automobile lessor proved them wrong. Armed with this example, CFLA lobbied on behalf of the industry. Ontario was first. In 2006, that province capped lessor and rental company liability at $1 million. In 2007, a CFLA delegation led by the presidents of the Ford Motor Company of Canada and of Ford Credit Canada met with the premiers of British Columbia and of Alberta. Later that year, B.C. followed the Ontario model, then other provinces: Alberta (2011), Nova Scotia (2013), and most recently Prince Edward Island (2014). Québec had a unique approach, which never held liable lessors with leases of a year or more. But, as noted by David Powell, "more work remains."

Clouds on the horizon

For almost half a century, leasing had combined innovation and carefully balanced risk-taking in a way that secured its place as an indispensable financing tool. Following rapid growth during the 1990s, the total value of assets financed by the asset-based finance and leasing industry in Canada was almost $200 billion at the end of the decade. By 2007, the industry was making healthy profits, with the total value of assets financed at $280 billion.

But that bright picture was about to darken as the U.S. subprime mortgage crisis reverberated across the world's financial markets.

Moe Danis, a CFLA board member known as the father of securitization in Canada, laid out a sombre scenario in his speech to the association's annual meeting at Mount Tremblant on September 15, 2008. The strains in financial markets were clearly evident, and Danis, then managing director of lease financing at Sun Life Assurance Company, told delegates that his phone had been ringing off the hook with panicked calls. He said that he needed to be clear about the impact of the widening market crisis on the leasing industry. Sun Life had been unable to come to the rescue of hard-pressed lessors.

"My presentation basically stated the obvious," Danis recalled five years later. "Liquidity was going to be an issue for all lease companies. I said that while Sun Life was considered a major provider of liquidity, this was a $100 billion industry and my book was only $2 billion. I pointed out to the audience that although Sun Life was not going to cut back on any of our clients and would honour its commitments, it would not be looking to add any new clients at that time. It was a harsh but honest statement."

"You could have heard a pin drop," recalled Angela Armstrong. "I'll never forget that moment of history in our industry." Two days before, the Wall Street investment bank Lehman Brothers had collapsed, sending shockwaves through the global financial system.

Not everyone took kindly to Danis's candour. Armstrong remembered talking with members afterwards. "People were saying, 'I run a good business and there's nothing wrong with my business. Surely my business isn't at risk?' Others said, 'This is a global problem. It's none of my making and outside my control, yet it's going to put my business out of business.'"

And that was exactly the fate that was to befall many once-proud and strong leasing businesses.

• *chapter 6* •

2007–10: Recession, Renewal, and Transformation

In the midst of the tumult in financial markets in 2009, Steve Hudson received several calls from Stanley Hartt, a former deputy minister of finance in the federal government in Ottawa.[77] Hudson was living in Wichita, Kansas. He had moved to the United States almost a decade earlier, following the sale of Newcourt Credit to CIT Group. The two men had known each other for many years. Hartt had long admired the way Hudson built Newcourt into North America's second-largest non-bank business lender. Despite the missteps that eventually cost Newcourt its independence, the company remained one of the biggest success stories in the Canadian asset-based finance and leasing industry.

Hartt, a lawyer by training, had spotted an opportunity that he thought might make a good fit for Hudson. The asset-backed market was in dire need of fresh players following the pullback of many U.S. companies in the Canadian marketplace. Even CIT had reduced its activity after filing for U.S. Chapter 11 bankruptcy protection as a result of steep losses tied to risky sub-prime lending. Hartt encouraged his friend to move back to Canada and to take another look at the leasing business.

"There weren't ten others who had Steve's experience with the Canadian asset-backed lending market," recalled Hartt. "He was a guy who had all the attributes of someone who could come in and fill the gap in the market. He knew how to find

his way around the industry without stepping on land mines. He knew what to do to get back into it and, most important, how to get access to capital. It needed to be an entrepreneur, someone who knew what he was doing but wasn't risk averse. Steve was a natural person to speak to, and I happened to think the world of him."

Hartt had spoken out on several occasions over the previous year about the threat that a credit crunch posed to the economy. His warning was heard at the highest levels of the Conservative government in Ottawa. Anxious to find ways of restoring liquidity to the Canadian economy after the deep freeze that began in 2008, Finance Minister Jim Flaherty had turned to the private sector for advice. After hearing Hartt speak at a conference, Flaherty asked him to chair a new advisory committee on financing.

The panel comprised eleven members, all leaders of large, successful enterprises, such as GE Canada, Enbridge, Bell Canada, Manulife, Great West Life, and Sobeys. Their mandate was to come up with ways of greasing the wheels of Canada's credit markets. Hartt decided to put out an informal feeler to Hudson.

As Hudson recalled, "There was almost a complete absence of people willing to finance all that ugly stuff on highways and construction sites, and it's hard to have recovery if people aren't buying new equipment. Stanley reached out to me and said that he and others had concluded that we can't have a recovery in Canada unless there are people willing to finance trucks, trailers, and yellow iron [construction equipment]. They convinced me to come back. After my nine-year walkabout, it was time to come home."

Hudson contacted members of his former team at Newcourt, urging them to join him. "I told them that the environment was better than it was in the mid-1980s and that we should do this, if for no other reason but to rewrite that last chapter.

I was pleasantly surprised that my partners re-formed, and we soon had backing from the life insurance companies."

So it came about that Element Financial Corporation, a small, Ontario-based equipment finance firm formed in 2007, caught Steve Hudson's eye. Hudson chose Element as the vehicle for his "second coming" in Canada, starting in April 2010. He recapitalized the company and expanded nationally, seeking to make a new beginning where others had stumbled. Having learnt a tough lesson at Newcourt, he avoided borrowing through the short-term commercial paper market.

Element began trading on the Toronto stock exchange in December 2011. Today, with assets totalling $2.7 billion, it is a leading North American independent equipment finance company, helping customers acquire car and truck fleets, helicopters, construction and healthcare equipment, and much else.

Stanley Hartt, now back in legal practice with Norton Rose Fulbright and a consultant for Australia's Macquarie Group, asserted that Hudson would have returned with or without his encouragement. "He clearly was going to enter the business anyway. I just gave him a tiny shove."

TO HIS ADMIRERS, Steve Hudson is as close to a superhero as it gets in an industry with its share of larger-than-life characters. Though he was eventually forced to sell Newcourt under a cloud to a U.S. rival, Hudson continues to draw wide admiration for the energy and far-sightedness that built Newcourt into one of the asset-based finance industry's most powerful players.

After a decade running U.S. businesses unrelated to asset-based financing, Hudson returned to the industry in Canada during the mid-2000s with money to invest. His high-profile return to Canada generated a buzz in and outside the industry.

Using Element Financial as his vehicle, he began to assemble many members of his old team, in the process garnering support from former Newcourt funders. Element has yet to reach the stature of Newcourt, but industry leaders constantly ask: What might Steve Hudson do next?

Asset-based financing was battered in 2008–09 by the most serious global recession since the 1930s, accompanied by a deep freeze in credit markets. Many players were forced to revisit their business models if they were to have any hope of surviving.

The story of Newcourt's rise and fall and the transformation of Element epitomize an attribute that has defined the industry from its earliest days in Canada: a determination to bounce back no matter what the challenge—whether tough economic times, regulatory changes, or foreign competition.

Hartt's move to woo Hudson back to Canada also underlined the importance of asset-based finance and leasing to the overall economy. The sector would end up overcoming the challenges of 2008 and 2009 to return to its significant role in corporate finance.

To understand these recent milestones and what they hold for the future, it is important to examine:

- events leading up to the 2008 financial meltdown,
- the global financial crisis and recession,
- the agony of the Detroit carmakers and their captives, and
- the ramifications for Canada's leasing industry from 2007 to 2010.

Leading up to a meltdown

The global financial crisis had its roots in the toxic world of U.S. sub-prime real estate mortgages, a segment of the larger asset-backed finance market.

U.S. mortgage lenders appeared to have found a pot of gold during the first few years of the twenty-first century. By methods fair and foul, they vastly increased their lending to homebuyers with sub-prime (in other words, risky) credit profiles, helping to fan a fire of speculation in the U.S. real estate market. By 2006, banks and other mortgage lenders were packaging these sub-prime mortgages into tradeable securities. The dubious value of these securities and the malpractices behind them were dramatically exposed as the real estate bubble burst and the economy slowed. Many borrowers were unable to meet their monthly payments, and the rate of home foreclosures rose steeply. Lenders—including investors in mortgage-backed securities—suffered massive losses.

The crisis initially centred on sub-prime real estate mortgages, but the malpractices in that sector soon cast doubt on the quality of many other types of lending, including asset-based financing. Questions were raised about the reputation of any broker behind a security—and about the creditworthiness of the ultimate borrower. With confidence shaken, investors stampeded out of the entire asset-backed securities market.

By the summer of 2007, the sub-prime crisis was spreading beyond the United States. Canada was not immune, in spite of the much smaller role of sub-prime mortgages in the real estate market and the relative conservatism of the domestic banking system.

The troubles in the United States and the slowing domestic economy caused a sharp contraction in availability of credit to consumers and business. Some of Canada's largest issuers of asset-backed paper were unable to find buyers, casting doubt on their ability to continue funding their day-to-day business. With capital in short supply, even the most successful players needed to make some tough decisions.

The federal government and the Bank of Canada joined central banks and governments around the world in a scramble for ways to revive the financing techniques that greased the wheels of trade and commerce. As a first step, the bank launched a special term-lending facility in late 2007 to inject extra liquidity into the markets and alleviate funding pressures. This initiative temporarily expanded the range of securities acceptable as collateral. Even so, the full repercussions of the financial landslide had yet to be felt.

Roman Oryschuck recalled late 2007, "I was a spectator in Europe. It was like watching a hurricane as it unfolded over North America."

Market crisis and recession

The enormity of the financial crisis became apparent on September 15, 2008, with the collapse of Lehman Brothers, once one of Wall Street's most respected investment banks. The news hit the headlines just two days before CFLA members were due to gather for their annual conference in Mont Tremblant, Québec.

"September 2008 was a hairy time for the leasing industry and financial services in general," recalled Moe Danis, who was in the thick of the crisis at Sun Life Financial. Danis gave his blunt assessment of the looming dangers in a presentation to the conference. "Securitization conduits were closing down, and other buyers exiting," he recalled. "I felt that the presentation was a good opportunity for me to get the message out that Sun Life could not be everyone's answer to their liquidity problem."

Crisis at Coventree Capital

Conduits were the vehicles that banks used to process the leases that they purchased from leasing companies. Most of the big banks had such conduits. They did not hold the assets on the balance sheet but instead used the conduits to sell asset-backed deals into the public market. The most prominent conduit to run into difficulty in Canada was Coventree Capital, which did business with several leading Canadian and international banks. Like others, Coventree was financing its lease receivables through the short-term commercial paper market, rolling over these loans every month. Coventree found itself in the crosshairs as rumours swirled that its securities might be tainted by toxic sub-prime mortgages. In fact, sub-prime mortgages made up only 4 percent of Coventree's portfolio. But the firm's plea to its investors fell on deaf ears and the market for its paper dried up. The banks, which were supposedly obligated to provide emergency liquidity in a market crisis, refused to honour that guarantee on the grounds that Coventree was a victim of a "Coventree crisis" rather than a "market crisis."

The crunch in global capital flows continued as nervous lenders and investors of all kinds pulled back. Equity and commodity prices tumbled. Stanley Hartt, who watched events progress from his position as chairman of the Canadian arm of Citigroup's global markets division, noted with only slight exaggeration that "people were so insecure that even the cash in their jeans was better left there than in the bank."

The Conference Board of Canada described the downward spiral as a "vicious cycle of credit withdrawal and halting of investment." Financial institutions shied away from their normal role as providers of capital, leading to higher funding costs and lower liquidity. As aversion to risk grew, the flow of credit to businesses, especially smaller ones, slowed to a virtual standstill.

One consequence of the credit crunch was that traditional funders of leasing and asset-backed financing pulled back from the securitization deals that had become the sector's lifeblood. The big life insurers, such as Sun Life, Canada Life, Manulife, and Great West Life, said they needed to direct their capital elsewhere. Funds that might otherwise have been earmarked for securitization transactions were needed to make up for losses on other investments, such as equities, as these institutions were forced to meet actuarial and regulatory obligations to depositors and beneficiaries. As often happens in uncertain times, they were also eager to boost cash holdings at the expense of almost any kind of investment.

"These were the companies that were creating conduits for credit to flow," explained Hartt. "They bought commercial paper from the equipment and vehicle lessors. They even could vouch for the value of that paper because they kept track of individual vehicle serial numbers. But suddenly they stopped buying the paper."

David Powell, the CFLA's president, was struck by the "precipitous collapse in confidence" across the financial sector. "The entire system virtually froze up, not just our relatively small subset," he recalled. "Our industry was caught in this turmoil along with every other. No one in the financial sector knew whom to trust anymore. Cash was hoarded by anyone who had it because you did not know when, where, or if it would be needed to meet some unexpected financial emergency. No one knew what the future held. No one knew how, when, or if the economy could be turned round—hence the unprecedented government intervention worldwide. Yes, there had been economic downturns before, but none this severe during the lifetime of those involved—from policymakers to bankers to lessors."

By the end of 2008, the disruption in the flow of credit to businesses and consumers had pushed the global economy into recession. Statistics Canada's chief economist, Philip Cross, pronounced that "the [Canadian] economy was clearly in recession for three quarters, from the fourth quarter of 2008 to the second quarter of 2009."

There was no doubt in Ottawa as to the severity of the crisis. By the third week of November 2008, Stephen Harper, leading a minority government re-elected only a month before, announced unprecedented stimulus and described the economic situation as potentially as dangerous "as anything we have seen since 1929." Canada's twenty-second prime minister recalled his conversation with finance minister, Jim Flaherty, when he spoke at his colleague's funeral in April 2014. "By November 2008, Jim and I had both concluded, not easily and certainly not what would have been expected, that the calamity befalling the global economic and financial system meant, among others things, that we had to run a deficit. That is, not merely allow a modest deficit, but deliberately engineer as large a deficit as could be reasonably run, as a response to a collapsing marketplace."[78]

Leasing loses its raw material

> *"Financing is the sine qua non for economic activity, like water is for life."*
>
> *Stanley Hartt*

Stable access to capital at a reasonable cost lies at the core of asset-based finance and leasing. Looking back over forty years of leasing in Canada, Ben Young, one of the early pioneers, observed, "Capital is our raw material. Without access to credit, a leasing operation simply cannot survive."

The capital to fund leases comes largely from securitization and bank credit. The annual amount of capital that flowed to Canadian businesses and consumers through asset-based finance reached $92 billion in 2007. Two years later, that annual number had shrunk to $72 billion. In other words, the dramatic drop in credit availability caused the asset-based financing business in Canada to shrink by almost a quarter.[79]

"If banks stop lending," noted Hartt, "then literally the economy has to grind to a halt because the oil in the working mechanism has been withdrawn."

Tom Pundyk at National Leasing was among those who watched the liquidity crunch take its devastating toll. "A pile of independent leasing businesses closed after 2008 because their funding taps closed. They had no more money, and it takes time find new funding sources. Many companies got terribly beaten up."

"There were all kinds of war stories," added Jeff Hartley at Foss National Leasing. "I would argue that virtually every leasing company came close to insolvency at some time. A couple just dodged the bullet, but more out of luck than good management."

Besides the difficulty of securing funding at reasonable cost, asset-based finance and leasing companies were hit on the other side of their business by their customers' financial woes. Lessees unable to meet their bills stopped paying their monthly fees, forcing lessors to repossess vehicles and equipment and sell them at bargain basement prices. Residual values plummeted.

"Independent leasing companies were struggling and getting killed with residuals," said Lease-Win's Ron Rubinoff. "We saw many companies and individuals just walk away from their leases rather than take the buy-out option and purchase the vehicles at the end of the lease term."

Rubinoff closed his company's leasing operations in 2008, not because of its own credit problems but because of the squeeze on existing and potential customers. As he explained, "Lease-Win was part of a public company, Chesswood Income Fund. As Lease-Win only represented a small portion of the public entity, we thought we would try and sell it. The problem was that the prospective purchasers—not us—had difficulty securing the necessary financing, so we elected to wind down the company."

Leasing companies take charge of their own fate

Large multinational corporations such as PHH were in a better position to weather the storm than smaller Canadian independents.

"We certainly saw a slowdown in business," said Jim Halliday, then president of PHH Canada, emphasizing that a cornerstone of his company's business philosophy is to help customers solve their problems. The value of this strategy became apparent during the recession, when PHH's customers were looking for ways to reduce expenses. During 2008 and 2009, PHH often found itself helping a business to downsize or "right-size" its vehicle fleet, or to make other equipment more productive. When corporate belt-tightening required cutbacks in in-house fleet operations, companies like PHH took on the role of fleet managers. It also helped that PHH was part of a global company. "Despite the tough times," said Halliday, "we were fortunate to be part of the larger PHH Corporation, which had capital to deploy, as well as other resources and systems to help us manage through a crisis."

Some other once-successful equipment lessors were forced to take more forceful action to survive, even to the point of finding new owners.

One of these was Vancouver-based Irwin Commercial Finance Canada, then the leasing division of Irwin Financial, a small U.S. regional bank based in Indiana. For ten years, Irwin had prospered in Canada, financing everything from cars and trucks to woodworking equipment. But in 2008, it was forced to look for a buyer for the leasing business. Scotiabank emerged as the successful bidder for its Canadian arm. The leasing assets were split between Roynat Lease Finance, a Scotiabank subsidiary, and a financial services subsidiary in the United States. Roynat is still part of Scotiabank, though it operates in many ways as a separate business, with its own product line specifically tailored to leasing customers. Irwin Financial, the Indiana bank, filed for bankruptcy.

Another notable change in ownership was at National Leasing, an independent family-owned business. The company had enjoyed double-digit growth every year since its formation in 1977 as a lessor specializing in the small- and mid-sized market. Even during the 2008–09 recession, National remained in the black. But management realized that the rapid growth of the past could not be sustained so long as it remained dependent on bank financing.

"When the securitization market was weakened and we were left to use bank financing to a greater extent, we knew it was time for a new treasury model," explained Nick Logan, National's president. "There were three roads to choose: become a deposit-taking institution, buy a bank, or join a bank."

Like many others, Logan and his advisers had no idea how much longer the credit crisis would last or, indeed, whether the crunch might get worse before it got better.

"At that time we felt that it would take too long to become a deposit-taking institution," Logan explained. "The banks for sale at the time were not the answer for us, so we went looking for the right partner." After interviewing several candidates, Logan and his team concluded that Canadian Western Bank would be a perfect match, in terms of both business and culture. Initially, the original owners retained a minority interest, but they subsequently sold all their shares to the Edmonton-based bank.

"To all intents and purposes our mandate and ambitions have remained the same," Logan said in 2013. "I think Canadian Western Bank would concur that we set National Leasing on an impressive track."

National's experience shows that bank ownership can work in the leasing business. Joining forces with a bank ensured a reliable source of funding supplied at the lowest possible cost through the bank's depositors. Under Canadian Western Bank's wing, the company continued to grow profitably. It also retained a corporate culture that stands out as a model in the industry, not only for its financial success but also for its management style, its approach, and how it treats employees. Long before it became a business trend, National took down the physical walls at its head office to flatten the corporate hierarchy, encourage communication, and increase employee engagement.

Banks like Scotiabank, Royal Bank, Toronto-Dominion, and Canadian Western Bank were eager to expand their interests in various sectors of the direct leasing business. Each found acquisition opportunities between 2006 and 2011. In most cases, the deals were initiated by the owners of independent companies who realized that, despite past success, they now had little choice but to find a new shareholder with deeper pockets and a wider reach. (Canada's three other big banks—CIBC, National, and Bank of Montreal—only engaged in indirect leasing, that is, they funded the independent asset-based finance and leasing companies that dealt directly with customers. Unlike the other four, they did not have leasing subsidiaries that dealt directly with customers.)

Following are some of the deals completed by the banks during this period.

2006

TD bulked up its leasing portfolio by acquiring VFC Inc., one of Canada's largest publicly traded indirect consumer finance companies. VFC gave the bank an opportunity to expand its non-prime vehicle financing business. The deal also gave the bank access to Web-based technology that enabled faster, more efficient financing decisions. TD paid $326 million for VFC, which represented an unusually high price of approximately 4.2 times book value and 18 times forecast 2006 earnings.[80]

2007

Following TD's acquisition of VFC, Scotiabank looked for a similar business specializing in the sub-prime vehicle market. In November 2006, it bought auto financing company Travelers Leasing Corporation. The purchase price was not disclosed, but the unit had $255 million in loans under administration.

2009

Scotiabank was the principal lender to Transportaction Lease Systems, whose offshoots included TLS Fleet Management, then Canada's fourth-largest fleet lessor. Nervous about its client's future during the credit crisis, the bank set out to acquire a majority stake. But there was a snag: the Bank Act barred a bank from owning a fleet leasing company.

Undaunted, Scotiabank found a way to move ahead. It used a special exception in the law that allowed a bank to own a vehicle leasing company temporarily, subject to approval by the Office of the Superintendent of Financial Institutions (OSFI). OSFI gave the green light for a long enough period—never disclosed, but rumoured to be five years—to put TLS on a more stable financial footing. Some believe the bank had hoped that the law would be amended in the meantime, allowing the deal to be made permanent. Such hopes, if they indeed existed, turned out to be forlorn. Scotiabank ended up selling the TLS business lines in 2012 to Steve Hudson's Element Financial.

2010

The same year that Canadian Western Bank acquired National Leasing, Royal Bank began negotiations with MCAP Leasing. With a track record of good corporate governance and prudent management practices, MCAP was an ideal choice to grow the bank's vendor financing activities. With MCAP equally interested in making a deal, the acquisition met with MCAP's strategy for growth. The deal was effective December 1, with MCAP Leasing later renamed RCAP. Everyone "won," said Eugene Basolini, president and chief operating officer of RCAP, now a wholly-owned Royal Bank subsidiary.

2011

Capital Underwriters, a commercial equipment leasing company, became increasingly concerned during the credit crisis that it needed a strong infusion of equity to remain competitive. It talked to numerous potential buyers before being snapped up by TD Bank's commercial banking division in 2011 and renamed TD Equipment Finance Canada.

U.S. companies go home

Steve Hudson estimated that prior to 2008, as much as 80 percent of the capital behind the Canadian leasing market came from U.S.- and European-based companies, such as Wells Fargo, CIT, Citigroup, and GE Capital. "When the crisis hit," said Hudson with only slight exaggeration, "they all went home, got smaller, or went bankrupt."

The retreat of the American banks from Canada was dramatic and, in some cases, sudden. Broker partners, vendors, and customers of Wells Fargo, the giant California-based bank, which opened its Canadian broker website on July 30, 2009, found that the login function and product information were gone. Mortgage Broker News reported the same day: "In a surprise announcement just minutes ago, Wells Fargo is discontinuing lending in Canada."

As Hartt saw it, the retreat was an inevitable reaction: "Wells Fargo did what every bank does in a crisis; it literally raced as fast as it could to get out of Canada, so they could protect the mother ship." The company that Hartt chaired at the time, a subsidiary of New York–based Citigroup, took a similar course. It sold its Canadian leasing business in late 2008 and stopped writing new contracts.

Another casualty was the 101-year-old CIT Group. CIT had grown aggressively for many years through acquisitions, including its 1999 takeover of Newcourt. But the expansion took a toll. For CIT, which was heavily reliant on funding from bond investors and the short-term commercial paper market, even a U.S. bailout and debt exchange were not enough to prevent it from filing for U.S. Chapter 11 bankruptcy protection in November 2009. It emerged reorganized and greatly downsized a month later.

Even GE Capital, the giant of the industry, took a big knock. During the crisis, many customers—individuals as well as businesses—delayed or defaulted on loan and lease payments. GE Capital suffered nearly $32 billion in losses from 2008 to 2010.[81] This dented the earnings of GE Capital, which constituted nearly half of the parent company's total earnings. By March 2009, the losses suffered caused Standard & Poor's to cut GE's triple-A credit rating down a notch.

Both CIT and GE Capital bounced back from the dark days of 2008–09, restructuring into more stable and profitable businesses. Under new leadership, CIT changed its funding model and trimmed expenses. General Electric made the strategic decision to reduce its dependence on financial services, cutting the size of GE Capital almost in half, while expanding its traditional industrial businesses. In the company's February 2013 letter to shareowners, GE chairman Jeff Immelt noted that "... we are creating a smaller, more focused financial services company—one that has a lower risk profile and adds value to our industrial businesses. We will continue to reduce the size of GE Capital from the $600 billion of assets it was in 2008 to a goal of $300–$400 billion in the future."

Survival and success

Not all leasing companies suffered the same fate. A few were able to push on with business pretty much as usual, adopting various prudent strategies to get through the leaner years. MCAP Leasing was one that had demonstrated the value of a strong portfolio, high standards, and good credit management. When Eugene Basolini reflected back on those years of tight credit, he described the time as lean but still profitable. "Was financing more expensive?" he asked rhetorically. "Yes, absolutely. We had to be selective in how we arranged it, and we ratcheted back our volumes. But during the crisis we were one of the only companies in Canada that was actually given a credit facility by our funder. We were proud of that."

Out west, Travelers Group expanded across Canada during 2008–09 and added a renewable energy financing unit to the company. "We had excess liquidity," said CEO Jim Case, "and the time was right for us to make a move." Québec-based Crédit-Bail Clé also chose to expand geographically, opening its Ontario-based subsidiary CLE Leasing in February 2008 without a hiccup. Crédit-Bail Clé depended on neither securitization nor the banks for capital. "Securitization was a method offered by many Ontario institutions," explained the company's president, Luc Robitaille. "But we were not dependent on it for capital because it was not available to us through our company's usual network." Robitaille noted that Québec companies that did rely on the securitization market were less fortunate.

CLE Leasing president Jack Marandola explained that his operation had already set aside capital for the first few years of operation and had benefited from the support of a strong group of shareholders. "CLE met its sales targets in 2008 and has continued to grow each year since," Marandola noted.

Others, such as Foss National Leasing, decided to shift focus. A year before the crisis peaked, Foss had both a leasing operation and a fuel and maintenance division. Fearing that funding conditions might become more challenging, it decided to shift its emphasis to the fuel and maintenance business. Foss bought Corp-Rate Card, a fuel card and maintenance company, in August 2007.

"We knew it would offset any losses we'd experience with the temporary downturn in leasing," explained Jeff Hartley. "We started selling our fuel and maintenance services without leasing. It turned out to be the best thing we ever did. We made money at it without having to buy or lease cars."

A few companies were able to expand by filling the gap left by the meltdown's casualties. Steve Akazawa described Jim Pattison Lease's performance during the recession as "spectacular." "The recession was one of the biggest opportunities for us," he said. "Our balance sheet was so powerful that we were the only car leasing company in Canada that continued to securitize through this time. We were not only able to continue to securitize our leases, but we were one of the few left that the banks would lend to."

Akazawa ascribed Jim Pattison Lease's continuing good health to his boss Jim Pattison's "ultra-conservative accounting and attention to the balance sheet, especially well ahead of what happened." He added, "We were the beneficiary of our owner's smarts in managing his business, so we actually grew substantially through that period because we took on business that our competitors couldn't fund."

The lessors' problems inevitably also hurt the brokers who brought them business. Debbie Sands acknowledged that times were tough for her brokerage firm, Polar Leasing. "We did limp along," she recalled. "Admittedly, it was Kraft dinner time, not steak, but we got the bills paid."

The Detroit carmakers in retreat

When Ontario's finance minister, Dwight Duncan, flew back from a meeting at Chrysler early in November 2008, the fate of those soon to be affected by the collapse of the North American auto industry and the global financial crisis weighed heavily on his mind. The lights of the homes and factories stretched from his home town of Windsor all along the 401 Highway corridor to Ottawa. He realized then that no one really knew what was coming, or how severe the depression in auto sales would be.

The North American auto manufacturers were among the most prominent casualties of the financial crisis. GM and Chrysler were forced into bankruptcy court, while Ford had to mortgage almost all its assets, including the famous blue oval logo. Ford was spared from bankruptcy thanks largely to a $25 billion loan that it negotiated in the nick of time, in late 2006.

The carmakers' problems were a long time in the making, and the financial crisis was the last straw. By 2007, bad debts were piling up at the manufacturers' captives, GMAC, Chrysler Financial, and Ford Motor Credit. All three were taking a knock from the slump in residual values, particularly for big pickup trucks and SUVs. With record-high gas prices, the market value of these gas guzzlers dropped way below the residual values projected in lease agreements. Because the leases were typically closed-end, customers were not on the hook for the shortfall at the end of the lease term. The carmaker was left to make up the difference, while the customer walked away.

The captive finance companies were forced to absorb huge losses. Ford wrote down the value of Ford Credit's leased vehicle portfolio by US$2.1 billion in the second quarter of 2008.[82] GMAC took a US$716 million pre-tax charge for residual value losses as part of its US$2.5 billion net loss in the same period.[83] Consumer leasing slumped from half of all new car leases in 2007 to just 7 percent two years later.

Adding to the captives' misery was the fact that their parents were steadily losing market share to Japanese, Korean, and European carmakers. The foreign manufacturers, notably Toyota and Honda, catered increasingly to the rising popularity of smaller, fuel-efficient cars. Furthermore, imports held their value better than Detroit-built models. Toyota's mid-sized Camry had become the undisputed leader in the U.S. sedan market since the late 1990s. Honda's smaller Civic was the number-one seller in Canada.

All the carmakers were hit by the loss of confidence in the asset-backed securities market, where their financing arms typically resold their lease portfolios. "The credit crisis froze the asset-based paper market, which is how most of the funders in the leasing space in Canada financed their business," explained Peter Andrew. "There was an immediate effect because of the trouble faced by automobile manufacturers."

GM, Ford, and Chrysler were among the United States' biggest corporations, and their troubles sent ripples of anxiety through the banking system. Banks became increasingly nervous about their loans to automakers, so the automakers that depended on banks for credit had no choice but to set aside hundreds of millions of dollars in provisions to cover their obligations. In 2006, GM was forced to sell 51 percent of its GMAC financial services arm to Cerberus Capital Management, a private equity firm. Cerberus also bought Chrysler Financial a year later.

Larry Baldesarra, president of Toyota Financial Services Canada, pointed out that the plight of the Detroit captives stemmed from the troubles of the parent companies rather than the captives themselves. "These were very good companies," said Baldesarra. "I knew them well; they were well managed, with good people."

Banks move in again

The plight of Detroit's captive finance companies presented some openings for Canadian banks. In December 2010, TD Bank Group acquired Chrysler Financial from Cerberus, forming TD Auto Finance, with a strong presence throughout North America. After being bailed out by the U.S. government, GMAC became a bank holding company and renamed itself Ally Financial in 2010. Ally Credit Canada Ltd. was acquired by Royal Bank of Canada in 2013.

Consumer leasing gives way to loans

A combination of the carmakers' troubles and heightened risk aversion among lenders brought consumer vehicle leasing to a virtual standstill. In August 2008, Chrysler Financial announced it was getting out of leasing. Ford Motor Credit and then GMAC said shortly afterwards that they were "scaling back." Tightened terms and higher monthly payments meant that, to all intents and purposes, their leasing business also ground to a halt.

Similarly, most foreign carmakers were forced to cut back their lease programs due to prohibitively high funding costs. Ford Credit's Primus Financial Services division, set up to service the import brands, stopped offering leases. Ford Credit also ended its affiliation with Mazda, leaving the Japan-based automaker without a lease program.

Toyota Financial Services Canada was an exception. According to Baldesarra, its financing programs, a fifty–fifty split between leasing and loans, remained intact. "Toyota never forgot the financial difficulties they experienced in the late 1940s and had remained a well-capitalized company ever since," Baldesarra said.

The captives found it more challenging to secure longer term funding during the height of the financial crisis. However, as conditions eased, they were able to leverage their global treasury operation to secure the funding they needed to continue leasing.

As the crisis unfolded, banks made it clear to auto dealers and auto manufacturers' captives that vehicle financing would, at least for the time being, need to take the form of loans, not leases. One important reason for the switch was that the residual risk always lay with the owner of the vehicle. In the case of a lease, the lessor was on the hook. But for a loan, it was the customer.

The three Canadian banks in the vehicle-financing business—Scotiabank, TD, and Royal Bank—adjusted the terms of their loans to make them similar to leases. Maturities were lengthened to bring down monthly payments and to include a large, end-of-term payment, known as a "balloon payment." As with all car loans, the deals were structured as conditional sales contracts under which a customer agreed to buy the vehicle at the end of the term. In order to hold monthly payments at roughly the same level as a lease, maturities were stretched to as long as six or eight years.

The shift from leases to loans may have had some drawbacks for car buyers and dealers, but it reduced the risk of losses for those providing the credit. A lease typically brought a customer back to a dealership after three to four years to choose another new car. On the other hand, customers with longer-term loans were more likely to hang on to their vehicles for longer and less likely to return to the same dealership for a replacement.

Another issue raised by a big balloon payment due at the end of the loan, was that such payments often exceeded the vehicle's residual value. Consumers are protected from balloon payments at the end of a lease-to-own because of legislation in place in most provinces. Consumer vehicle leases typically include a stated residual value, which consumers *may* choose to pay if they want to buy the vehicle at the end of the lease. Or the consumer can return the vehicle and walk away. No such protection applies on loans.

Crisis of confidence

Through the fall of 2008 and into 2009, it was clear to policymakers and analysts that the Canadian economy was set for a long period of stagnation unless ways could be found to get credit flowing again. Rob Wright, then the deputy minister of finance, noted that banks and credit unions had provided conventional lending of $271 billion, or only 24 percent, of the $1.125 trillion in outstanding business credit in Canada in 2007. In other words, more than three-quarters of business credit came from other sources: $306 billion from the equity markets and $458 billion from non-equity financial markets (including an estimate by the Centre of Spatial Economics of up to $100 billion from finance companies and the asset-based finance subsidiaries of the banks and credit unions).[84]

The banks really were the last man standing. Bond and equity markets essentially closed down, and the other non-bank finance companies had nowhere to go to access funds. The banks stepped up, but not sufficiently to appease all critics. There were segments of the market that complained that they could not get access to funds (at least not from their traditional providers). Some may not have had a strong relationship with banks before the crisis. But once the crisis hit, the banks definitely were not in the mood to take on anything that could be perceived as high risk.

The asset-based finance and leasing industry faced a serious challenge. Investors had been unnerved by worthless—often fraudulent—sub-prime real estate mortgages passed off in the United States as legitimate and even blue chip investments. The industry urgently needed to differentiate its sound products from those tainted by the financial crisis. It needed to offer reassurance that equipment and vehicles could back safe and profitable investments.

"The equipment and vehicle assets securitized by the asset-backed financing and leasing industry were totally different," said Angela Armstrong. "Unfortunately we got tarred with the same brush."

David Powell outlined the dilemma facing the industry: "Essentially, securitization as a financing method for both real estate mortgage–backed securities and asset-backed securities was similar, but the quality of the assets secured as collateral was totally different. These were equipment and vehicle assets that were being used and paid for by real customers. The cost and availability of funds in no way reflected the risk that the industry or its business represented. Rather it reflected a system-wide 'capital rationing.' Traditional funders were deploying their cash elsewhere to meet the pressures they were experiencing because of the global crisis."

CFLA takes action

The asset-based finance and leasing industry, with the CFLA in the forefront, was determined to step up to the plate and demonstrate that it could be part of the solution. But it faced a particular problem of its own making. In this largely unregulated industry, people had deliberately avoided much contact with governments in the past. As a consequence, most policymakers knew little about the sector, what it did, and how it functioned. The CFLA had a double challenge: first, to educate politicians and government officials on how the industry should be part of the solution to stimulate the recovery and, second, to reassure them that there was minimal risk to taxpayers. Discussions with Finance Department officials revolved around ways to temporarily "replace" private funding for the industry until market confidence returned.

Industry leaders realized that they needed to convince the government that:

- asset-based financing was a direct, efficient, and effective way to stimulate the recovery by getting credit rapidly back to Main Street Canada;
- their sector was such an important source of financing for consumers and business that the sector merited temporary support; and
- their businesses were fundamentally stable and profitable.

"We needed to let the government know that in stepping into the shoes of absent private investors, government investment would not only be safe but also profitable," Powell said.

The federal budget was set for January 27, 2009. In a sign of the gravity of the situation, it would be tabled a month earlier than usual. That gave the CFLA only a very small window to convey the urgency of the situation and to promote a simple policy solution to key players both in and outside government.

Powell went to Ottawa in early December 2008 to press the industry's case with senior officials at the Finance Department. He made a return visit on December 18, with a full CFLA delegation of leading industry representatives, including the presidents of Ford Credit Canada, Toyota Financial Services Canada, and Foss National Leasing, and senior executives from GE Capital, National Leasing, and MCAP Leasing. Rick Gauthier, president of the Canadian Automobile Dealers Association, asked to join the group at the last minute, fortuitously as things turned out.

The delegation's message, put forward in a presentation titled "Getting Credit to Main Street Canada for Small and Mid-Sized Enterprises and Consumers," was that government funding was urgently needed to support the asset-based finance and leasing industry. Such support, it argued, would help restore liquidity and stability to the wider financial system, while profiting taxpayers in the long term.

Two days later, at the invitation of the government, Gauthier, the car dealers' representative, found himself in the company of Prime Minister Stephen Harper, Ontario premier Dalton McGuinty, and two senior federal cabinet ministers— Minister of Finance Jim Flaherty and Minister for Industry Tony Clement. The five men were together in a back room awaiting a call to go on stage to announce $4 billion in emergency federal and

Ontario aid to support the Canadian subsidiaries of Chrysler and General Motors. The meeting gave Gauthier the unique opportunity to make a twenty-minute pitch for the CFLA proposal to the key political decision makers.

The CFLA remained in constant contact with Finance officials, who asked a stream of questions. Despite it being the holiday period, members of the CFLA delegation were quick to provide responses and advice. In parallel, Powell did the rounds of the three opposition parties, the Liberals, NDP, and Bloc Québécois.

The association's lobbying efforts were complicated by the unsettled political climate at the time. Stephen Harper's Conservatives had been re-elected in October 2008, but again with less than a clear majority in the House of Commons. The first session of the new parliament was prorogued just two months after the election to forestall a no-confidence vote by the Liberals and the NDP.

The CFLA was eager to win support for its proposal from all parties to ensure that it was not sidelined by political acrimony. "Given the volatile political environment," said Powell, "we needed the opposition to understand what we had asked for, why we had asked for it, and how it would be a positive step toward supporting Canadian businesses and consumers."

The proposal was also run past Bill Robson, president of the C.D. Howe Institute and a respected independent expert on the economy and the financial services industry. Robson was supportive and offered to convene a full-day private discussion with key players, including investors, financial institutions, dealers, brokers, and government policymakers. This gathering would be held on March 6, 2009. In mid-January, Powell also met with two senior executives of the Canadian Bankers Association, who indicated that the banks would not object to the CFLA proposal.

The CFLA's efforts bear fruit

Go big or stay home

Looking back at what was going on in Ottawa at the beginning of 2009, the government had a very small window in which to take action. The uncertainty around the world had not abated, Canada had promised the G20 it would do its part to keep markets functioning, and Jim Flaherty needed to put together a budget that would allow the minority government of the Conservatives to stay in power. Everyone agreed that stimulus measures were required. The debate focused on the size of the spending package and what it would include. Five years later in an interview with BNN (Business News Network), Flaherty recalled his discussions with Prime Minister Harper: "We listened to business people, small, medium size, tell us how grim things were.... We decided we'd have to run a big deficit. At first I was hoping we would get away with something more modest but the more I listened the more I realized we could either go big or stay home ... so we went big."[85]

As part of the January 27, 2009, budget, Flaherty unveiled an initiative known as the Extraordinary Financing Framework, which included a $12 billion package, called the Canadian Secured Credit Facility (CSCF), targeted specifically at the asset-based finance and leasing industry.

Under the overall federal rescue plan, the government agreed to pump $200 billion into the economy, in addition to its contribution to the GM and Chrysler bailouts. A major portion of the funds ($125 million) would be earmarked for an Insured Mortgage Purchase Program, designed to buy real estate mortgages from banks to stabilize the Canadian mortgage-backed securities market and free up capital for lending. The CSCF was allocated up to $12 billion to fund the equipment and vehicle asset-based finance companies so that they could resume financing consumers and business customers across Canada. The facility would be administered by the Business Development Bank of Canada, a Crown corporation, which would be authorized to buy securitized auto and equipment loans and leases.

"This was the second-proudest moment in my time with the CFLA," Powell said. (The first had been the membership's support for the association's submission to the Mackay taskforce on the future of Canada's financial services sector in 1998.) "The 2009 federal budget confirmed that the government understood and accepted that this industry was an important source of financing for consumers and business, meriting government support in an extraordinary time."

Stanley Hartt described the actions taken by Finance Minister Jim Flaherty as "truly heroic." Flaherty also set up an Advisory Committee on Financing, chaired by Hartt. The members of the group, all CEOs of major companies, met from April 2009 to March 2010. They agreed to accept a nominal salary of one dollar plus expenses. "Our mandate," Hartt said, "was to ensure that anyone who was creditworthy had access to funds so they could do business."

CFLA representatives including Powell, Hugh Swandel, Jeff Hartley, and Serge Mâsse met several times with the committee to keep the industry's interests squarely in the sights of policymakers and business leaders. The association also kept reminding politicians of the importance of the leasing industry, so that the CSCF program would not be in jeopardy if the minority government fell. Powell appeared before the House of Commons standing committee on finance in March 2009. He explained, "We needed to show support for the government's budget proposal to create the CSCF and to make MPs aware of the importance of the industry and its role in getting the economy moving again."

Red tape stymies the CSCF

To the industry's frustration, the secured credit facility got off to a very slow start. One reason was that the Business Development Bank (BDC) had little advance warning that it would be responsible for designing and implementing the program. The CFLA offered assistance to the BDC throughout 2009 in an effort to start funds flowing to credit-starved businesses as quickly as possible. As part of the association's efforts, a large group of CFLA members participated in the March 2009 C.D. Howe policy conference on shaping a secured credit facility with government policymakers and the BDC leadership.

CFLA also commissioned Hugh Swandel and Murray Derraugh of the global consultancy Alta Group to prepare a detailed blueprint demonstrating how a workable private securitization funding model could be created and implemented. The sixty-two-page report was sent to the BDC. No response was received back.

CFLA and Hartt's advisory committee tried to keep things moving. In the end, however, the response was disappointing to the point that many hard-pressed leasing companies gave up waiting. They downsized operations, sought financial support elsewhere, or simply closed their doors.

The first transaction backed by the CSCF was not consummated until December 2009. The deal involved an injection of $300 million into CNH Capital Canada Ltd., the captive financing arm of CNH Industrial, a maker of farm and industrial equipment. Another four deals followed, but the program was terminated at the end of March 2010, having used only about $3.4 billion of the $12 billion at its disposal.

Despite the modest results, Hartt noted that, "overall, the government got first-class marks for recognizing that financing is the heart of the entire economy. They did quite well by the larger originators in the vehicle and equipment loans." But, he added, "they were extremely slow to come to the assistance of the smaller originators, and the method they chose was inapplicable. When it did start to trickle out financing, other market players who were finance providers, such as Steve Hudson, had started to fill the gap. A number of the players fell by the wayside. They couldn't fund themselves and couldn't use an external vehicle to take their paper. So they had to sell."

Powell and CFLA members reviewed the program and reached a similar conclusion, namely, that, in addition to being hampered by red tape, the government-backed credit facility was not suited to smaller finance companies with leasing volumes under $100 million a year.

To address this subsector's concerns, the 2010 federal budget set up a new program, known as the Vehicle and Equipment Finance Partnership (VEFP). It was launched in March 2010, at the same time as the ill-fated Canadian Secured Credit Facility was terminated.

Like the CSCF, the VEFP was funded and managed by the Business Development Bank, with an initial allocation of $500 million. Its purpose was to provide financing options for small and mid-sized finance and leasing companies and to expand the availability of credit at affordable rates for smaller dealers and users of vehicles and equipment. Separate from the VEFP, the Bank and TAO Asset Management set up a joint venture to facilitate access to funding. This partnership, known as the Funding Platform for Independent Lenders (F-PIL), remains intact today.

CFLA's "eyes and ears" in Ottawa

Effective government relations was never so important to the CFLA as during the 2008-09 financial crisis. Kudos go to Huw Williams, president of Impact Public Affairs in Ottawa. Williams and his team have been the association's government relations advisers for over fifteen years.

"Huw has provided wise advice and effective guidance on a number of key federal issues, not least the efforts to convince the government to invest in the industry during the 2008–2010 financial crisis," said CFLA president David Powell.

A former acting chief of staff to the deputy prime minister of Canada, a senior special assistant to the minister of constitutional affairs, and a legislative assistant to the speaker of the Alberta legislative assembly, Williams, with his intelligence, political acumen, unfailing good humour, and "get-it-done" character, has served the association well.

Williams continues to be a very popular regular speaker at CFLA conferences.

Credit starts flowing again

Canada weathered the global financial crisis relatively well. The Canadian banks had been more prudent than their U.S. counterparts and had little exposure to the sub-prime real estate mortgage market. They also benefited from a strong regulatory system and, more generally, from sound management of the economy. The banks remained well capitalized, stable, and secure. None required a direct bailout. Even so, they became much more averse to risk, pulling in their horns and severely slowing down bank lending in 2008 and 2009.

In response to this credit freeze, the Bank of Canada followed the lead of the U.S. Federal Reserve, pumping massive amounts of liquidity into the economy and holding interest rates at very low levels. On other fronts, the federal government provided support, first with the CSCF, then with the VEFP.

One measure of these policies' success was that all four financing companies that benefited from the Canadian Secured Credit Facility had repaid every penny of their government funding—plus interest—by November 2013. The *National Post* praised the program as "one of the federal government's key emergency responses to the global credit crisis," and one that "may be the most financially successful government program in recent history."[86]

Powell was especially heartened by the successful, if belated, outcome of government support. "At the time, the industry knew that its proposal was sound, but officials were politely skeptical," he recalled. "Now the government had tangible proof. The history of the CSCF can only reinforce the strong positive public image of the industry, its professionalism, and the quality of the assets it finances in Canada."

As the CFLA saw it, the program reinforced its argument that the securitization freeze in the depths of the financial crisis was caused more by the ripple effects from other corners of the financial markets than by any inherent defect in asset-based financing.

Alexandre Laurin, associate director of research at the C.D. Howe Institute, confirmed as much in November 2013, telling Powell in a note:

> *At the time of the 2009 federal budget, when the facility was announced, you were very forceful in insisting that irrational fears or contagion spreading from other asset classes in the global securitization market were the main cause behind the rise in spreads, and that the poor economic outlook and inherent business risks could not explain the market collapse in your industry. Developments since have shown the validity of your argument.*

Transformed but not defeated

The financial world changed in 2008, and Canada's asset-based finance industry changed with it. In particular, the concept of risk took on new meaning. As Moe Danis put it, "We learned that we couldn't structure risk away." It would be several years before investors fully trusted the concept of securitization again, or before consumers realized once more that leasing a new car might be a better proposition than snapping up a zero-deposit loan.

Even so, as Richard McAuliffe at Key Equipment Finance noted, "Change brings opportunity, which brings change again." And with new global regulations on the horizon and some of the biggest players in the world either pulling out of the industry or ramping up their interests, there was plenty of change to come.

A year after the watershed moment in CFLA's history when Moe Danis had spelled out the impending dangers, three hundred delegates gathered for the association's 2009 annual meeting at Ottawa/Gatineau. This time, the conference theme was "Capitalizing on our Transformed World." The keynote speaker was Finance Minister Jim Flaherty.

The association's chairman, Fred Booth, president of ARI Financial Services, opened the meeting with a trenchant observation and a timely word of advice: "We are working through a period of unprecedented challenge touching every aspect of the asset-based finance and leasing world. In these challenging times, CFLA members need their association more than ever—to connect with their peers, to understand what is impacting their business and why, and how others are responding. These are all invaluable benefits that only an association can offer."[87]

Flaherty then took the floor. He started off by thanking CFLA members for their tenacity during the financial crisis, then went on to underline the critical role that the industry had played in the drive to put the economy back on an even keel. Most important, he pinpointed the industry's enduring hallmark—a determination to transform crisis into opportunity. "As your conference theme indicates," Flaherty concluded, "you are planning to succeed because of it and capitalize on the transformations that you have lived through. I have no doubt whatsoever that, having survived hard times, you have everything it takes to excel in better ones."

· *chapter 7* ·

Unstoppable

Leasing has made a meaningful contribution to the Canadian economy for a long time. A goal for all of us in the industry is to remember to tell our story.

Joe LaLeggia, senior vice-president, Scotiabank Leasing Group

IN THE AFTERMATH of the 2008–09 recession, the Canadian economy entered a period of slow to moderate growth. In contrast to the volatility in some European credit markets, Canadian financial institutions enjoyed steadily improved confidence and, once again, adequate access to wholesale funds. By 2010, consumers were back in the market for new cars, SUVs, and pickup trucks. Canadian businesses were also finally seeing unmistakable signs of an upturn and starting to replace aging machinery and equipment. From the head office of Element Financial at BCE Place in Toronto, Steve Hudson noted in 2013 that "this represented a huge replacement cycle that was overdue, and a huge opportunity for companies that could take advantage of it."

The recovery meant that asset-based finance and leasing could start to move forward again, albeit cautiously. After four consecutive years of decline, the leasing market[88] bounced back by 5 percent in 2011.[89] The number of new leased vehicles more than tripled, from 91,000 in 2009 to 279,000 by 2012.

Those willing and able to invest, such as Element, took advantage of gaps in the market. As Hudson noted, "there was a complete absence of people willing to finance that stuff on highways and construction sites." But with the financial crisis fresh in everyone's minds, many players remained uncertain whether they could find adequate funding for expansion or come to terms with a shift in culture that put a greater emphasis on risk management and transparency.

Moe Danis portrayed the prevailing mood as one of "wait and see." As he put it, "Wait and see if the economy is truly in recovery, or still very fragile and subject to the happenings in the United States, Europe, and Asia."[90]

Richard McAuliffe described the post-recession years as a time for reflection. He noted that "2008 and 2009 were a wake-up call for many industry players.... The approach after that became more strategic, more opportunistic. Whether a regulated financial institution, independent or privately owned organization, everyone asked: 'Is this the kind of market I want to be in? Does it fit my risk profile? Does it provide returns acceptable for that risk profile?'"

There was certainly no question of a quick return to the swashbuckling days of the 1990s and early 2000s. BAL Global Finance Canada Corporation's manager, Doug McKenzie observed, "In the end, I don't think business returned to normal. A new normal emerged and would continue to evolve."

Nonetheless, some of the industry's basic pillars remained firmly in place. Access to capital remained its lifeblood. Knowledge of the assets being financed was indispensable. Leasing still enabled businesses to improve productivity by gaining access to the most modern technology through a source of capital other than traditional bank lending. The tried-and-tested concept of vendor financing that had emerged in the early 1960s—namely, the ability to provide financing at the point of sale—took on a new importance among manufacturers as an effective way to build customer loyalty.

Tightened regulations with more rules

One immediate outcome of the financial crisis was growing pressure from governments and regulators around the world for tighter rules on bank capital to ensure that banks would be in a better position to withstand future shocks. The Basel Committee on Banking Supervision, a group representing nearly thirty countries that sets international regulatory standards for banks, hammered out new rules to mitigate the risk of another meltdown. Known as Basel III and finalized in 2010, the agreement built on two earlier initiatives, Basel I and Basel II. In essence, the latest rules aim to improve the banking sector's ability to deal with financial and economic stress, enhance its risk management, and strengthen transparency.

Canada's big banks began the six-year phase-in period for Basel III in January 2013. Among other requirements, they will need to meet a "leverage ratio" of 3 percent by 2018, meaning their cash reserves must equal at least 3 percent of total assets.

However, such rules could make it much harder for some banks to earmark extra capital for longer-term financing such as leases. CFLA members and other industry players have lost no time considering the potentially far-reaching ramifications of these stricter capital requirements.

"When Basel III is fully implemented," explained David Powell, "banks will be obliged to hold more money in reserve. Once they do that, they will have to relook at how they allocate money for funding various activities. If returns from the asset-based finance business do not appear to be attractive, companies may find themselves cut off from bank support. This includes even the bank-owned equipment finance companies, as well as independents that have relied, at some level, on banks for financing."

Hugh Swandel, senior managing director at The Alta Group, echoed Powell's sentiments. "Tighter pressure on banking capital will force some banks to review their commitments to equipment leasing and vehicle leasing," he said. Swandel noted that ING, the big Dutch bank, closed its U.K. leasing operation at the end of December 2011 after reviewing the impact of the Basel III rules.

In keeping with the industry's resilience, some saw Basel III as an opening for independent lessors to pick up accounts from the banks. "While banks were looking seriously at their product mix in the context of Basel III, there was a whole category of people considering entering the leasing market," commented Roman Oryschuk, now chief executive of Global Change Leaders and adjunct professor at the business schools of the Université de Montréal and McGill University.[91]

The tighter capital requirements also rippled through to the securitization market, which had been shaken by the financial crisis. While securitization deals returned, stricter disclosure rules did not entirely overcome investors' wariness. Moe Danis, one of Canada's securitization pioneers, observed in the fall of 2013, "Securitization is still a four-letter word to many who never really understood what it was. But conduits are moving paper again, just in much smaller amounts than in 2008."

Fewer, larger players become the norm

The industry entered a period of consolidation after the recession, resulting in fewer and larger players. For some, the onset of the recovery was a perfect time to take advantage of gaps in the market. Perhaps the most closely watched player was Steve Hudson's Element Financial, which began expanding in late 2011 with the acquisition of Montreal-based Alter Moneta, an equipment-leasing company catering to mid-market businesses. Alter Moneta was well placed to capitalize on a void in the market created when foreign-owned leasing firms retreated from Canada and smaller independent lessors withered during the 2008 credit crisis.

When Hudson was at the helm of Newcourt Credit in the 1990s, GE Capital was his chief rival. Once the largest player in the global equipment leasing and financing market, GE Capital's assets had halved by 2013 as it shed some businesses and shrank others. Element, for one, wasted no time circling GE Capital's cast-offs, with Hudson declaring that "it was a sweet position where the most dominant player in the industry became smaller."

Element acquired GE Capital's Canadian aerospace team in early 2010 to provide an entrée into big-ticket transactions. It followed up over the next couple of years with the purchase of, among others, GE's Canadian fleet operations, TLS Fleet Management, CoActiv Capital Partners, and the technology finance arm of Nexcap Finance Corporation. By early 2014, Element was expanding into leasing railcars and helicopters servicing North Sea oil platforms. By the time of this book's publication, Element had agreed to buy PHH Corp's auto fleet leasing business for about $1.4 billion (U.S.) in cash—and for a time, answered the question on everyone's mind, "what will Hudson do next?" According to Hudson, the move was part of an overall strategic and financial objective to expand Element's domestic fleet management business into the U.S. market.

Among other deals during this period of consolidation:

- Hitachi Capital, a 100 percent owned subsidiary of Hitachi Capital America Corp., signed a share purchase agreement to acquire the shares of CLE Canadian Leasing Enterprise Ltd.
- Two successful companies with western Canadian roots, Ritchie Bros. Auctioneers Inc. and Travelers Financial Corporation, created the joint venture Ritchie Bros. Financial Services to provide lease and financing services to buyers at Ritchie Bros. auctions.

- TCF Commercial Finance Canada, a subsidiary of Minnesota-based bank holding company TCF Financial Corporation, acquired Arctic Cat Floorplan Financing from Textron Financial Canada.
- Lease Link Canada Corp., a Canadian-owned financial services company and subsidiary of Credicor Financial, bought Lease Plus Financial from Lease Plus Services.
- U.S.–based computer maker Dell Inc. expanded its global empire in 2011 with the acquisition from CIT Group of the shares it did not already own in Dell Financial Services Canada. The deal ended a pioneering, fourteen-year partnership originally set up between Dell and Newcourt. CIT had inherited the stake as part of its acquisition of Newcourt.

Global players also continued to expand their networks, serving large, worldwide market niches. De Lage Landen Financial Services Canada Inc., a Canadian subsidiary of a Netherlands-based parent, De Lage Landen (DLL), was described by president and CEO Peter Horan as the world's "only truly global vendor finance company." Originally set up to offer asset financing and leasing to the Dutch agriculture industry in 1969, today DLL is a fully-owned subsidiary of the Dutch Rabobank, with representation in thirty-eight countries.

Captive finance companies bounce back

The captive finance arms of such manufacturers as Caterpillar, John Deere, and the carmakers were badly bruised by the liquidity crisis and the subsequent economic downturn. But although they were down, they were by no means out. Indeed, most of the captives not only survived but set about capturing market share at the expense of banks and independents.

The captives took decisive action to address past missteps. One of their most obvious weaknesses had been their dependence on outside funding. The degree of that dependence varied. For example, Caterpillar had a separate financing subsidiary but kept all its business on its own books. Others offered their customers financing options through a small division or department, and then syndicated some or all of their commitments to a funding partner. The 2008–09 credit crunch drove home the heavy cost of tumbling sales and a dependence on outside funding.

"During the turbulent years, manufacturers had trouble getting their funding partners to be consistently reliable," explained Paul Frechette, senior managing director at The Alta Group and an expert on vendor and captive finance. "These captives and their parents decided they needed to be ready for the next time—because they knew there would be a next time. So many made the decision to control more of their customer financing themselves."

The strategy was smart from a sales perspective too. By offering financing through its own captive, a manufacturer had a better chance of retaining the customer at the end of a lease term. While an independent lessor might recommend a different brand—thereby steering the customer to another supplier—a captive stood a much better chance of winning the business again in three to four years.

Manufacturers also learned that their financing products needed to be packaged with other services that set them apart from competitors. "It's no longer enough simply to provide financing," Frechette wrote in the June 2013 issue of the *Monitordaily*, a newsmagazine for the U.S. equipment finance industry. "They must also deliver speedy turnaround, a single point of contact and an impressive amount of product expertise."[92]

Captives went to work streamlining their operations. They still controlled customers' financing programs, but increasingly outsourced the administration to process management specialists like Genpact, formerly a GE unit called GE Capital International Services.

"Captives have learned a lot over the past couple of decades and now make a strong contribution to their parent companies' bottom line," observed Alta's Hugh Swandel. "They also have become a core part of the international expansion strategy of companies such as Caterpillar, John Deere, IBM, Microsoft, and Case New Holland. The key to continued success will be access to cheap capital and good leverage."

In Canada, manufacturers' captives (including the carmakers' financing arms) are the second-largest segment of providers of asset-based finance. But they remain well behind the banks when measured by the value of assets financed.

Although reliable data is scarce in Canada, the Centre for Spatial Economics estimates that banks and credit unions accounted for between 50 and 60 percent of all asset-based finance and leasing transactions in 2013, with the captives making up about 25 percent and the balance provided by independent finance companies and government financial institutions. (See Appendix II for details on how these figures were calculated.)[93]

The banks and credit unions boost their stronghold

The Canadian banks and credit unions, which had tended to jump in and out of the leasing business depending on economic conditions, returned with a vengeance in the wake of the recession. This was particularly true for Royal, TD, Scotiabank, and Canadian Western, which came to covet leasing not only for short-term profits but also as part of their long-term growth plans. The equipment financing and leasing companies they had acquired over the previous decade gave them not only a strong foothold in the marketplace but also an opportunity to market extra banking services to hundreds of small and mid-sized businesses across the country.

"Before the crisis," observed Swandel, "if you were an independent leasing company going to an equipment dealer, you would compete with other independent companies. You almost never saw a bank rep calling on that account. But now, as the banks have acquired many independents, they are very present at equipment dealers. That's a big change."

The secret of the banks' success was to allow their new acquisitions to "stick to their knitting," in other words, leasing rather than banking. Thus, when Canadian Western Bank bought National Leasing, there was an understanding that National would operate as if it were an independent entity. "We had a thirty-five-year track record, so there was a high degree of autonomy," said Tom Pundyk.

RCAP Leasing's Barb Hannesson noted that "for years, banks bought leasing firms and said, 'The heck with how they've been run; now we're going to dictate our policies and procedures.' But in recent years, banks have changed their tune. They had to change their ways because they failed miserably with that attitude. Royal Bank has been very conscious about leaving the back shop alone and only enhancing it."

Other banks signalled that they also planned to expand their presence in direct equipment financing. By 2013, CIBC was promoting its securitization group for such assets as motor vehicles, industrial equipment, credit cards, and trade receivables. Some industry experts predicted that CIBC might step up its activity in the vehicle leasing market too. Laurentian Bank announced in late 2013 that it was adding leasing to its financing choices for commercial clients, and for the first time, Laurentian signed up to attend the CFLA's annual conference. In April 2014, Canada's second-largest credit union, Coast Capital Savings, consolidated its subsidiary, Coast Capital Equipment Finance Ltd. with the assets of Travelers Financial Corporation, making TFC now part of the Coast Capital Group of Companies.

The auto financing battle

The banks moved aggressively to strengthen their foothold in the auto loan business before the carmakers' captives—previously the dominant players—had a chance to get back in that game. The main players—Scotiabank, Royal, and TD—broadened their dealership financing products to include mortgages for new bricks-and-mortar facilities, commercial lines of credit, and floor plan (inventory) financing. Others, such as Bank of Montreal, CIBC, and Québec-based Desjardins Group, also enhanced or introduced new dealership financing options.

In an especially bold move in early 2013, Royal Bank bought the Canadian arm of Ally Financial, General Motors' old financing arm. It reportedly beat out TD Bank. At the time of the deal, Ally provided financing for six hundred dealerships across Canada. The acquisition propelled Royal into the number-one spot in Canada's auto loan market.

The banks were generally successful both in expanding their reach and in keeping customers happy. Dealers still turned to the captives to subsidize the loan rates they were promoting, known as subvented deals. But their loyalty was waning, and they were increasingly willing to do business with a bank if it offered better terms. A 2012 dealership survey compiled by J.D. Power and Associates noted: "Banks are continuously improving their offerings and improving the dealer lending experience. This is putting competitive pressure on all automotive lenders to focus on providing outstanding service to dealers in order to maintain or grow their share of the business."[94]

The car companies, through their finance captives, fought back against the banks. "Even though Toyota had always maintained its level of leasing," noted Larry Baldesarra, president of Toyota Financial Services Canada, "as the market shifted, we also promoted auto financing to compete."

Monthly payments for consumer auto loans were stretched beyond what anyone would have predicted a few years earlier. By 2010, 57 percent of all new vehicles sold in Canada were financed with loans offered largely by banks offering repayment terms of six years (seventy-two months) or longer. Having no captive finance affiliate, Hyundai was funded by a bank. In 2013, it advertised a fifty-year anniversary special of "0/96"—a tag line for zero percent financing over ninety-six months, or eight years. Commonly known as "buying down the rates," these bargain basement incentives' costs were borne by manufacturers, not dealers.

So tempting were these deals that they set alarm bells ringing among those worried about Canadian consumers' soaring debt. A Postmedia news story revealed in mid-2013 that the Finance Department was "closely monitoring the huge growth in popularity of long-term vehicle financing in Canada." With loan maturities stretching out to seven years and beyond, many consumers were rudely surprised when halfway through the financing term they realized that they still owed more on their loan than their car was actually worth. Such shocks served as a reminder that leasing could still be a good choice for those who do not drive much, prefer to drive a relatively new vehicle, or want to avoid a big down payment.

According to the Canadian Automobile Dealers Association's 2013 annual report, "Leasing continued its slow march back to past glories by grabbing just over 20 percent of new sales in 2012 after bottoming out at just over 7 percent in 2009 when leases almost went extinct." Loans made up 62 percent of new vehicle purchases in 2012, and 18 percent were bought for cash.[95]

Retail leases accounted for a peak of 45 percent of all vehicles sold in Canada in 2005, rising to almost 50 percent in 2007. The share shrank to 24 percent in 2008 and 7 percent in 2009 but bounced back to 20 percent by 2012.

The dominant captives fighting for market share in the consumer leasing market were Toyota Financial Services Canada, Honda Canada Finance, Nissan Canada Financial Services, GM Financial, Mercedes-Benz Financial Services, VW Credit, and BMW Financial Services. Ford Motor Credit kept its focus on financing and remained a less aggressive player. Chrysler Canada unveiled a new national leasing program in 2013.

General Motors and Chrysler return to leasing

GM completed the disposal of its subsidiary Ally (formerly GMAC) in 2006, leaving Detroit's number-one carmaker without its own captive financing company. But GM returned to auto financing in October 2010 with the acquisition of U.S.–based AmeriCredit, which was renamed GM Financial. Six months later, it bought FinanciaLinx, Canada's largest independent vehicle leasing company, forming the nucleus for the new GM Financial Canada. Headquartered in Toronto, GM Financial provides GM dealers with a leasing program, a retail sub-prime option, and full-scale commercial lending.

After a five-year break, Chrysler Canada also returned to the leasing market, in the spring of 2013. Chrysler differed from other major automakers in that it no longer owned a captive finance company, so it needed to work through third parties. The new leasing program was set up in conjunction with B.C.–based Westminster Savings Credit Union and its leasing division, WS Leasing.

One way for a lessor to gain market share is to set residual values higher than those of its competitors, thereby lowering monthly payments. Luxury carmakers such as Mercedes-Benz, Audi, and BMW dangled this carrot in front of buyers to stimulate demand for high-end vehicles. By 2013, a consumer could lease an Audi at a monthly rate equal to or lower than many run-of-the-mill models. It was an offer too good to refuse. The approach created a high lease penetration—Audis seemed to be everywhere—and paved the way for the driver to return to the same luxury brand when the lease expired in three or four years. The practice of constantly adjusting residuals also helped carmakers stimulate demand for specific models. As Tom Simmons explained, "The captives play with their gross margin. If they want to move the sale of a certain model, they just adjust the calculation."

Dealer consolidation

One consequence of the meltdown in the North American auto industry in 2008 and 2009 was a massive scaling back of dealerships, especially by the Detroit carmakers, and an accelerating trend toward dealer groups, each comprising multiple outlets. Chuck Seguin, writing in the *Canadian Auto Dealer,* compared the trend to a Pac-Man video game: "The consolidation started before the recession, as larger auto groups with huge resources bought up smaller independent businesses."[96]

The move was fuelled by automakers' demands for costly capital investments in showrooms, sophisticated technology, and management systems. During 2012, the number of single dealerships in Canada dropped from 2,109 to 1,876. The growth of the dealer groups is illustrated by Auto Canada (with thirty outlets) and GO Auto (over twenty-five outlets), both based in Edmonton.[97]

Most of the remaining dealer-owned leasing companies were unwilling or unable to go head-to-head against the deep-pocketed automakers' captives. As explained by John Carmichael, whose family owned City Buick, now part of the twenty-three dealership, Toronto-based Humberview Group, "The financial resources required to fund such an organization made it extremely difficult, or for that matter impossible, for a single dealership operation to set up its own leasing company or division." As the dealer groups have gained in strength, some predict that that they may eventually take on the manufacturers' captives by setting up their own lease operations.

By 2013, consumer leasing had rebounded, but the business was confined almost entirely to a handful of big carmaker captives. Independents with more limited resources were unable to compete. As Mike Collins at DealerTrack Technologies saw it, these moves placed consumer auto leasing in Canada at risk. "When you remove dealers, banks, and some manufacturers from the lease supply," he observed, "you're taking away hundreds of thousands of transactions."

Vehicle-leasing veteran Tom Simmons also took the view that the market had benefited from having both the banks and captives as active players. Dealerships could fund their business through their own portfolio as well as through lease and loan programs offered by the manufacturers and loans offered by the banks. Carmakers' captives that competed with banks also depended, in many cases, on the same institutions for additional financing in order to offer lower rates.

Even so, Toyota Financial's Larry Baldesarra remained confident that captives such as his would continue to dominate the consumer vehicle leasing market. "We don't try to be all things to all people," he noted. "We are expert in setting residuals for our own brands so we can better manage the residual risk and promote our products. Toyota's promise is to provide customers a choice that suits them, whether it be leasing or loan. The road to ultimate customer satisfaction is to enable our customer to get the vehicle they want with the financial product that they want."

Fleet leasing: A triumph of technology

Fleet leasing, which makes up about 10 percent of the total vehicle leasing business (which includes sales by manufacturers to both fleet companies and rental companies), went through a dramatic shift in the mid-2000s.

When Jim Halliday joined the global fleet management company in the early 2000s, he was not a typical "car guy." Instead, his background was in research, data management, and analysis—skills that were becoming increasingly prized in the fleet management world. Telematics (or GPS vehicle tracking) was emerging as a popular way for fleet managers to monitor the location, movement, status, and performance of their vehicles. And so it has remained.

"Our hiring profiles today," said Halliday, "are scientists trained to analyze the amount of data available and make sense of it for their customers and those with deep domain expertise, such as spec'ing and upfitting a certain kind of truck. It's all expertise a majority of our clients don't have."

Huge changes that have taken place in the past decade, for instance, in the area of vehicle maintenance. "We have always helped fleet departments in our clients' companies manage the purchase and maintenance of vehicles," said Halliday. "A decade earlier, in-house fleet managers would log on and run reports on what vehicles they had, when to replace them, and when they sold them." After the recession however, outsourcing fleet management to companies like PHH became increasingly popular. This practice meant that companies could focus on their core business. It also reflected the growing complexity of the fleet management business in a digital and mobile world.

PHH's systems and contact centres can now focus not just on reporting but on proactively enhancing the productivity of the fleet driver. The system sends automated preventive maintenance notifications to fleet drivers, telling them it's time to get an oil change or other work done. PHH call centres use "virtual hold" technology that reduces the time drivers spend on the phone when they have a vehicle issue or question. The company has migrated to use of email, Web, and mobile communication tools in addition to the traditional phone call. PHH's online system for interacting with maintenance and repair facilities streamlines the repair transaction process, ensuring the driver gets back on the road quickly. And when telematics are employed, PHH can access remote information on engine diagnostics and productivity, that is, how much time a driver is spending with clients and prospects. For safety purposes, such data also tells a manager how the driver is actually behaving behind the wheel.

"With mobile device in hand," explained Halliday, "customers now use an app to tell them in real time what vehicles or drivers aren't performing well, as well as why, and how the problem can be solved."

The benefits of telematics go far beyond solving fleet customers' problems. Tighter regulations now demand that securitized transactions include more comprehensive information on the packaged assets, including where they have been and their second-hand value. GPS systems make it possible to provide this data almost instantly. Cars and trucks can be precisely tracked, making it possible for a fleet management company to estimate more accurately the value of each one at any time.

But the complexity and cost of telematics have posed an insurmountable challenge to smaller fleet lessors, making it more difficult for them to stay afloat. By 2013, fewer than a dozen large fleet management companies remained in Canada, the top six being ARI, PHH, Element, Foss National, Jim Pattison Lease, and EMKAY.[98] By the summer of 2014, the list had been further reduced, with the acquisition of PHH's auto leasing unit by Element Financial.

Two Canadian-owned companies carved out a spot in the market. Rather than competing with the very large U.S. fleet managers that each have as many as 25,000 vehicles under their wing, Jim Pattison Lease focused on mid-sized fleets of fifteen to thirty vehicles apiece. "We don't go after everyone," said Steve Akazawa. "The requirements for an ideal Pattison customer are credit—number one; the right type of vehicle; and a reliable history for resale value."

Foss National Leasing found a different way to sharpen its competitive edge. It signed a licensing agreement in 2013 with Netherlands-based LeasePlan, one of the world's leading fleet management companies. As a unit of a Dutch bank of the same name, LeasePlan could not enter Canada directly due to restrictions imposed by the *Bank Act*. Through a licensing agreement, however, LeasePlan could extend its reach into North America. Foss now serves all LeasePlan customers requiring fleet management services for their Canadian operations.

The "unbundling" of leasing services

The size and complexity of asset-based finance and leasing led to various specialized services in the industry. Lease Administration Corporation, which had its start liquefying the assets of Pacific National Leasing, moved post-recession into outsourced lease administrative and management services for companies engaged in consumer leasing.

Consumer leasing—apart from vehicles—began its heyday with hot-water tank leases being sold door to door in the early 2000s. Both Direct Energy and Reliance Home Comfort aggressively competed against each other to get homeowners to sign a lease. LAC stepped in as the "back office" to ensure that lessors were compliant with consumer rights and disclosure requirements.

LAC deepened its experience around the *Consumer Protection Act* so that funders could confidently finance contracts, minimizing their risk of consumers exiting their contracts. As the market moved to other home comfort items, such as furnaces, LAC grew its business, fuelled by a plethora of government incentives to help consumers replace HVAC systems with newer, greener options.

In addition to cars, there is almost no limit today as to what consumers in Canada can lease for their homes, from hot-water tanks, furnaces, air conditioners, windows (for a house renovation), water purifying systems, even swimming pools. "As long as there is enough volume for these relatively small assets, then you can offset the cost," said Ginter Baca, president and CEO of LAC.

Baca estimated that serving the consumer leasing market represents over half of LAC's business.

A new frontier: Technology leasing

Like so much other business spending, investment in technology was curtailed and delayed during the recession. But by the time the recovery was underway, much of the thinking behind those investments had changed. This included decisions about when and how to replace equipment. Doug McKenzie observed that by 2013 the typical lease term for laptops was four years, instead of two or three prior to the recession.

"Although in '08 and '09 companies pushed out their upgrades and renewals, particularly for laptops," McKenzie explained, "companies realized through the recession that there was no downside to keeping the gear in service longer."

New habits unrelated to the recession also affected the use of technology in unexpected ways. "Within eighteen months of the recession," said McKenzie, "companies moved away from laptops and went back to desktops for the office, with extra tablets for portability. This trend impacted leasing volumes as the combined spend for a desktop and a tablet was less than for a laptop."

The bottom line was that information technology was becoming a pervasive part of the leasing business, no matter what the sector. IT comprised 85 percent of BAL's portfolio in 2013, centred on computers (desktop, laptop, and tablets), data storage, software, and network switches.

Another significant part of the technology leasing business today is the "re-marketing" of used software and hardware, including the disposal of unwanted gear. Fuelled by increased pressure on business to embrace "green strategies," demand for IT disposal services grew steadily. By the early 2010s, most major computer makers, such as Dell, Hewlett-Packard, Oracle, and IBM, had leasing and re-marketing divisions. IBM reported in 2011 that no less than 99.7 percent of all IT equipment returned to it through its Global Asset Recovery Service was either reused, remanufactured, or recycled. By 2013, it had set up equipment reprocessing centres on six continents. It prepared three-quarters of a million units of IT equipment that year for reuse or resale.[99]

Technology assets "taken apart" have also created a secondary market for the re-marketing departments. The precious metals recovered from hardware, even smart phones, is usually more valuable than if the asset were repurposed or scrapped.

The *Bank Act* ... again

Surprise, surprise ... the domestic banks did not push their perennial request to gain direct access to vehicle leasing during either of the regular five-year reviews of the *Bank Act* in 2007 and 2012. Their new-found reticence stemmed from two post-recession realities: Basel III and the disappearance of residual risk insurance.

The banks have been forced to reconsider their priorities ahead of the tighter Basel III requirements, which include limits on the amount of capital they can invest in specific market segments. Their ambitions to enter direct vehicle leasing were also dealt a blow by a move among insurance companies to discontinue residual risk coverage, a type of policy that protected against falling vehicle values at the end of a lease term. The banks had previously contended that the risks of direct auto leasing would be offset by residual risk insurance. The challenges of the 2008–09 recession and the end of this coverage undercut any lingering support that the aggressively risk-averse Finance Department may have had for allowing banks to enter the vehicle leasing business.

The next *Bank Act* review is due to take place in 2017, and leaders in the auto leasing sector will be watching closely to see whether the banks renew their interest in the business. Jeff Hartley, for one, is confident they will not return to the fray. Recalling Scotiabank's decision in 2010 to sell its stake in Transportaction, a large vehicle lessor, to Element Financial, he noted, "There will always be clouds on the horizon as we wonder what the banks are going to do. But in my opinion, this tells me that they've pretty much given up, otherwise the bank wouldn't have sold Transportaction."

Present and future challenges

Leasing undoubtedly has an exciting future. That said, the CFLA, with its membership of almost 250 firms or corporations, has identified several issues critical to the industry's well-being.

International accounting standards

For more than a decade, the International Accounting Standards Board (IASB) (the body responsible for global financial reporting standards in countries other than the United States) and the U.S. Financial Accounting Standards Board (FASB) have cooperated on a project to align the world's accounting rules for lease transactions. Their work is part of a far-reaching drive begun in the 1990s to improve financial reporting.

The lease-accounting project has proved to be a tough nut to crack. The industry has questioned the feasibility of developing common standards and reporting methods. After all, so its argument goes, what do photocopiers, aircraft, cars, and software have in common? How does a lessor account for the wide range of services that often accompany a lease, from vehicle fuel cards to software upgrades? To complicate matters, the joint IASB–FASB project lumped real estate transactions with equipment and vehicles even though the two types of leasing have different objectives. Most lessees of real estate are tenants. They do not intend to buy their leased premises, while those who lease equipment or vehicles either intend to buy or at least want to have the option to do so.

The CFLA has followed the accounting standards debate for almost two decades, consulting with members on how to respond to proposed changes. Canada's accounting standards were set for many years by the Canadian Accounting Standards Board, but the profession agreed to cede that authority to the IASB as of January 2011. Meanwhile, the CFLA has chaired an international group of leasing associations to coordinate their message on accounting standards. The task has grown increasingly complicated. "The first paper that was issued on the subject was twenty-five pages," Powell notes. "The most recent ran to about one hundred and fifty." Although not opposed to common standards in principle, the industry sees little value in standards that are too complex and therefore too expensive to implement. Burdensome accounting rules, it fears, could end up driving businesses away from leasing in favour of other forms of financing.

The IASB and FASB finally published a new draft in May 2013, but progress has stalled again since then. "The boards have had a tremendous amount of pushback from the industry, including the CFLA, but also from neutral bodies like the European Union," reports Powell. "Even a high-level investor advisory committee of the FASB has come out against it, saying that what is being proposed is too complicated and does not have sufficient benefit to merit the cost of transforming the system. The industry, not only in Canada but also around the world, is waiting to see what happens next. The expectation is that something will happen, but no one knows what."

The Alta Group's Paul Frechette is unfazed, displaying the optimism that has long marked leasing industry leaders: "So accounting laws change and all this stuff has to be on the books now? Okay, we'll figure it out. We'll be resilient!"

CFLA's lease education program

Canadian Lease Education On-Demand (CLEO) was introduced in 2008. With the help of several volunteer industry veterans, CFLA offered 11 two-hour online sessions designed to enhance a general understanding of asset-based finance and equipment and vehicle leasing in Canada.

The CLEO program follows the life of a lease, from sales, marketing, and pricing to credit adjudication, vendor relationships, collections, and lease company management. Participants learn about the basic legal, accounting, tax, and insurance issues that affect the industry.

This initiative began with acquiring the rights to the Certified Lease Professional (CLP) Program, an existing education course developed by the United Association of Equipment Leasing in the United States. With the assistance of Hugh Swandel and his colleague Murray Derraugh, CLEO's editor-in-chief, the detailed operational chapters, slides, and instructor notes were adapted to the business in Canada.

CLEO has since moved to a pre-recorded, on-demand Web format.

Passing the baton

A curious aspect of asset-based finance and leasing is the number of early pioneers who came to the business by accident and then stayed for the rest of their careers. Those same people—many retired or soon to be—are pushing to bring in fresh blood. It is a safe bet, after all, that not many kids would declare at their school's career day that they are dreaming of a job in asset-based financing when they grow up.

Tom Hopkirk, now retired from Barclays Canada Leasing, expresses concern about a potential shortage of future leaders but also excitement at the prospects that the industry offers. "I would tell students about to graduate that they should consider a career in the leasing industry," he says. "I'd explain that it would mean they were not going to be sitting in a bank, opening up safe deposit boxes. Instead they'd be participating in something that goes on every day of every week of every year at the very heart of Canadian business."

The CFLA and its members have launched various initiatives in recent years to attract young talent. The association has set up focus groups to scope out the sector's needs, the types of jobs available, and student attitudes toward the industry. It piloted a co-op program in 2013 with Wilfrid Laurier University in Waterloo, Ontario, matching member companies with students. The plan is to expand the program to more universities and colleges across Canada. Other initiatives have included on-campus career days with member companies and a drive to encourage business schools to teach students about leasing's invaluable role in the financial services sector.

Spreading the leasing message

Asset-based finance and leasing leaders often express frustration that policymakers and regulators do not fully appreciate the benefits of their business compared to traditional lending. "Policymakers tend to understand financing as banks do it," says Powell. "There's always the risk that they will try and shoehorn the leasing industry into the same category and deal with it in the same way they deal with loans and banks."

Scotiabank Leasing's Joe LaLeggia echoes that sentiment: "Our biggest challenge has always been helping Ottawa to understand the industry and how meaningful it could be. This problem never goes away. If we in the industry take a nap, we risk that a new government comes along with some new regulation." Or, as Serge Mâsse quips, "if you're not at the table, you're on the menu."

Although great strides have been made in differentiating loans from leases, the problem, in LaLeggia's view, "never goes away." His point is underlined by the lumping together of real estate leasing with asset-based finance in the 2013 draft proposal for international accounting standards.

"The industry is continually evolving," echoed Eugene Basolini, current chairman of the CFLA. "We have to continue to educate that this type of financing is available to Canadian companies."

Industry leaders dream of the day when the world will see leasing through the same lens as both the 2004 and 2014 *Asset-based Financing, Investment and Economic Growth in Canada* reports—that "commercial lending and leasing are different products, each with an important role to play. Both offer alternative forms of financing to Canadian businesses and consumers, but leasing is a very separate commercial discipline and must not be confused with lending."[100] Not only does asset-based financing support business spending on machinery, equipment, and commercial vehicles (see figures below), but it is integral to the success of the economy, contributing to the GDP, job creation, and Canada's economic competitive edge.

As LaLeggia puts it: "The key to raising the standard of living of Canadians is to improve productivity. By facilitating the acquisition of productive assets by Canadian businesses and consumers, the asset-based finance and leasing industry is enabling Canadians to work smarter."[101]

The "used-car salesman" tag

Asset-based finance and leasing has suffered over the years from a form of the "used-car salesman" syndrome. With a business model that is not always easy to understand and made even less so by sometimes arcane terminology, outsiders all too often draw a blank at the mention of leasing. Even those with some familiarity with leasing tend to equate it only with cars and real estate. David Powell jokes that the industry often reminds him of comedian Rodney Dangerfield's famous line: "I don't get no respect."

Paul Frechette, who has witnessed these attitudes from the perspective of the North American industry, explains that "even as late as the 1980s, if you mentioned the word *lease*, it was often interpreted as, 'Do you mean you can't afford it?' But today the sentiment is, 'Do you mean you're paying cash?'"

There are many signs that the tide has changed. The Canadian Secured Credit Facility unveiled in the 2009 federal budget may not have achieved its goals in terms of dollars and cents, but the program was indisputably a vote of confidence in the industry. The CFLA's own research has come up with persuasive data on the industry's sizeable contribution to the Canadian economy. The association publishes an annual survey of industry activity, which details the size and growth of its three segments—equipment, fleet, and consumer vehicle leasing. The most recent report, released in the spring of 2014, confirmed the industry's contribution to the Canadian economy. The figures speak for themselves. Over time, business spending on machinery, equipment, and commercial vehicles adds to Canada's GDP, supports new job creation, and adds to government revenue.

Ongoing contributions of the asset-based finance and leasing industry

	2013 (first year)	Each year, going forward (projected)
Amount added to Canada's GDP	$14.2 billion	$8.9 billion
Number of jobs supported	100,000	27,000
Additional revenue directed to governments	$4.3 billion	$0.7 billion

Source: The Centre for Spatial Economics, 2014

On a wider front, former finance minister Jim Flaherty showed a greater understanding of the industry than many of his predecessors. He did not hesitate to promote its importance throughout his eight years in this role. "Asset-based financing is an important part of our financial system," Flaherty told the CFLA's annual conference in 2009. "After traditional lenders your industry is the largest provider of debt financing in this country. This type of lending provides a boost to the living standards of Canadians every day. With your help families can more easily afford to improve their homes or buy newer and more reliable vehicles. You give businesses a greater opportunity to innovate and invest, to hire people and grow our economy."[102]

Such endorsements have undoubtedly enhanced the reputation of asset-based financing. "The industry no longer feels like a second-class citizen," says Angela Armstrong, president of Prime Capital Group. "Business owners and CFOs now know about leasing and understand it. It has become mainstream."

CFLA's heart and soul

CFLA members unanimously respect and admire David Powell. He is described as "the heart and soul of the organization" and credited by many for uniting the association coast to coast. One person said he is like "glue, making sure it focuses on what can be done that is good for the industry and good for the association."

Powell's many skills include a rare combination of advocacy and diplomacy, two critical ingredients during times when the industry's very existence was threatened.

"The contributions of David Powell as a leader to the CFLA cannot be understated," commented Hugh Swandel. "His ability to manage the complex relationship of industry competitors and define key issues is nothing short of brilliant."

"Without David I am certain we would not have succeeded in changing proposed legislation at the federal and provincial level that could have critically impaired the ability of our industry to survive," said Swandel.

On numerous issues Powell rallied the industry to a successful lobbying effort, whether it be vehicle vicarious liability, tax policy, or international accounting standards. The CFLA's finest hour was the lobbying with Ottawa during 2008 and 2009. Led by Powell, the association never let up on its efforts to bring credit relief to the industry, never missed an opportunity to remind government and policymakers of the quality of the assets it finances and of the industry's professionalism.

Swandel and Jeff Hartley, who accompanied Powell on several of his Ottawa visits, saw first-hand the effect of his leadership. "His stewardship during the credit crisis was critical to bringing government focus to our industry and organizing a very effective campaign to win our industry support and mention in the federal budget."

Powell is also lauded for having the insight to put the right resources in place at the right time, transforming the industry's voice into one that was strong, respected, and effective. "Over the years David has contributed to Canada's public finance policy and by doing so has increased our industry's importance to the Department of Finance, no easy task," commented Nick Logan.

Serge Mâsse recalled that the association was in reactive mode until it became infused with Powell's vision for a Canada-wide presence, with both large and smaller players. "Today, the industry is welcomed and listened to across the country," said Mâsse. "By monitoring changes that could potentially impact the industry in all fields, such as fiscal, accounting and legal, CFLA is able to intervene in the early stages of legislation and make a real difference. Because of David, CFLA is now *the voice* of the industry in Canada."

Coming full circle?

An April 2014 *Wall Street Journal* article informed of a growing trend of "larger companies [in the United States] becoming financiers for their smaller suppliers and customers who often have had trouble getting conventional business loans ... balance sheets show that 80 companies in the S&P 500 are big lenders, almost double the number in 2006."

According to the *WSJ*, "Instead of beating up on their suppliers to drive down costs, large companies seem to be stepping up to the plate to finance their suppliers and customers, shoring up their relationships and getting a return on otherwise idle cash ... companies are saying, 'I'm sitting on piles of cash, and let's see if we can trade each other's relative cost of capital.'"

"It looks remarkably like what Hamilton Cotton initiated all those years ago," reflected CFLA president David Powell. In thinking about the example set by the Young family at the beginning of the 1960s, "everything old is new again."

Looking back over his almost twenty years with the association, Powell observed how the asset-based finance business moved in cycles, shape-shifting with the ups and downs of the economy.

When the economy contracts, the banks and credit unions have to carry the bulk of the burden of providing capital and credit, absorbing many of the other players in the financing marketplace. But when the economy is growing, well-capitalized manufacturing and servicing companies with substantial earnings often leverage their own financial means and core competencies to establish their own financing arms. Or they partner with independents who manage it for them to finance their suppliers and customers. When this happens, the relative market share of the non-banks grows too.

Powell asked, "Are we witnessing the beginning of a rebirth in non-bank financing options for both suppliers and customers?" Hamilton Cotton used its credit strength and strong relationships with funders to offer short-term financing to its textile customers who needed to bridge the time it took to transform basic textiles into saleable products. Then, reinvented as The Hamilton Group, it offered financing to vendors of dental, medical and office equipment.

As noted earlier, financial historian Ron Chernow observed that financing is "a mere by-product of the world of trade.... Commodity merchants often advanced farmers money against crop deliveries or extended loans against the security of merchandise for safekeeping. The natural progression from commerce to finance is worth mentioning, for it left open the possibility that clients of merchant banks with surplus lendable funds might someday become rival banks themselves."

The phenomenon is a natural outgrowth of economic activity. According to Powell, it is nothing new. "It has happened before. If the traditional banking and financial institutions of today were created a century or two ago in this same way, what we are experiencing is simply part of a continually evolving process."

The qualities that guide us: Confidence and innovation

> *Innovation is at the heart of economic growth ... financial services are at the core of the innovation system.*
>
> *Statistics Canada*

Those who have toiled in the financing trenches present a picture of enduring confidence. Whatever the obstacles and setbacks they have faced in the past—and there have been many—they have always bounced back. Determination and innovation have been the order of the day.

One reason is that Canada's asset-based finance and leasing industry has pulled out the stops to keep abreast of technological change, helping both its customers and itself remain competitive. The idea that innovation is embodied within new equipment has been around since the mid-twentieth century.[103] By enabling businesses to acquire new equipment and vehicles, Canada's asset-based finance and leasing industry has helped promote innovation and technological change.

When Bill Bell started work at NABEL in 1962, he encountered the latest marvel in office equipment—the IBM Selectric line of electric typewriters. At the heart of these new-fangled machines was what IBM described as "a single printing element" that looked like a revolving golf ball. By tailoring an affordable financing package, NABEL helped IBM put Selectrics on desks in law firms across the country, boosting the productivity of lawyers and their typists.

In one sense, nothing has changed since the early 1960s: successful businesses still need to maintain a competitive edge with the latest equipment and technology. Thus, the U.S. Equipment Leasing and Finance Association named the move toward cloud computing as one of the top leasing trends in 2013.[104] What many outsiders may not realize is that asset-based finance and leasing makes it possible for even the smallest businesses to gain access to these vast, virtual storage pools.

"Leasing has completely changed since I got in, and it will change again," said National Leasing's Tom Pundyk. "Those who recognize that and can apply their know-how to meet the changes that are coming will thrive. Those who say 'We've always done it that way' and continue to do it that way will get swallowed up."

Asset-based finance and leasing has adapted as Canada has made the transition from an industrial to a knowledge-based economy. It has not only faced up to changes in regulations, banking policies, and accounting rules that sought to whittle away its advantage over traditional lending; it has also uncovered new ways to bring value to consumers and businesses. The industry emerged from the credit freeze of 2008 and 2009 wiser and more confident of its vital role in Canada's financial sector.

Reflecting his colleagues' ever-present determination to come out on top, Jeff Hartley began his chairman's address to the CFLA's 2012 conference with this question: "So how do we find opportunity in unprecedented times?" He was echoing Ben Young, the Hamilton Group pioneer now well into his eighties, who noted that from its earliest days "there simply never was a period in the leasing business when it was business as usual."

Embracing opportunity at every turn, leasing has taken advantage of a long list of technology breakthroughs—from postage meters to telematics—to help Canadian businesses improve their efficiency and compete globally. "The photocopier sector led the industry," Angela Armstrong notes, "because the copier showed that you don't necessarily want to buy a piece of equipment even though you are using it to make money."

It has also displayed an unwavering commitment to customer service seldom matched by traditional financial institutions. As Doug McKenzie puts it: "My money is the same as your money; prices are all within the same basis point. The difference is how fast we can say 'yes' to finance what you need."

Steady, reliable, and uncomplicated have been the watchwords for success. "Leasing provides a huge benefit to small and medium-sized businesses where finance is the number-one, the number-two, and the number-three issue," says retired PricewaterhouseCoopers partner Ralph Selby.

Asset-based finance and leasing have carved out an indispensable place as vital tools for the sustained prosperity of Canadian business. Tom Hopkirk sums up the gutsiness that promises to keep the industry moving forward in the future: "Rather than put their heads in the sand, the leasing guys have always been able to sit down and say, 'What can we do now?'"

No doubt about it. The momentum is unstoppable.

What the future holds

Industry leaders see opportunities galore

- Angela Armstrong, president, Prime Capital Group: "In Western Canada, where growth has been steady, the need for capital has never been greater. Leasing finds its way into all manner of transactions, filling needs ranging from multimillion-dollar drilling rigs, down to small conventional office equipment. Building a business is expensive work. Any means by which business can defer the costs of growth while gaining revenue is good for the entire Canadian economy, because it means there is more money to channel into growth projects, which benefit sectors coast to coast."

- Steve Hudson, chairman and chief executive, Element Financial Corporation: "Leasing has always been driven by expertise. Today's office equipment is highly specialized and mechanized. Smaller players that finance $5,000 to $10,000 pieces of equipment, usually in the office equipment and technology sectors, can do very well."
- Jim Halliday, president, PHH: "The people who will win in the fleet leasing space are the ones who figure out what the real value is of data and the great decisions you can derive from it. Telematics has allowed us to do that. Business today is about predicting what a client should do in the future, then prescribing it without a lot of people actually 'touching it.'"
- Moe Danis, vice-president, Pacific & Western Bank of Canada: "The investment community is being very cautious, even though the markets have bounced back since 2008. But there are trillions of dollar on the sidelines—in corporate balance sheets or in bonds—waiting to be invested. Corporate balance sheets, in fact, are the best they've been in years. Right now, companies still are not spending the money for productivity-enhancing equipment. But once they do, the leasing business will start to get really stronger again."
- Peter Horan, president and chief executive, De Lage Landen Financial Services Canada: "The future of

leasing is very blurry and strongly linked to changing accounting standards and increased governance created in the aftermath of the financial crisis in recent years. Governance issues in many western countries that place significant obligations on lessors relative to privacy, compliance, and electronic communications are adding new layers of cost that may further pressure the value of lease products.

"Major trends in leasing are centred on managed service type offerings, where customers get one-stop shopping for a single payment, which includes equipment, maintenance, software, services, and consumables. It is anticipated that leasing will explode in the Asia Pacific region as countries like India and China adopt the usage of the product."

- Tom Pundyk, chief operating officer, National Leasing: "Reputation is everything in this industry. It takes years and years to build up and minutes to destroy. You can't be considered a fly-by-nighter or a quick-fix guy. You need a reputation for delivering what you say you're going to do."
- Hugh Swandel, senior managing director, The Alta Group: "Usually after the industry has gone through these cycles of consolidation, businesses can't find a certain product or can't find a company that will finance their industry. So when you get to the next cycle of unmet needs, independents come to the rescue because they are the ones that identify pockets of risk that are acceptable but have just fallen out of style with the major players. The number of independent finance companies is currently smaller, but I do foresee more independents developing again,

especially five to ten years out. It is a strong, vibrant industry."

- Eugene Basolini, president and chief executive, RCAP Leasing: "I'm an old-school guy, so I've seen the ups and downs of the industry. The companies that stuck to their knitting survived—that is, the ones that were well run and well managed, with prudent risk management practice and fundamental leasing procedures."
- Jim Pattison, founder, chairman, and chief executive, The Jim Pattison Group: "The industry keeps changing all the time. I like that because that's where the opportunities are. One thing you do know for sure is that things will be different ten years from now, and you have to be ready."

Glossary

Asset-based finance

Asset-based finance refers to a secured loan, conditional sales contract, lease, or line of credit used to acquire an asset. The asset—whether equipment or vehicles—becomes the principal security for the customer's obligation to repay. For the business customer, the income generated by using the asset finances it, while the inherent value of the asset being financed serves as the essential collateral for the transaction.

Compared with traditional lending: Asset-based finance offers access to financing for those businesses that either do not have a significant collateral base or whose collateral base is largely committed to others, such as banks and other traditional lenders. Banks have much broader powers to secure wider security and normally do so. When acquiring an asset, a conventional bank loan requires security greater than simply the asset itself. But for an asset-based financing company, the equipment or vehicle is generally the only collateral available.

Advantage to business: Approval for the financing typically hinges on the customer's ability to generate cash flow from business operations to service the instalment payments. Because the financing company retains legal ownership of the asset, a business can qualify on the basis of generated cash flow rather than the net worth lending formula typically applied for traditional loans. For businesses that do not have a lengthy credit history or a significant collateral base, this form of financing becomes particularly advantageous.

Unique three-way relationship: An asset-based finance company generally finds itself between a vendor (typically a manufacturer, distributor, or dealer) and the end-user customer. To do its job, a finance company must possess a multitude of talents far beyond those of traditional lenders, including sales and marketing experience; multiple relationship-building skills relating to vendors and customers; a thorough understanding of the value of the asset financed over its useful life; credit analysis and adjudication skills; contract administration, collections, and repossession specialists; and asset re-marketing and resale know-how.

Complementary, not "instead of": The services of the asset-based finance industry are complementary to traditional banking and other financial lending. Each provides incremental capital to increase the pool of available credit in Canada and offers a vital competitive alternative in the financial services sector.

Big-ticket, mid-ticket, small-ticket leases

Leases are classified as small-ticket, mid- or medium-ticket, and big-ticket based on the value of the equipment being leased. Big-ticket leasing in Canada involves the financing of $1 million or more; small-ticket, generally up to $75,000 to $100,000; and mid-ticket, in between. In the early days (1960s and 1970s), "big-ticket" was largely confined to acceptance companies that arranged large leases to industrial and transportation companies for such assets as mining equipment, ships, shipping containers, and rail cars. In recent years, the terms are not used as much because large financing companies and the finance and lease subsidiaries of bank are organized to deal with transactions as large as aircraft and as small as a single piece of office equipment.

Automated credit decision-making is a critical component of modern financing. Small-ticket deals are typically "high-tech, low-touch" transactions. That is, automated credit decisions are based on sophisticated algorithms requiring little human intervention. As credit requests rise in value to big-ticket deals, the balance shifts to less tech and more (human) touch.

Capital cost allowance (CCA)

CCA is an annual deduction of the cost of certain assets based on their depreciation. Depreciation is a reduction in the value of an asset through age, use, and deterioration. In accounting terminology, depreciation is a deduction, or expense, claimed for this decrease in value.

In Canada, a business taxpayer cannot deduct from income tax the full cost of an asset, such as a building, vehicle, or equipment, used to earn income. But because this type of asset wears out or becomes obsolete over time, a taxpayer can deduct a percentage of the asset's cost each year. The part of the cost deducted, or claimed, is called depreciation or, for income tax purposes, capital cost allowance (CCA).

Closed-end versus open-end vehicle lease

Most consumer vehicle leases are of the closed-end type. In a **closed-end lease**, the customer makes a set number of lease payments during the term of the lease and returns the vehicle to the leasing company at the end of the lease term. The customer is not required to make any additional payments unless there is physical damage to the vehicle or the customer exceeds the number of kilometres driven as set out in the lease.

At the end of the lease, the options are:

- return the vehicle,
- buy the vehicle (if there is a purchase option), or
- lease a new vehicle.

Most leases for vehicles used for business purposes are the open-end type. In an **open-end lease**, the customer makes a set number of lease payments during the term of the lease and returns the vehicle to the leasing company at the end of the lease term. Then an adjustment is made. The customer is required to make an additional payment covering the difference between the actual value of the vehicle at the end of the lease and the residual value stated in the lease contract. (This is also known as the estimated wholesale value of the vehicle at the end of the lease term.) If the value of the vehicle is more than the residual value stated in the lease, then the customer is entitled to the difference.

For example, if the residual value in the lease is $8,000 and the leasing company can only sell the vehicle for $7,500, the customer pays the leasing company $500. If the vehicle is sold for $8,500, the leasing company pays the customer $500.

Fleet or commercial versus consumer vehicle lease

Fleet or commercial vehicle leasing involves the leasing of groups of motor vehicles to a business or government through a third-party leasing company. The vehicles are then made available to stipulated employees for the purpose of carrying out their job (for example, delivering goods or being part of a sales team).

Typically, under a consumer vehicle lease, a vehicle is leased directly to an individual consumer, who selects the vehicle at a dealership and signs a lease contract at the dealership. That contract is then assigned to an auto manufacturer financing company or to an independent financing company. While the consumer maintains a relationship with the dealer for maintenance and repairs, the financing company assumes all administration of the lease, including the collection of monthly payments.

Lease

There are many definitions and interpretations of a lease. Accounting, tax, legal, and financial advisers all have different perspectives on leasing, as do government regulators and the users of leased vehicles and equipment. In the end, however, it all comes down to a very simple concept.

A lease is an agreement whereby an owner of equipment or vehicle(s)—the lessor—conveys to another party—the lessee—the right to use that equipment or vehicle. The lease is arranged for a predetermined length of time and a negotiated payment.

Very generally speaking, there are two kinds of leases. A capital, or finance, lease and an operating lease.

In both cases, the leasing company typically purchases the equipment or vehicle from the manufacturer, distributor, or dealer and then provides use of the asset to the lessee under the terms and conditions of the lease.

The distinction between a capital, or finance, lease and an operating lease is important for a number of reasons.

From a business perspective, a **capital**, or **finance**, **lease** (similar to an open-end vehicle lease) is generally used to finance an asset for the major part of its useful life such that the lessee ultimately acquires title to the asset. Lease contract payments enable the lessor to recover its entire investment in the asset over the term of the lease, together with the desired yield on that investment, without relying on the resale value of the asset.

In general, the largest portion of such payments consist of the straight write-down of the repayment of the cost of the asset. Much of the balance is composed of the interest cost to the lessor for the money used to fund the cost of the asset and administrative costs. The lessor's profit is the final component part.

For accounting purposes (information current as of at the time of publication of this book) a capital or finance lease is capitalized in the lessee's financial statements as a liability and reported as a financial receivable in the lessor's financial statements.[105]

In contrast, an **operating lease** (similar to a closed-end or consumer vehicle lease) is generally defined as a lease that is not a capital or finance lease. An operating lease usually finances an asset for less than its useful life, and at the end of the lease term the lessee can either buy the asset or return the asset to the lessor without further obligation. The lessor may then re-lease it or sell it at auction.

In an operating lease, the remaining—also known as "residual" or "wholesale"—value of the asset when the lease comes to an end is very important to the lessor because it safeguards the lessor's financial position. At the outset, the lessor takes the risk and purchases the asset for the lessee. The lessor structures the lease to ensure that it recoups its costs and makes a profit from the payments made by the lessee and the eventual sale of the asset at the end of the lease either to the lessee or to a third party.

For accounting purposes, again at the time of publication of this book, an operating lease is not capitalized in the accounts of the lessee. In this way, unlike a traditional loan or a finance lease, an operating lease offers an "off–balance sheet" financing alternative. Lease payments are treated as an annual expense for the lessee and revenue for the lessor.

Who are lessors? In most cases, lessors are corporations specializing in financial services. They can be privately owned or publicly traded companies, manufacturing companies or dealer/distributors, subsidiaries of domestic or foreign banks, trust companies, or insurance companies.

A lease is not a loan

With a loan, an asset (equipment or vehicle) is purchased with some money down, followed by regular and set payments. From the beginning of the transaction, the asset is considered the property of the borrower. The asset may or may not be the sole collateral for the loan.

With a lease, an asset (equipment or vehicle) is not purchased outright. Use of the asset is provided by the lessee through monthly payments. The payment amounts can be structured according to the cash flow needs of the customer, and there may or may not be a down payment. If it is a capital lease, there's an assumption that at the end of the term, the company will acquire the asset. If it is an operating lease, the lessor owns the asset throughout the transaction and is responsible for its disposal or re-marketing at the end of the lease term.

Leases uphold the idea that one doesn't need to own an asset in order to use it. For most small businesses, therefore, the principal motive for leasing is cash flow—the ability to get equipment now without a major expenditure of cash.

Sale-leaseback

An arrangement whereby equipment is purchased by a lessor from the company that owns it and plans to use it. As the owner, the lessor then leases it back to the original owner, who continues to use the equipment.

Securitization

Securitization is a principal means by which the asset-based finance industry funds its activities. Customers make regular payments to a financing company under each loan or lease contract. A large number of contracts are pooled together by the financing company into a single bundle. The bundle has value—the combined revenue to be generated by the contracts.

The process of securitization consolidates all the pooled customer indebtedness and converts it into securities. These are financial instruments that can be readily bought and sold in financial markets—the way stocks, bonds, and futures contracts are traded—so that investors may buy interests in the pool rather than in the individual assets. The credit reliability of the customers is rated to assure outside investors of the quality of the investment, that is, the predictability of the original contracts being fully paid.

The principal and interest on the debts underlying the security are paid to the investors on a regular basis, though the method varies based on the type of security.

A Short History of Leasing[106]

Wealth does not lie in ownership but in the use of things.

Aristotle, circa 350 BC

LEASING IS ONE of the world's oldest professions. The ancient Sumerians evidently produced leases on clay tablets for agricultural tools, land and water rights, as well as oxen and other animals. Clay tablets excavated at the site of the ancient Sumerian city-state of Ur in Mesopotamia predate 2000 BC, although leasing may have been transacted earlier. These are the oldest known "hard evidence." There is a record of Babylonian leasing law, introduced by King Hammurabi, dating back to 1700 BC (the Code of Hammurabi).

Many ancient societies used leasing as a financing tool, including the Greeks, Romans, Egyptians, and Phoenicians. These people found leasing to be the only viable and affordable way to finance equipment, land, and livestock. The Phoenicians, who were shipping and trading experts, used a "ship charter," which closely resembled today's pure equipment lease, to obtain the use of a crew and ship. The longer-term ship charters covered the economic life of the ship and required the lessee to assume the benefits and obligations of ownership. Today, lease negotiations deal with issues similar to those encountered in those long-ago ship charters.

The concept of leasing was contained in the Code of Justinian, one part of the codification of Roman law ordered by the Emperor Justinian. Known as the Corpus Juris Civilis (body of civil laws), it completely revised imperial laws, becoming a landmark in legal history. From 533–34 AD, the Code was established as the legal authority of the Roman Empire, ultimately serving as the basis for modern civil law systems.

At the beginning of the Middle Ages, various types of agricultural, industrial, and even military equipment were leased. In 1066, two invasion fleets, sent to England by the Norwegians and the Normans, respectively, involved forms of lease financing to obtain the use of the ships and crews. Leasing was subsequently limited mostly to horses and farming equipment. The leasing of personal property in England was not recognized under English common law, but long-term leasing of real property was allowed. In 1284, however, the Statute of Wales introduced the English common law system to Wales, and it dealt directly with the leasing of personal property. It was further clarified in 1571 by a statute that defined who actually owned the leased equipment.

The onset of the Industrial Revolution in the United Kingdom and North America brought more opportunities for leasing, particularly relating to the railroads. These opportunities followed the same pattern. New equipment was needed for manufacturing or transportation, and investors provided the capital. Most of the early railroad companies were only able to afford the laying of the track, so they sought financing from private entrepreneurs for the locomotives and railcars. In the 1700s in the United States, liverymen leased horses, buggies, and wagons.

It was the railroad industry, however, that brought the first real growth of leasing to the United States and Canada, as it had to

Europe. Investors provided financing for locomotives and railcars through equipment trusts. Banks or trust companies set up and administered these trusts, issuing an equipment trust certificate. The certificate represented the right of the holder to receive a return of principal and interest on the invested funds. The trust administrator would pay the manufacturer for the equipment and then sell these trust certificates to investors. The administrator collected the rentals from the railroad company, which covered the cost of the equipment and the interest. The most common form of the trust certificate provided for the transfer of ownership of the equipment to the railroad company at the end of the term. These railroad finance plans resemble the modern conditional sales contract and money-over-money leases.

According to the United Nations in 1994, one-eighth of the world's private investment was financed through leasing; in one-third of the OECD countries[107] private investment is financed through leasing; and in both middle- and low-income countries, leasing doubled between 1988 and 1994.[108]

Asset-Based Finance by the Numbers

A major change in how industry statistics are calculated

The Canadian Finance & Leasing Association (CFLA) has compiled statistics on the activities of its member companies since the early 1990s to provide members with information on their collective performance and to provide public policymakers with an overview of activity in the sector. This data was originally limited to the lease and loan activity of member companies involved in financing the purchase of machinery, equipment, and motor vehicles in Canada where the finance company retained ownership of the asset for the life of the contract. This type of credit—asset-based financing—differs significantly from traditional lending in the structure of the finance contract and in the credit assessment formula used by the finance company.

Over time it became evident that other companies and agencies outside the CFLA membership were also providing asset-based financing of vehicles and commercial equipment.

With the onset of the financial crisis in 2008 in particular, their importance in the marketplace was growing. The CFLA decided it was important to try to estimate the overall value of asset-based financing in Canada. The asset-based finance market has now been redefined to include leases, secured loans, lines of credit, and conditional sales contracts provided by banks, credit unions, insurance companies, government agencies, the finance subsidiaries of manufacturers (the so-called "captive finance companies"), independent finance companies, and by vendors themselves. The key feature of this market is that the finance company retains title to the asset for the life of the contract.

Sources of information

As discussed above, a survey of CFLA member company activity was no longer sufficient to provide an estimate of asset-based finance activity in Canada. In 2012, the CFLA initiated a comprehensive review of available statistics to (i) identify existing sources of information and (ii) determine areas that would require additional research. Information was required for the financing of new machinery and equipment and commercial (fleet) vehicles by public and private organizations and for the financing of consumer (retail) motor vehicles by households for both the value of new financing (originations) on an annual basis and the overall value of assets financed in that year (financed assets).

Statistics Canada surveys provide comprehensive information on the purchase of new machinery, equipment, and motor vehicles. Along with the Bank of Canada, Statistics Canada also produces information on the value of credit provided to businesses and households. Unfortunately, this information does not reveal the purpose of this financing in sufficient detail to allow us to estimate the value of the asset-based finance sector.

Table 1: Gathering Asset-Based Finance Statistics: Then and Now

	What was included in CFLA statistics (until 2013)	What's been added to the data	What's included in current statistics (as of 2013)
Assets	• Public and private spending on machinery and equipment • Fleet motor vehicles • Retail motor vehicles	• None	• Public and private spending on machinery and equipment • Fleet motor vehicles • Retail motor vehicles
Credit instrument	• Lease (operating and capital) • Conditional sales contract • Secured loan	• Lines of credit	• Lease (operating and capital) • Conditional sales contract • Secured loan • Lines of credit
Credit provider	CFLA membership within: • Banks (Schedule I, II, III) • Credit unions • Captive finance companies • Foreign and independent finance companies • Vendor finance	Balance of activity within: • Banks (Schedule I, II, III) • Credit unions • Captive finance companies • Foreign and independent finance companies • Vendor finance *plus* • Government finance agencies • Insurance companies	• Banks (Schedule I, II, III) • Credit unions • Captive finance companies • Foreign and independent finance companies • Vendor finance • Government finance agencies • Insurance companies

The CFLA turned to PMG Intelligence (www.pmgintelligence.com), a market research firm, to conduct a set of surveys of equipment-financing patterns by businesses in Canada. The data provided a detailed picture of the factors driving equipment finance, which was used to determine the size of the sector in 2013. Corroborating these results was analysis from The Alta Group (www.thealtagroup.com), an international equipment leasing and asset finance advisory service that tracks companies active in the Canadian commercial equipment finance industry and compiles estimates of new financing and finance assets by provider.

Information on fleet and retail vehicle financing was obtained from DesRosiers Automotive Consultants Inc. (www.desrosiers.ca), Canada's leading market research firm specializing in the automotive sector.

Methodology

The information collected from the sources described above was compiled by the Centre for Spatial Economics (www.c4se.com) and, combined with data from previous CFLA surveys, used to generate estimates of asset-based finance new business and the value of assets financed in Canada from 1990 to 2013.

New machinery and equipment segment

Information from the PMG Intelligence surveys was combined with Statistics Canada's information on the number of business establishments in Canada to estimate the value of new machinery, equipment, and commercial vehicles financed by the private sector in 2013. These surveys provided information on the proportion of companies that acquired new machinery, equipment, and commercial vehicles in 2013; the proportion that was financed; and the average value of the equipment financed by lease, conditional sales contract, secured loan, or line of credit. A set of seven different market-size estimates were generated based on aggregating the survey results by company size or by industry sector. The estimates ranged from a high of $39.3 billion to a low of $17.3 billion, with the bulk of the estimates between $25 billion and $30 billion. The average of all the estimates was $27.1 billion, and this value has been used as the CFLA's estimate of new financing of private sector machinery, equipment, and commercial vehicles in 2013.

The PMG Intelligence survey did not include machinery, equipment, and vehicles purchased by public sector organizations (i.e., governments, municipalities, universities, schools, and hospitals). The use of asset-based financing for the acquisition of machinery, equipment, and vehicles by the public sector was assumed to be the same share of total spending as estimated for the private sector. The value of new public sector asset-based financing of machinery, equipment, and vehicles in 2013 was $7.1 billion, which is 32 percent of Statistics Canada's estimate of the $22.5 billion of public sector purchases of machinery, equipment, and vehicles that year. The combined public and private sector is estimated to have used asset-based financing to acquire $34.3 billion of new machinery, equipment, and commercial vehicles in 2013, or 32 percent of all public and private sector spending on new machinery and equipment in that year.

New public and private machinery, equipment, and commercial vehicle financing from 1990 to 2012 was estimated using the CFLA's previous estimates of new financing by member companies and adjusted to reflect the full set of asset-based finance market participants identified in Appendix III. Table 1 provides a summary of the change in coverage of asset-based finance statistics from the previous CFLA member-based approach to the current economy-wide coverage approach. While there is no change in the type of assets included in the statistics, lines of credit have been added to the list of credit instruments. Lines of credit using equipment as the main collateral have long been common for key segments of the industry, particularly in the farm sector, and are now growing in importance for mid-ticket business where all of a customer's equipment financing needs can be met by providing them with a line of credit secured against the equipment acquired with that credit. Finally, the list of credit providers is now an economy-wide, comprehensive list that includes government finance agencies, insurance companies, and providers that were not CFLA members in the past.

The value of commercial or fleet vehicles acquired by public and private sector organizations is removed from the equipment and commercial vehicle total to generate the machinery and equipment segment. So, for purposes of this analysis, machinery and equipment excludes passenger vehicles and light trucks used for commercial purposes but includes heavy trucks and other transportation equipment.

The Centre for Spatial Economics estimated that the value of machinery and equipment financed assets using a stock-flow relationship in which the current value of financed assets (end of year) is equal to new financing that year plus the value of financed assets from the end of the previous year less payments made on those assets over the year. The average finance term is assumed to be 3.5 years for all years.

Fleet vehicle segment

DesRosiers data includes the number of new passenger vehicles and light trucks sold in the fleet market from 1990 to 2013. The Centre for Spatial Economics assumed that all fleet vehicles are financed and are, therefore, part of the asset-based finance market. The average cost per unit was assumed to be 80 percent of the average retail market unit price. Combining this information yields an estimate of the value of new financing for the fleet vehicle market segment from 1990 to 2013.

The centre also estimated the value of financed assets using a stock-flow relationship in which the current value of financed assets (end of year) is equal to new financing that year plus the value of financed assets from the end of the previous year less payments made on those assets over the year. The average finance term is assumed to rise from 2.9 years in 1990 to 3.8 years in 2013. The value of financed assets from the previous year is further adjusted to account for 2 percent vehicle losses from theft, accidents, and bad debts.

Retail vehicle segment

The retail vehicle segment includes both new and used vehicles sold to households. DesRosiers provides data on the value of loans and leases for both new and used vehicles in the consumer market from 2000 to 2013. The Centre for Spatial Economics extended this data back to 1990 by making assumptions about the trends in the share of new vehicles financed by lease or loan combined with new vehicle prices plus the trends in the total sales of used vehicles financed by lease or loan combined with used vehicle prices.

The centre again estimated the value of financed assets for both new and used retail vehicles using a stock-flow relationship in which the current value of financed assets (end of year) is equal to new financing that year plus the value of financed assets from the end of the previous year less payments made on those assets over the year. The average finance term for new retail vehicles is assumed to rise from 3.6 years in 1990 to 4.7 years in 2013. The value of new retail vehicle financed assets from the previous year is further adjusted to account for 4 percent vehicle losses from theft, accidents, bad debts, and accelerated payment of consumer loans. For used retail vehicles, the average finance term is assumed to be 2.75 years. The value of used retail vehicle finance assets from the previous year is further adjusted to account for 6 percent vehicle losses from theft, accidents, bad debts, and accelerated payment of consumer loans.

Estimated asset-based finance market size

Asset-based finance new business volumes are heavily influenced by trends in the economy. The recession of the 1990s led to a decline in new business volumes, as did the financial crisis starting in 2008 and the subsequent great recession. The new business volume estimates are divided between public and private sector new machinery and equipment, the fleet vehicle market, and the retail vehicle market. For purposes of this analysis, machinery and equipment excludes passenger vehicles and light trucks acquired by public and private enterprises (the fleet vehicle segment) but includes heavy trucks and other transportation equipment.

The fleet vehicle segment consists of motor vehicle sales (passenger vehicles and light trucks) to fleet lessors/management companies, car rental companies, other commercial customers, and the government sector. The fleet vehicle segment is reported separately to allow users to combine it either with machinery and equipment to generate the equipment and commercial vehicle market or with retail vehicles to generate the total vehicle market.

Estimated current new business volumes

Total annual new business volumes rose from an estimated $43 billion in 1990 to $107 billion in 2013. New business volumes are dominated by the retail vehicle segment, which accounted for 67 percent of the total in 1990 and 68 percent in 2013. The fleet vehicle market's share of total new business has fallen from 11 percent in 1990 to 7 percent in 2013, so the overall motor vehicle share of the market slipped from 78 percent in 1990 to 75 percent in 2013. The equipment and commercial vehicle segment was 33 percent of the total in 1990 and 32 percent in 2013.

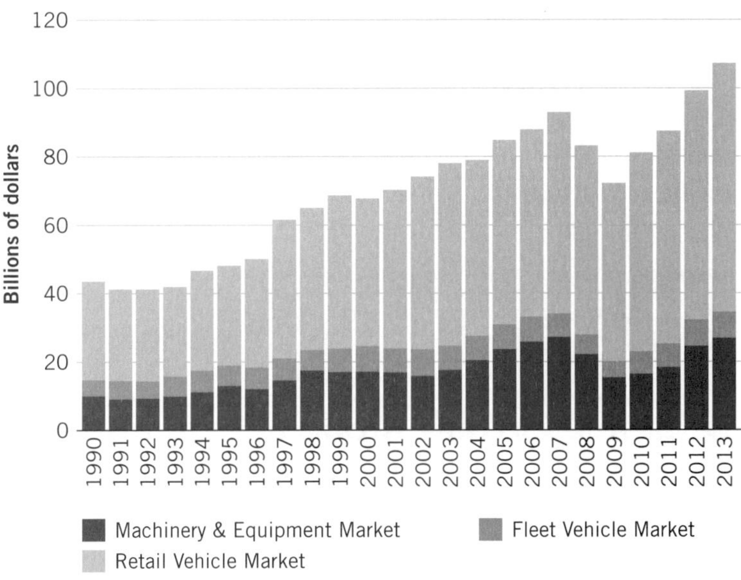

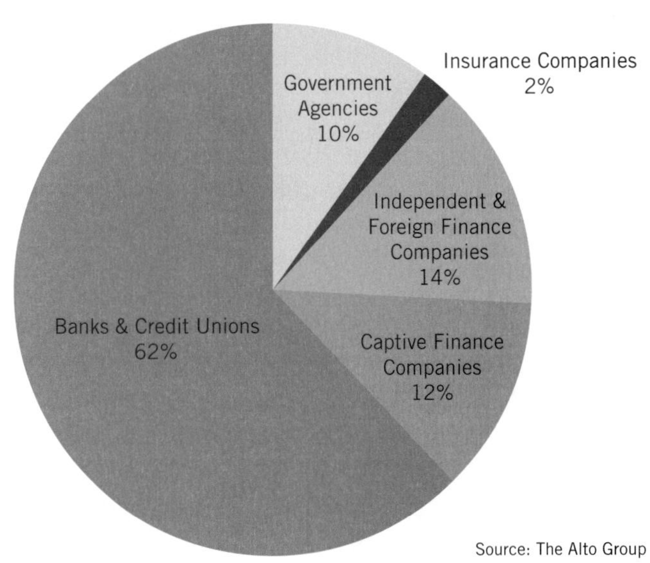

Source: The Alto Group

The Alta Group produces an independent set of estimates of new asset-based financing of equipment and commercial vehicles in Canada. Their research estimates the volume of new business in 2013 to be $34.7 billion, corroborating the $34.3 billion estimate generated by the CFLA. The Alta Group also provides a breakdown of this new financing by provider. Banks and credit unions account for 62 percent of new business, government agencies for 10 percent, while independent and captive finance companies combine for 26 percent of the total. Definitions of each of these sectors are provided in Appendix III.

Estimated current total value of all asset-based finance assets

The total value of all asset-based finance assets in Canada is estimated to be $314 billion in 2013, up from $138 billion in 1990.

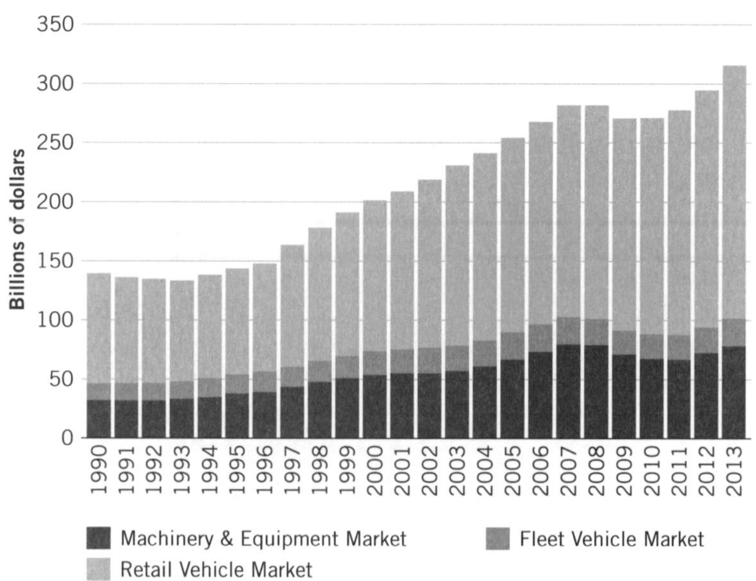

Banks, credit unions, captive finance companies, and independent finance companies are all involved in financing new and used asset acquisitions. Although reliable data is scarce in Canada, the relative shares of the total asset-based finance market in Canada for new and used consumer vehicles, fleet vehicles, and commercial equipment appear very similar to those reported for new business volumes. The centre estimates that the banks and credit unions account for between 50 and 60 percent of all asset-based finance transactions in 2013. Manufacturers' captives, including the carmakers' financing arms, are the second-largest segment of providers of asset-based finance, but they remain well behind the banks: accounting for about 25 percent of the value of assets financed in 2013.

The reader is cautioned that the statistics presented here are estimates based on extensive research conducted on behalf of the CFLA. While every attempt has been made to ensure that they are representative of activity in the market, it is possible—perhaps even likely—that additional research will allow further refinement and improvements to these estimates in the future. In fact, it is the hope of the CFLA that this analysis will stimulate further contributions from stakeholders in the industry.

Robin Somerville, director
The Centre for Spatial Economics
Milton, Ontario

Who Offers Asset-Based Finance?

THE ALTA GROUP has identified the various key organizations offering asset-based financing in the Canadian marketplace.

Banks

There are three categories of chartered banks. The Schedule I banks are the biggest, providing the largest share of financing generally to the Canadian economy. Banks offer asset-based equipment financing either directly or through wholly-owned subsidiaries, such as National Leasing, RBC Equipment Finance, RCAP Leasing, and Roynat Lease Finance. Because of restrictions contained in the federal *Bank Act,* banks may only offer indirect funding to the auto sector—to finance manufacturers, auto dealers, and fleet management companies.

Schedule II banks are foreign bank subsidiaries that take deposits and lend in Canada. For example, both HSBC and Bank of America fund equipment transactions.

Schedule III banks are foreign bank subsidiaries that do not accept deposits but actively lend in Canada, such as Deutsche Bank, Wells Fargo, and Société Générale.

Credit unions

Credit unions are co-operative financial institutions, owned and controlled by their members. Canada has the world's highest per capita membership in the credit union movement, with more than 10 million members, or about one-third of the Canadian population. While the sector is active in all parts of the country, it is strongest in Québec and in the western provinces. In 2012, 70 percent of Québécois belonged to a caisse populaire, while in Saskatchewan close to 60 percent of residents belonged to a credit union. Examples include Caisses populaires Desjardins, Coast Capital Equipment Finance, Concentra Financial, and WS Leasing.

Captives

The so-called "captives" are the finance company subsidiaries of the auto and equipment manufacturers, such as Caterpillar Financial Services, Cisco Systems Capital, Daimler Truck Financial, Ford Credit, General Motors Financial, Honda Canada Finance, IBM Global Finance, John Deere Financial, PACCAR Financial, and Toyota Financial Services.

Government financial institutions

Government sources of commercial equipment financing include Alberta Treasury Branch and a broad range of federal agencies: Farm Credit Canada, Business Development Bank of Canada, Western Economic Diversification Canada, Atlantic Canada Opportunities Agency, and the Canada Small Business Financing Program.

Crown corporations: Filling market gaps or unfair competition?

Federal and provincial Crown corporations and their agencies provide approximately 10 percent of all asset-based financing in Canada.[109] Farm Credit Canada (FCC) and the Business Development Bank of Canada (BDC) are two of the largest federal participants. These and other such government bodies started with a common policy goal: to fill market gaps and assist marginal borrowers so more could qualify for private sector financing. Over time, however, most of these organizations outgrew their initial mandates. With their significant cost advantages, many have become unfair competitors in the asset-based financing market.

Today, for example, FCC is one of the biggest financiers of equipment for the agricultural sector in Canada. According to a 2013 C.D. Howe study, FCC's share of farm debt was less than 15 percent twenty years ago. By 2011, it was 29 percent (or $23.8 billion), compared with 36 percent for *all* chartered banks and 16 percent for *all* credit unions.[110]

With the cost of capital being considered "the life-blood" of the industry, even highly rated private sector financing institutions have difficulty competing with these government bodies. Most pay no corporate income taxes so they do not need to generate the market pre-tax return on equity. They do not have to raise equity on open markets. They borrow either by obtaining funds directly from government at preferred rates or by issuing debt guaranteed by the government. There is also the issue of risk. When Crown corporations overextend themselves and need bailing out, it is the taxpayer who provides the funds.

Pushed by an internal appetite to grow and with government pressures to be "self-financing," Crown corporations and other public agencies offer below-market financing to an ever-broadening customer base. As the C.D. Howe Institute pointed out in a 2013 *Commentary*, it is not difficult to understand how this happens.

> Farm debt held by FCC has, in the past decade, grown sharply faster than the total farm debt market and, accordingly, far faster than farm debt issuance by banks and credit unions.... The dynamic at play is not only the fact that FCC was permitted to expand its activities and enlarge its capital base to do so, but that it was able to build its lending share in a market where private sector competitors ... historically have been very active.
>
> Clearly, FCC has been successful in building its market share because of the institution's low capital costs.... Its capital has in part been provided directly by government and, again, as an agent Crown corporation it is able to borrow directly from the federal government on term's that reflect Ottawa's credit quality. It does not face the same regulatory capital requirements as financial institutions and ... does not pay corporate income tax.[111]

Through the years, the CFLA has intervened each time the activities of federal Crown corporations are reviewed, and the industry consistently opposes efforts to increase their mandates. The C.D. Howe Institute is unequivocal on the matter. Crown corporations "have no clear public policy rationale. At the same time, private ownership within a market-oriented economy is usually considered the best way to ensure an efficient allocation of scarce resources. In other words, the private sector tends to be better than the government at running a business."[112]

This, too, is the CFLA's position. An open marketplace with free and fair competition is always in the best interests of Canadians and the Canadian economy.

Foreign finance and leasing companies

Firms outside Canada have established operations in Canada, such as ARI Financial Services, CIT Financial, De Lage Landen Financial, GE Capital, Macquarie Capital, and PHH Arval.

Independent financing companies

Domestically owned financing companies that are not owned by financial institutions include Bennington Financial Services, Element Financial Corporation, Foss National Leasing, Jim Pattison Lease, Maxium Financial Services, Somerville National Leasing and Rentals, and Travelers Financial.

Insurance companies

Canadian insurance companies such as Sun Life offer securitization funding. Insurance companies are involved in financing large transactions (such as wind turbines and rail systems).

Vendor finance

Vendor finance involves manufacturers, distributors, and dealers of vehicles and equipment who use their own financing services to sell their products directly to customers. Examples include Johnston Equipment (forklifts), OE Canada (office equipment), Henry Schein (medical, dental, and veterinary supplies), Ingram Micro Canada (technology solutions), and Akhurst Machinery (wood processing, metalworking, and grinding/sharpening machinery).

CFLA Chairmen

2013–15	Eugene Basolini, RCAP Leasing
2011–13	Jeffery Hartley, Foss National Leasing
2009–11	Serge Mâsse, FinTaxi sec/lp
2007–09	Fred Booth, ARI Financial Services Inc.
2005–07	Joseph LaLeggia, Irwin Commercial Finance
2002–05	Mike Goddard, PHH Arval
1999–2002	Nick Logan, National Leasing Group
1997–99	Tom Simmons, Newcourt Credit Group
1995–97	Tim Hammill, AT&T Capital Canada Inc.
1994–95	Peter Kidd, AT&T Capital Fleet Services
1993–94	Hugo Sørenson, Triathlon Leasing

CFLA Members of the Year

2012–13	Paul Zalesky (AllWest Insurance Services)
2011–12	Angela Armstrong (Prime Capital Consulting and Forest Leasing)
2010–11	David Dalziel (Deloitte & Touche) Rishi Malkani (Deloitte & Touche) Loraine McIntosh (Deloitte & Touche)
2009–10	The volunteer instructors of Canadian Lease Education On-Demand (CLEO) Angela Armstrong (Prime Capital Consulting and Forest Leasing) Kevin Bowman (Equirex Leasing Corporation) Michael Burke (Blake, Cassels & Graydon LLP) Jason Cooper (PricewaterhouseCoopers LLP) Murray Derraugh (The Alta Group) Michel Lévesque (Group Credit Lease) Stuart Sherman (Morrison Acceptance Corporation) Judy Smiley (Maxium Financial Services) Hugh Swandel (The Alta Group) Michael Stewart (KPMG LLP) Steve Weisz (Blake, Cassels & Graydon LLP) Robin Wilks (HUB International HKMB)

2008–09 Michael Collins (DealerTrack Technologies, Inc.)

2007–08 The CFLA Education & Program Committee
Chairman: Richard McAuliffe (Key Equipment Finance Canada Ltd.)
John Barraclough (Maxium Financial Services Inc.)
Gary Batchelor (Travelers Financial Corporation)
John Estey (Stonebridge Financial Corporation)
Douglas McKenzie (BAL Global Finance Canada Corporation)
Alan Morgan (RBC Equipment Finance Group)

2006–07 Ford Motor Company of Canada Ltd. and Ford Credit Canada Ltd.

2005–06 Hugh Swandel (Swandel & Associates)

2004–05 Peter Freill (Securcor Group of Companies)

2003–04 Mark Robinson (DaimlerChrysler Financial Services Canada Inc.)

2002–03 Diane Sekula (CIT Financial) and Bob Westlake (GE Capital Canada)

2001–02 David Chaiton (Chaitons LLP), Tom Hopkirk (HKMB Capital Solutions), and Raja Singh (Pitney Bowes Global Credit Services)

2000–01 Brian Stevens (MFP Financial Services)

1996–97 Serge Mâsse (Crédit-Bail Findeq)

1995–96 Tom Simmons (Commcorp Financial Services)

1994–95 Greg Korsos (Sako Leasing Inc.)

1993–94 Tom Hopkirk (Barclays Bank of Canada, Leasing Division)

Endnotes

1. See Appendix II, "A Short History of Leasing."
2. Telecom Decision CRTC 82-14, issued November 23, 1982.
3. *Asset-based financing, investment and economic growth 2004,* a study prepared by the Centre for Spatial Economics, Milton, Ontario, December 15, 2004. An updated study will be published in summer 2014.
4. Ibid., pp. viii, 61.
5. Email sent to David Powell following the release of the report in 2004.
6. *Asset-based financing, investment and economic growth 2014,* a study prepared by the Centre for Spatial Economics, Milton, Ontario, to be published summer 2014.
7. Email sent to the author, March 19, 2014.
8. *Asset-based financing, investment and economic growth 2004,* p. ix.
9. Ibid. pp. 34, 99.
10. CFLA online glossary. www.cfla-acfl.ca

11. Although some refer to these as similar to leverage leasing deals, others noted that the deals were not the same because of restrictions by Canadian laws.
12. "Decades of Innovation." Archived website copy for Wheels Inc. http://archive.today/RUp32
13. CIT was originally called Commercial Credit and Investment Company, founded in St. Louis, Missouri, in 1908, and then renamed Commercial Investment Trust, or CIT, in 1915. http://www.cit.com/about-cit/our-history/index.htm
14. *Encyclopedia of American Business History*, "Charles R. Geisst," p. 219.
15. General Electric History. https://www.ge.com/about-us/history/1925-1934
16. Richard Knight, *A Brief History of Investor Relations Investor Relations Society*, UK, 2010, p. 1. www.irs.org.uk/files/A_brief_history_of_investor_relations1.doc
17. Independents are defined as domestically-owned financing companies that are not owned by financial institutions.
18. "Equipment Leasing Now a Billion Dollar Business," *The Beaver County Times*, San Francisco (October 22, 1975): p. C2.
19. Hamish Smith, "Memoirs: Ethics and Dealmaking in Canadian Asset Finance," unpublished and undated memoirs.
20. This is a market segment generally represented by lease financings over $1 million (over US$2 million in the United States).
21. Roger Graham and Arthur Meighen, *No Surrender*, Vol. III, Toronto, Vancouver: Clarke, Irwin & Company Ltd., 1965, pp. 4, 5, 38.
22. The Honourable Michael Meighen, former Chair of the Senate Standing Committee on Banking, Trade and Commerce, and 19th Chancellor of McGill University 2014–2017.
23. Ontario Royal Commission Appointed to Inquire into the Failure of Atlantic Acceptance Corporation, Limited, the Hon. S.H.S. Hughes, September 12, 1969.

24. Irvine Duncan Weeks, *The Collapse of Atlantic Acceptance Corporation and Its Effect on the Structure of Liabilities and Quality of Reporting of Canadian Finance Companies*, Vancouver, University of British Columbia MBA Thesis, 1968.
25. "First City," *Montreal Gazette* (August 16, 1972): p. 26.
26. Numbers provided by John Carmichael, who at this time was working in his father's dealership, City Buick, and was given the assignment of making a list of the current companies and fleet sizes ahead of the vehicle leasing lobby. Lend Lease numbers provided by Fred Booth.
27. Not even Ford Motor Company has a record of the exact founding of FALS. Ginter Baca recalled that it was around 1960, which is consistent with marketing copy at the time promoting the new program.
28. Budget Papers, May 1976, Department of Finance, Government of Canada, p. 76.
29. Israel Mida and Kathleen Stewart, "The Capital Cost Allowance System," *Canadian Tax Journal* 43: 5 (1995), p. 1256.
30. Ralph F. Selby, *Leasing in Canada, A Business Guide*, Third Edition. PricewaterhouseCoopers LLP / LexisNexis Butterworths, March 1999, p. 88.
31. Approximately 50 percent.
32. DesRosiers Automotive Consultants Inc., *Background Report on Extending Bank Powers to Include Light Vehicle Leasing*. Task Force on the Future of the Canadian Financial Services Sector, Department of Finance: Ottawa, September 1998).
33. Ibid, p. 43.
34. *Bank Act* (S.C. 1991, c. 46).
35. Minutes of House of Commons Standing Committee on Finance, Trade and Economic Affairs, June 12, 1980, p. 9:16.
36. CFLA Backgrounder on the Asset-based Financing, Equipment & Vehicle Leasing Industry in Canada, CFLA document, Toronto, August 2006, p. 5.
37. GE press release, January 1, 1994.

38. Five years later, Lloyds Bank of Canada took over ownership of the Continental Bank. Lloyds was acquired by the Hong Kong Bank of Canada in 1990.
39. 1988 or 1989, date unconfirmed.
40. IBM Annual Report, 1997.
41. Onex Corporation, Annual Information Form for the Year Ended December 2005.
42. Name changed in 1987 to General Electric Capital Corporation, a subsidiary of General Electric Company.
43. Tim Smart, "GE's Money Machine," *Bloomberg Businessweek* (March 7, 1993). http://www.businessweek.com/stories/1993-03-07/ges-money-machine
44. Newcourt Credit, Canadian Encylopedia. http://www.thecanadianencyclopedia.ca/en/article/newcourt-credit/
45. Ibid.
46. Doug Alexander, "Element Avoids 'Market Heroin' for Leasing Business," *Bloomberg*, April 10, 2013. http://www.bloomberg.com/news/2013-04-10/element-avoids-market-heroin-for-leasing-business.html
47. Boyd Erman, "Steve Hudson: The Comeback Kid Returns to His Roots," *The Globe and Mail* (October 26, 2012).
48. Source asked not to be named.
49. William Donald Rankin, "Newcourt Credit Group: A Case Study of Employee Ownership," Thesis submitted for the degree of doctor of education, OISE, University of Toronto, 2003.
50. "Donlen Celebrates 25 Years of Fleet Service, *Automotive Fleet Magazine* (September 1990). http://www.automotive-fleet.com/article/story/1990/09/donlen-celebrates-25-years-of-fleet-service.aspx
51. "Ford Credit's Red Carpet Lease," advertisement in *The Milwaukee Sentinel* (January 26, 1984).
52. Later, Mutual Life was taken over by Clarica when Mutual Life was "de-mutualized." In turn, Clarica was acquired by Sun Life Financial.

53. Ling Chu, Robert Mathieu, and Ping Zhang, "Why Firms Lease Short-Lived Assets: A Tax-Based Explanation," *Canadian tax journal / Revue fiscale canadienne* 56(3) (2008): pp. 639-60.
54. Inspired in part with ideas from *Market Unbound: Unleashing Global Capitalism* by Lowell Bryan and Diana Farrell (New York and Toronto: John Wiley & Sons, Inc., 1996).
55. Ron Chernow, *The Death of the Banker* (Toronto: Vintage Canada, 1997): p. 17. This book resulted from a Barbara Frum Lectureship presentation, April 1997.
56. "Canada's Economic Future: What Have We Learned From the 1990s," speech by Gordon Thiessen, governor of the Bank of Canada, to The Canadian Club of Toronto, Royal York Hotel, January 22, 2001.
57. Ibid.
58. GE Capital's acquisitions included McCullough Leasing, Greyvest Financial Services Inc., and the lease financing operations of National Bank of Canada.
59. With the addition of Mexico in 1994, the FTA was superseded by the North American Free Trade Agreement (NAFTA).
60. Bank of Montreal 1999 Annual Report: p. 9.
61. According to Ginter Baca, president and CEO at Lease Administration Corporation.
62. Pacific National Leasing, Pacific National Vehicle Leasing, and Pacific National Lease Holding.
63. David Chaiton, "The Leasing Fraud Fiasco," *Fraud Report* 7(6) (May 2005): pp. 8, 9.
64. Advertisement in *Automotive Leasing* placed by Chrysler Motor Corporation, October 31, 1994.
65. "Consumer Spending," *Consumer Trends Report* (Ottawa: Industry Canada). http://www.ic.gc.ca/eic/site/oca-bc.nsf/eng/ca02117.html
66. *Task Force on the Future of the Canadian Financial Services Sector, Change, Challenge, Opportunity: Report of the Task*

Force (September 1998). Also known as the *MacKay Task Force Report.*

67. Maryanna Lewycky, "Leased – or fleeced? Is auto leasing giving you help or getting you hooked?" *Chatelaine* (September 5, 2003). http://www.chatelaine.com/living/leased-or-fleeced/
68. Consumer Trends Report, Chapter 9, Industry Canada, p. 178.
69. *The Final Report of the RIM Park Financing,* City of Waterloo Judicial Inquiry, p. 230.
70. Ibid, p. 231.
71. *The Final Report of the Toronto Computer Leasing Inquiry and the Toronto External Contracts Inquiry,* Volume 1: Facts and Findings, p. 445.
72. Ibid, p. 101.
73. "Choice. Financial Services into the 21st Century," A Submission to the Task Force on the Future of the Canadian Financial Services Sector, CFLA, October 31, 1997, p. 3.
74. Ibid. p. 3.
75. Ibid. p. 3.
76. According to David Powell, Peterson made the comment to the CFLA delegation meeting with him in Ottawa and then repeated his comments at a January 13, 1999, CFLA dinner meeting in Toronto attended by about 100 members.
77. Stanley Hartt O.C. began his career as a lawyer, practising labour law at Stikeman Elliott in Montreal for twenty years. From 1985 to 1988, he was the deputy minister in the federal department of finance, under the Hon. Michael Wilson. From 1989 to 1990, he was chief of staff to Prime Minister Brian Mulroney. Among other things, he participated actively in negotiating the Canada–USA Free Trade Agreement (he was one of eight Canadians in the room when the agreement was signed). From 1990 to 1996, he was chair, president, and chief executive of Campeau Corporation, a real estate and retailing enterprise. He became

chair of Salomon Brothers Canada Inc., later renamed Citigroup Global Markets Canada Inc. (1996–2008), and then served as chair of Macquarie Capital Markets Canada Ltd. (2008–13). From April 2009 to March 2010, he chaired the federal Advisory Committee on Financing, a committee of chief executives appointed to advise the minster of finance on financing conditions, access to credit, and gaps in the credit markets. In September 2010, he gave the keynote speech at the CFLA annual conference in Vancouver, titled "The credit crisis and its impact on the Canadian economy." He is now Toronto-based counsel to the international law firm Norton Rose Fulbright.

78. Text of Stephen Harper's eulogy for Jim Flaherty. http://pm.gc.ca/eng/news/2014/04/16/statement-prime-minister-canada-honourable-jim-flahertys-state-funeral-0
79. CFLA letter to the Canadian Securities Administrators, August 31, 2011.
80. James Langton, "TD Bank to acquire VFC," *Investment Executive News* (February 16, 2006).
81. GE Is Creating a Smaller, More Stable and Profitable Financial Business (September 17, 2013). http://www.trefis.com/stock/ge/articles/205937/ge-is-creating-a-smaller-more-stable-and-profitable-financial-business/2013-09-17
82. Matthew Dolan and John Stoll, "Ford Credit to Cut Back On Leasing, Citing Risks," *Wall Street Journal In-Depth* (August 9, 2008).
83. Greg Bensinger and Jeff Green, "GM Has $15.5 Billion Loss on U.S. Sales Drop, Leases (Update4)," *Bloomberg* (August 1, 2008).
84. Federal Deputy Minister of Finance Rob Wright spoke about the 2009 federal budget to the C.D. Howe Institute on February 3, 2009. In his presentation he noted, "Outstanding business credit in 2007 in billions of dollars: $271B to the chartered banks, $306B in equity, $458B non-equity financial markets, $90B other."

85. Nick de Bass, int., "The Daily Wrap: Flaherty remembers the financial crisis," BNN (September 17, 2013). http://www.bnn.ca/News/2013/9/17/The-Daily-Wrap-Flaherty-remembers-the-financial-crisis.aspx
86. Barry Critchley, "Ottawa's $3.7-billion credit crisis bailout actually made money," *National Post* (November 12, 2013). http://business.financialpost.com/2013/11/12/ottawas-3-7-billion-credit-crisis-bailout-actually-made-money/
87. Fred Booth, CFLA chairman, from the Chairman's Report to the 2009 National Conference, Gatineau, Québec, September 21, 2009.
88. In this context, the leasing market includes machinery and equipment, commercial vehicles, and retail (consumer/personal) vehicles.
89. *Global Asset and Auto Finance Survey*, Quarter 4, 2013, published by White Clarke Group and Asset Finance International Ltd. UK. (White Clark Group, 2013). http://www.whiteclarkegroup.com/knowledge-centre/category/global_leasing_report
90. Ibid.
91. Founder, president, and CEO of Global Change Leaders, a consultancy group of former GE leaders advising on change initiatives, organizational integrations, and business mergers and acquisitions to clients in Europe and North America. Adjunct professor at the business schools of the Université de Montréal and McGill University.
92. Paul W. Frechette, The Alta Group, "A New Lease on Life, The Captives Take Control," 2013 *Monitor* 100, June 2013. http://www.monitordaily.com/new-lease-life
93. Robin Somerville, The Centre for Spatial Economics, Milton, Ontario, document prepared for Appendix II, April 24, 2014.
94. Lubo Li, senior director and financial services practice leader at J.D. Power and Associates, Toronto. As reported in a press release "J.D. Power and Associates Reports: Dealer

Financing Satisfaction with Banks in Canada Increases As Captive Share of Auto Financing Business Declines," Westlake Village, California, May 24, 2012.

95. Ibid.
96. Chuck Sequin, "Dealership Pac-Man," *Canadian Auto Dealer* (November 2012).
97. Greg Keenan, "Big Dealers Remodel Canadian Car Lots," *The Globe and Mail* (February 12, 2013). http://www.theglobeandmail.com/globe-investor/big-dealers-remodel-canadian-car-lots/article8535918/
98. *Canadian Automotive Fleet Fact Book*, 2013.
99. Happy Earth Day: The Role of IBM Global Asset Recovery Services. http://greateribm.wordpress.com/2013/04/18/happy-earth-day-the-role-of-ibm-global-asset-recovery-services/
100. *Asset-based financing, investment and economic growth 2004*, a study prepared by the Centre for Spatial Economics, Milton, Ontario, December 15, 2004, pp. 34, 99.
101. Joe LaLeggia, CFLA chairman, from Chairman's Report to the 2005 CFLA national conference, Vancouver, B.C., September 15, 2005.
102. Speech transcript, Minister of Finance Jim Flaherty, P.C., M.P., keynote speaker at the CFLA Conference, September 21, 2009, Hilton Lac Leamy, Gatineau, Québec.
103. Nicholas Kaldor first put forth the concept of technical progress function in the late 1950s. Nicholas Kaldor, "A Model of Economic Growth," *The Economic Journal* 67: 268 (Dec. 1957): pp. 591-624.
104. U.S. Equipment Leasing and Finance Association, Top 10 Equipment Acquisition Trends for 2013. http://www.equipmentfinanceadvantage.org/articles/10Trends.cfm#sthash.oMVd8xgE.dpuf
105. As is described in greater detail later in this book, lease accounting standards have been under review for more than a decade by the International Accounting Standards

Board and the U.S. Financial Accounting Standards Board. Changes to the accounting for leases, both by lessors and by lessees, are expected.

106. Sourced in part from "The History of Equipment Leasing," a chapter in the *Certified Lease Professionals Handbook*, with permission from the Certified Lease Professional Foundation (CLP Foundation), Northbrook, Illinois.
107. The thirty member-states of the Organisation for Economic Co-operation and Development (OECD) include Canada, the United States, the member countries of the European Union, Japan, Korea, Australia, the Czech Republic, Poland, Hungary, and Mexico.
108. "Leasing—Lessons of Experiences, The United Nations Economic Commission for Europe." A conference room paper prepared within the framework of the Regional Advisory Services Programme of the Coordinating Unit for Operational Activities of the United Nations Economic Commission for Europe for the Project Group on Financial Policies for Strengthening SMEs through Microcredit and Credit Guarantee Schemes of the Southeast European Cooperative Initiative (SECI), Geneva, (June 1997): p 4.
109. See "Appendix II: Asset-Based Finance by the Numbers."
110. Philippe Bergevin and Finn Poschmann, "Reining in the Risks: Rethinking the Role of Crown Financial Corporations in Canada," C.D. Howe Institute *Commentary No. 372* (February 2013), p. 12.
111. Ibid.
112. Ibid., p. 3.

Index

About the CFLA

THE CANADIAN FINANCE & LEASING ASSOCIATION (CFLA) represents the asset-based finance, vehicle, and equipment leasing industry in Canada. Members range from large multinationals to national and regional domestic companies, crossing the financial services spectrum from manufacturers' finance companies and independent leasing companies to banks, insurance companies, and suppliers to the industry.

The CFLA advocates on behalf of the industry, creates networking opportunities for members, delivers timely business-relevant information, and offers a unique Canadian industry education program. **www.cfla-acfl.ca**

About the Author

BETH PARKER writes for business and organizations in Canada and the United States. Her clients range from Fortune 500 companies to start-up entrepreneurs. Beth has an English specialist degree from the University of Toronto (Victoria College) and an MA in journalism from the University of Western Ontario.